NOTHING COULD BE FINER

by
Michael Myerson

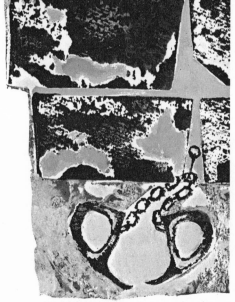

International Publishers, New York

Library of Congress Cataloging in Publication Data
Myerson, Michael, 1940-
 Nothing could be finer.

 Includes bibliographical references.
  1. Afro-Americans—Civil rights —North Carolina.
2. Civil rights —North Carolina. 3. North Carolina—
Politics and government -1951- 4. Chavis, Ben,
1948- 5. Clergy —North Carolina —Biography.
I. Title.
E185.93.N6M93   323.4′09756   78-17407
ISBN 0-7178-0553-0
ISBN 0-7178-0498-4 pbk.

Contents

This one's for Charlene, of course

Acknowledgements

NATURALLY the author accepts full responsibility for the words you are about to read, but credit must be shared by many people, too many to list here. Still, special mention should be made of the staff of the National Alliance Against Racist and Political Repression, whose patience in the face of great impatience allowed this work to proceed. Under the leadership of executive secretary Charlene Mitchell, they include Kay Anderson, Linda Edwards, Lucia Faithfull-Stevenson, Sandra Frankel, Malvice Jefferson, Bonnie Kanter, Frederica Lawson, Anne Mitchell, Stefanie Mitchell, Maria Ramos, Marj Sutherland, Nancy Sutula and Ruth Yates.

So many folks in North Carolina were generous with their time and knowledge, showing their famous hospitality to this Northern boy. The entire Chavis family and the Paul family have been particular inspirations.

Finally, I owe enormous debts to Henry Winston, Laura Brown, Elaine Markson and my parents who, each, in very special ways, made this book possible.

NOTHING COULD BE FINER

Introduction

Esse Quam Videri [*To Be Rather Than to Seem*]
North Carolina state motto

BY THE time Ben Chavis and the Wilmington 10 entered prison in February 1976, it had come to this in North Carolina: the state's license-tag slogan, "First in Freedom" was meeting with protest. Some local folks, appalled by the nation's largest death-row population at Raleigh's Central Prison, taped over the slogan. For which they were arrested. Misdemeanors in North Carolina bring sentences as high as two years at Central.

With the first Southern president of this century now in the White House, new national attention has been paid the South. Much has been written about the New South, how the tradition of racist terror has been abandoned by a new breed of public officials ushering in a bright era. Discrimination is now an occasional occurrence, lynching a distant memory. North Carolina, it is said, best exemplifies this reformist spirit. But, like rouge on a corpse, the New South is little more than cosmetic to prevent the reality of North Carolina from showing through.

The gap between "to be" and "to seem" in this state suggests some of that same eerie incongruity that the Polish writer Tadeusz Borowski portrayed of life in Auschwitz—the Red Cross van transporting gas to the "showers," the German-occupied cities with stores filled with books and religious objects while smoke from the crematoria hovered over the trees. In this sense alone, the New South doesn't seem as repressive as it really is.

Barbara Howar finds symbolic of North Carolina the tragedy of a childhood friend, "the daughter of old Monty," who became a drug addict and now lives out her days in the attic of the family mansion, spaced out on morphine. Her father is on the boards of the state hospitals and will tell the curious that his daughter has "back trouble."[1]

In 1584, two English settlers published a booklet, extolling the beauties of what is now North Carolina. They called it "the goodliest land under the cope of heaven," a description used today by the tourist merchants to drum up business. Business seems good: Tourism, the state's third largest industry, accrues about a billion dollars a year. By mobile home and backpack, the citizenry comes to sup on the goodliest land's Blue Ridge with its azalea, rhododendron, mountain laurel and wild orchids; the Outer Banks with the largest coastline of any state, after California and Florida; the stockcar racetracks that originated in the mountains with enterprising young moonshiners who had to flee the "revenooers." The fauna and flora of North Carolina are seductive. Valleys are misty in the dawn, willows weep for us in the East. Tear off the page, it's already September. The more alert tourist in the Great Smokies will discover increasing air and water pollution and land erosion as this eastern tip of Appalachia becomes the "second-home" center for developers like former NATO commander, General Lauris Norstad. In some mountain counties, more than 75 percent of the land is now owned by resort developers from outside the state.[2]

Some come as tourists and decide to settle. Whereas a postwar exodus sent Black farmworkers and white mountain people to the cities of the North, there has been a more recent influx of whites into the state, looking to staff the executive suites and research laboratories of the new industries and expanded government apparatus. One such settler began as a news reporter for Raleigh's paper of record, The *News and Observer,* and moved into state government promoting tourism. He likes North Carolina because of the affection among the people: "I've never seen a place where people are quite as warm and friendly." Another Northerner, David Flaherty, who calls himself a "Boston Irishman," became the state's Secretary of Human Resources and Republican candidate for governor in 1976. Flaherty came south as a salesman for Broyhill Furniture, settled, became a state senator and now devotes himself to Little League baseball and the boy scouts. "This is a good environment for bringing up kids," he says. "They can get as good an education here as anywhere."[3] Where he sees salad, others see weeds: North Carolina has the fourth highest drop-out rate in the country, and more juveniles in prison per capita than any other of these United States.

In the North Carolina Museum of History, a block away from the state capitol, not one Black person is identified in three floors of exhibitions. In one corner hang three oil paintings of unidentified Black women, one of whom is a maid, peacock fan in hand, standing over a dinner spread. There are two paintings of Black men, one a cook preparing a meal.

Thirty photos alone are exhibited of David Marshal Williams, the white man who designed the U.S. .30m caliber carbine. Nearby are a dozen oil paintings depicting "Plantation Scenes from Life" of unidentified Black slaves. Schoolchildren and tourists by the busload troop through these rooms each day to receive "as good an education as anywhere."

Visitors and native Carolinians drive on the largest state-maintained highway system in the United States, some 75,000 miles of roads which have given North Carolina the nickname, "The Good Roads State." Only the more curious will discover that until 1973 the roads were built and maintained by convict labor in chain gangs.

So much camouflage is required to cover the past of the New South. Fayetteville, the state's fastest growing community, is the off-base town for Fort Bragg, the nation's largest military base. In the center of Fayetteville sits its major tourist attraction, the "Old Market House." Erected in 1838, the building is identified to the thousands who annually pass by as a former town hall, former house of worship, former bank and former school. Left unmentioned is that it was built and served as the largest slave auction block in the state until emancipation.

To prevent that emancipation from ever coming to pass, enlightened North Carolina furnished more men to the Confederate cause than any other state.[4] North Carolina honors Confederate Memorial Day on May 10 each year with the official flying of the Stars and Bars. Known to tourists and basketball fans as the Tarheel State, it took that name from a compliment by Robert E. Lee for the refusal of its soldiers to retreat during the Battle of Gettysburg. Lee, commander of the only army that ever tried to overthrow the government of the United States by force and violence, is regarded as the most wonderful of heroes in this state which prides itself on vigilence against subversion. Thus does the New South hold onto "a dream remembered, a civilization gone with the wind," as Margaret Mitchell would have had it.

It doesn't exactly harken one back to the Burma Shave days of yore, but North Carolina's famed highways aren't without their Ku Klux Klan billboards, urging drivers to "Help Fight Communism and Integration, Join and Support the United Klans of America, Inc." Or, accompanied by a picture of the flag, handbills declaring: "Old Glory. If Anybody tries to tear it down, shoot him on the spot." But most of those in authority deny the existence of the Klan or consider it, at most, a handful of crackpots. Nightriders have become, if not a relic of the past, at least a seldom-used albeit effective method of delivering a message. Black families are occasionally run out of previously all-white neighborhoods upon receiving a 12-gauge "salute" from hooded bullies down the block.

Whatever one's guess of Klan influence, the cross burns bright in many a white Carolinian's heart. The notion of evangelical Christianity leads to suspicion of others as "less than Christian." One needn't travel far to view outsiders as doing the Devil's work. In the town of Oxford until recently, the Klan rallied its forces after church services on Sunday. With God and R.J. Reynolds on their side, preachers in Winston-Salem admonish the heathen and the believers in the tobacco plants against joining trade unions. One Tarheel native, the Reverend Billy Graham, allows as how the "signs are now in place" for the second coming of Christ. Among those signs are such things as worldwide rebellion, greed and "problems for which there are no human solutions."[5]

Many years ago the Brothers Grimm turned a scum-laden toad into a lovely prince for the benefit of children the world around. And more recently the National Rifle Association has grown to mammoth proportions on the premise of shooting as a form of peaceful recreation. But sorcery in the form of public relations has no equal to the power structure of North Carolina. In 1963, eight years after the censure of Joseph McCarthy by the United States Senate, the North Carolina legislature passed a bill banning from state-supported schools speakers who 1) were members of the Communist Party; 2) advocated the overthrow of the U.S. Constitution; or 3) pleaded "the Fifth Amendment of the Constitution in refusing to answer questions with respect to Communist or subversive activities."[6]This peculiar legislation, which adroitly "protected" the Constitution against potential overthrow, and simultaneously overthrows the Constitution itself, perfectly illustrates the unitarianism of the Old-New South. Dr. Herbert Aptheker, a Communist leader with a long history of campus speaking engagements, recalled his experiences at the University of North Carolina at Chapel Hill, "the Harvard of the South" and the single institution most responsible for the state's progressive image. Aptheker remembered, "I had spoken at Chapel Hill as early as 1946 and 1947 as a Party spokesman. At the time there was no speakers ban but UNC was all white. I argued that any all-white institution could not be a university, that this was a contradiction in terms. I was waylaid and physically assaulted for mere exercise of the Constitution. By the time I spoke there in 1964, I was waylaid by the law. Banned from speaking on the campus, I had to speak onto it from a Chapel Hill sidewalk."[7]

The First and Fifth Amendments are not the only ones to experience mayhem at the hands of North Carolina justice. In late 1974, three high school students carted off two dozen bottles of soda without paying, from a gas station near Elizabeth City. The students, all first offenders, were sentenced to a five-year waiver of Fourth Amendment guarantees against illegal search and seizure. Under the sentence, their homes, automobiles and persons may now be stopped, searched, and entered without warrants or probable cause by any law enforcement officer. The Pasquotank County district attorney said that waivers of the Fourth Amendment are common in that part of the state. They are used "to encourage folks to walk the straight and narrow," he said. In another 1974 case, the state Court of Appeals ruled valid the deprivation of the Fourth Amendment.[8]

Stern indeed is discipline in this bastion of progressivism. A major controversy developed in the 1974 General Assembly over a bill to limit spanking of students by teachers in the schools. A compromise bill was finally submitted to a House education subcommittee which called for spanking "only as a last resort," limited the number of school personnel allowed to spank, required a witness be present during corporal punishment, and required record-keeping of punishment. The bill never got out of committee. After public arguments favoring spanking as a method of relieving tension and establishing good rapport with pupils, Representative Sam Bundy of Pitt County pronounced the clinching argument: "Teachers file enough reports already," he said.[9]

Recalling bygone days of posses and bounty hunters, North Carolina is the only state in the union that retains a statute that deputizes the citizenry and allows officers to shoot a designated felon on sight. Enacted in 1868, the law tells the outlaw that any citizen "may slay him without accusation or impeachment of any crime." Moreover, a felony suspect may be declared an outlaw before he has been convicted if a judge deems "convincing" evidence of his guilt. Any judge or any two justices of the peace can declare a suspect an outlaw. While prison guards are only allowed to shoot felons, not misdemeanants, a misdemeanant becomes a felon if he tries to escape.[10] In "the goodliest land under the cope of heaven," it is estimated that at least half the adult population maintains a private collection of arms.

Still, it would be a serious miscalculation to believe that the problem of North Carolina and the New South is a population made up of what H. L. Mencken sneeringly described as "howling yokels" and "homo boobiens."

One

I would invite those who have criticized us to look at North Carolina. Look at our people. People, working side by side for common goals. Look in our schools, look in our factories, look at what's happening in our neighborhoods and our communities.

Governor James B. Hunt, Jr.

IF you drive along Interstate highway 85 heading north from Durham, about 18 miles out you will pass a large red, white and blue billboard that reads: "Welcome to Granville County. Ku Klux Klan Country. Help Fight Integration and Communism." The billboard pictures a white knight atop a white horse. On I-95 outside of Benson, another highway sign announces, "You are Now Entering the Heart of Klan Country. Welcome to North Carolina." Until 1977, a similar billboard would welcome you to Johnston County, with the added feature of a border of red and white blinking lights. The Granville County Klan is not so ostentatious.

Just past its billboard, as you turn off I-85, you come onto the Jefferson Davis Highway which brings you into Oxford, seat of Granville County. One of the 5 counties in North Carolina with more than 10,000 slaves, Granville was one of 16 in the state with majority Black populations during the Reconstruction years. Consequently it was one of the 26 Republican counties. Today, only 40 percent of the county is Black; half the county's families earn less than $4,000 a year. Granville has been known for a century for its ideal soil, which produces the finest Bright leaf tobacco in the entire country, a reputation that caught the notice of Buck Duke, R.J. Reynolds and the other captains of the industry in the nineteenth century. Hence Oxford and nearby Henderson were the sites of the first expansion of the emerging Carolina Power and Light Company at the turn of the century.

Entering Oxford today, you first pass the spinning plants of Burlington Mills, which are said by the townsfolk to run Granville County. Just past the mills is the Welcome Gas Station, a combination filling station-general store-gun shop, said to be a local gathering place for members of the United Klans of America, Inc. Just north of Oxford, Robert G. Teel, a local Klan leader, owned a mini-shopping center in a Black community called Brown-town. Here it was that Teel, his son and his stepson set upon Henry Lee Marrow, a Black Vietnam veteran, whom they accused of insulting Mr. Teel's wife. After shooting Henry Marrow just above the kneecap, the Teel men beat in Marrow's skull as he lay bleeding on the ground. Finally young Larry Teel ended the business by blowing Marrow's head off.

A block and a half after you pass the Welcome Gas Station you come to Oxford's town square which contains—as do the town squares in the seats of most of the state's 100 counties and the state capital square—an obelisk with the inscribed dedication, "To Our Confederate Dead." A few blocks north of the obelisk is what appears to be a small New England college campus. This is the Oxford Orphanage—officially the White Orphanage until 1971—which raised white parentless children from all over the state at the expense of the Duke Endowment. But if you drive south of the town square and head out beyond the Oxford town limits, you will come to a cluster of red-brick buildings in need of repair, standing in a field of patchy grass and weeds. This is the Central Orphanage, formerly the Colored Orphanage, set up separately and unequally, also by the will and with the largesse of James B. Duke.

For years, Mrs. Elizabeth Chavis taught at the Colored Orphanage. Mrs. Chavis lives right down the road in a sprawling Victorian house which has belonged to her family since Reconstruction, as testified to by some two dozen gravesites a couple of hundred yards into the pine woods in back. Mrs. Chavis was born Elizabeth Ridley, her people originally having been brought as slaves from Africa via the West Indies to Granville County. In the backyard of the house is a well, now covered over, which, Mrs. Chavis remembers being told as a child, served as a watering hole for hooded Knights of the Ku Klux Klan, to refresh their horses after returning from Oxford's Lynch Hill.

Elizabeth Ridley received her education at the all-Black North Carolina Central College in Durham and became a schoolteacher. Her husband Ben, a graduate of St. Augustine College, a Black Episcopalian school in Raleigh, also taught school for a while, although he was a brick mason by trade. Ben Chavis was a descendent of John Chavis, said by historian John Hope Franklin to be "the most prominent free Negro in North Carolina." Born in Oxford in 1763, John Chavis was educated at Princeton as a Latin and Greek scholar. As W.E.B. Du Bois wrote, "In 1802, his freedom and character were certified to and it was declared that he had passed 'through a regular course of academic studies' at what is now Washington and Lee University." John Chavis returned to North Carolina in 1805, where he became a preacher in the Presbyterian church. "His English was remarkably pure," wrote Du Bois, "his manner impressive, his explanations clear and concise." His career as a minister ended in 1832 when, following Nat Turner's insurrection, free Negroes were prohibited from preaching. John Chavis turned then to teaching—white children by day, Black children at night. Among his former students were a U.S. senator, two sons of a Supreme Court justice, and Charles Manley, later governor of the state. Eventually North Carolina passed a law banning Blacks from teaching, so John Chavis set up an underground school in the town of Hillsborough, near Chapel Hill.

After retiring from the school system in the early 1960s, Ben Chavis built the Ridley Drive-In restaurant on the family property. The town of Oxford being shy of recreational facilities for Black folks, people came from all over to the Drive-In as a place to hang out and socialize. In back of the Drive-In and before you come to the graveyard in the woods, sits an empty lot which serves as the Black baseball field for Oxford's young people. Before he died in 1965, Ben Chavis was the local Black scoutmaster and baseball coach, his troops and his teams using the Drive-In as their center.

Mrs. Chavis's immaculately furnished living room is filled with pictures of her children, and with relics of the Episcopal Church in which they were raised. The eldest, June, converted to Catholicism when she married, and moved to Charlotte where she too is a schoolteacher. Helen, the second daughter, received her PhD. at the University of Wisconsin, and now is also in Charlotte where she chairs the Humanities Department at Johnson C. Smith University. The youngest of the Chavis children, Francine, attended the University of North Carolina at Greensboro but was forced to leave in the middle of her senior year because of her involvement in civil rights activities. Francine is now studying medicine in the German Democratic Republic.

In the corner of Francine's old bedroom stands a shotgun which, before she went abroad to study, she had needed more than a few times to protect her mother from Klansmen who drove by the house to shout insults and taunts. For Mrs. Chavis is also the mother of Francine's older brother, the Reverend Benjamin Franklin Chavis, Jr. Growing up a boy scout in his father's troop, assistant coach to his father's baseball team, product of Oxford's "colored" school system, and lifelong friend of the murdered Henry Lee Marrow, the Rev. Chavis made the 1972 volume of *Outstanding Young Men of America*. His biographical sketch in the book tells us the following: "Born January 22, 1948. Education, University of North Carolina, B.A. 1970. Labor organizer AFL-CIO, 1967–68. Southern Christian Leadership Conference organizer, 1968–69. Commission for Racial Justice, Director, United Church of Christ Community Program, 1970. First African Temple of the Black Messiah, founder, pastor, 1971. American Chemical Society, 1969. Granville County Democratic Party precinct chairman, 1970. SCLC Education Fund, board of directors, 1972. President, founder, Black Student Union, 1968. President, UNC Student Union, 1968. Candidate, City Council, Charlotte, N.C., 1969." Perhaps unbeknownst to the compilers of *Outstanding Young Men of America*—the volume was Foreworded by Richard Nixon's presidential press secretary Ronald Ziegler—was that, at the time of publication, Rev. Chavis was serving the first of 34 years in prison on conspiracy charges growing out of his defense, together with nine co-workers, of a church in the Black community of Wilmington, N.C., under a four-day armed siege by the Ku Klux Klan and other racist fanatics.

At the Oxford house, Mrs. Chavis stores every issue of *Chemistry News* for her son while he sits in prison. She once told an interviewer about Ben, Jr. as a child, "My, yes, he was always trying to put something together."

In the New Dixie, old times there are not forgotten. "In its grand outlines, the politics of the South revolve around the position of the Negro," wrote Professor V.O. Key back in 1949. "The hard core of the political South—and the backbone of southern political unity—is made up of those counties and sections of the Southern states in which Negroes constitute a substantial proportion of the population." In these areas, which make up what was once called "the Black Belt" and which include the eastern third of North Carolina from the Virginia stateline to South Carolina, "The situation resembles fundamentally that of the Dutch in the East Indies or the former position of the British in India. . . . As in the case of the colonials, that white minority can maintain its position only with the support, and by the tolerance, of those outside—in the home country or in the rest of the United States."[1]

A quarter-century after those words were written their essence remains true. One cannot hope to understand the United States, the South, North Carolina or Ben Chavis, without the knowledge, firmly grasped, that Black people today are descendants of slaves, and white people are not.

Even in the course of the colonial revolution that formed the United States, that power relationship held. North Carolina historians still proudly proclaim that among the 13 original colonies, theirs had more loyalists to the Crown than any other. In the course of the revolution against British rule, these loyalists held nothing more dear than the King, with the single exception of the institution of chattel slavery. In the summer of 1775, while the colonies were in revolt against the King, slaves in North Carolina were in revolt against their bondage. Hundreds, possibly thousands, of slaves in Beaufort, Pitt and Craven counties were executed, whipped, branded or had their ears cut off in a wave of repression against these slave revolts.[2] Elsewhere, some slaves were allowed to join the colonial army in exchange for which they won their freedom.

As throughout the South, the spirit of freedom in North Carolina expressed itself in numerous slave rebellions in the decades before and following independence from England. Groups of maroons—fugitive slaves engaged in guerrilla warfare against the "peculiar institution"— roamed through North Carolina in the early nineteenth century. In the area near Wilmington, runaway slaves gathered under the leadership of a man called the "General of the Swamps" at the turn of the century. Another Black fugitive, Tom Cooper, led bands in the region of Elizabeth City. In his seminal work, *American Negro Slave Revolts,* historian Herbert Aptheker estimates that in the year 1802, at least 15 slave rebels were executed, scores arrested and tortured as a result of reported "slave conspiracies" in 10 North Carolina counties.[3] Later in 1804, slaves rose up in Johnston, Sampson and Wayne counties, for which some 20 slaves were arrested. One, a woman, was burned alive, 3 or 4 others were hanged, one "was pilloried, whipped, his ears nailed down and then cut off," one was banished, the others lashed.[4] Maroon detachments in Onslow, Carteret and Bladen counties mounted a rebellion in 1821, led by a Black called Isam, "alias General Jackson," who was later captured and lashed to death in a public execution.[5]

In 1829, David Walker, born the son of a slave in Wilmington, issued his "Appeal to the Colored Citizens of the World," a manifesto for the "total abolition of slavery" which became the catalyst for the embryonic abolitionist movement. Published in Boston, the Appeal found its way into Walker's home state. Copies were reported to have been found by police in Fayetteville, Wilmington, Chapel Hill, New Bern and Hillsborough. Spies were used by the governor to try to discover who were its distributors, among them the Reverend John Chavis. In 1830, the state passed a law to forbid the teaching of reading and writing to slaves. Laws were passed requiring heavy penalties—death for slaves—for those engaged in distributing anti-slavery materials. The state required all Blacks emancipated after 1830 to leave North Carolina within 90 days.[6]

The state legislature convened secretly to develop methods of subduing the growing disaffection of the Black population. In the end, increased repression in the form of strengthened militias was all the established order was able to come up with. Slaves suspected of insubordination were arbitrarily executed. The slaveholders saw insurrection from every quarter. A state judge rendering an opinion in 1852 demonstrated the siege mentality: "What acts in a slave towards a white person will amount to insolence, it is manifestly impossible to define—it may consist in a look, the pointing of a finger, a refusal or neglect to step out of the way when a white person is seen to approach. But each of such acts violates the rules of propriety, and if tolerated, would destroy that subordination, upon which our social system rests."[7] Clearly, when push came to war over whether to maintain or break up the slave system, North Carolina would be voted among those most likely to secede.

When the Confederacy was defeated on the battlefield, President Andrew Johnson of North Carolina, successor to the murdered Lincoln, received a petition from Blacks in his home state who had fought alongside the Union army. The petitioners prayed for "the privilege of voting" for they who were "willing on the field of danger to carry the Republic's muskets, in the days of Peace ought to be permitted to carry its ballots."[8] In September 1865, four months after the petition was submitted, the first freedmen's convention in North Carolina met at Raleigh. About 350,000 Blacks in the state had been freed by the Thirteenth Amendment and, at great personal risk, their 120 delegates now came in secrecy under cover of night, some receiving safe-conduct papers from the federal military authorities. This convention of former slaves hailed the passage of the anti-slavery amendment to the Constitution, the recognition of Liberia and Haiti by Washington, and the admission of a Black attorney to the state bar. More, it demanded wages for labor, free education for the children, protection of the family, and the repeal of all discriminatory legislation.[9]

The next year, the state legislature, in a bid to be received back into the federal union, enacted a code legalizing Black marriages and safeguarding the rights of Blacks in making contracts. Still, they were denied the right to vote or the right to testify in court. Late in the year, the legislature voted overwhelmingly against the Fourteenth Amendment, which would grant Blacks citizenship and deny public office to anyone who had supported the Confederacy. Support of the amendment was the congressional requirement for admission back into the union. Congress then passed the Reconstruction Acts over the protests and veto of President Johnson. Southern state governments were temporarily suspended, pending the adoption of new state constitutions. Military law was imposed to implement Reconstruction. After the occupation of Raleigh, President Johnson appointed William W. Holden as provisional governor to replace Zebulon Vance, who was arrested and imprisoned for several weeks. The reaction was predictable. Governor Jonathan Worth, who defeated Holden in the subsequent election, declared: "I abhor the Democratic tendency of our government. I use the word in its proper, not its party, sense. The tendency is to ignore virtue and property and intelligence—and to put the powers of government into the hands of mere numbers... Men will be governed by their interests. The majority in all times and all countries are improvident and without property."[10]

The Republican Party was organized in 1867 and chose Holden as its gubernatorial candidate in 1868. Running on a platform of support for the Fourteenth and Fifteenth Amendments, and for universal public education, Holden won the election, the first in which the state legislature was chosen on the basis of population per district, not wealth.

With the Republican victory, the Ku Klux Klan rose up in 1868, particularly in Alamance and Caswell counties where the Republicans showed increasing strength. Called the Constitutional Union Guard (CUG) in Lenoir County, the Klan was led by Jesse Kennedy, a wealthy mill owner and by deputy sheriff A. Munroe. Among its activities were stealing horses from Black farmers, preventing whites from working alongside Blacks, and assassinating Republican leaders, particularly Black Republicans. Lynchings became commonplace; ears were taken from the victims as proof of their accomplishments. A public barbecue was given to celebrate the assassination by the CUG of Jones County Sheriff O.R. Colgrove, a Northerner who supported Reconstruction. In Moore County, in which both the sheriff and superior court clerk were Klan members, numerous houses and barns were burned down to drive out Black and white Republicans. One Black woman and her five children were shot before their house was set afire. One participant in the lynching admitted to having "killed one of the children by kicking its brains out with the heel of his boot," according to a local news story. In Alamance County, a Black man was given 150 lashes and his baby was clubbed to death. Black farmers were kidnapped and hanged by gangs of 75 or 100 Klansmen. County Sheriff Albert Murray, all of his deputies and Alamance's representative in the legislature were members of the White Brotherhood. Frederick Strudwick, an Orange County lawyer, led a party of Klansmen in a plot to assassinate a Republican state senator who had drafted a law permitting the governor to proclaim a state of insurrection in areas of Klan terrorism. Strudwick failed in the attempted murder, but he was soon elected to the legislature where he led a movement which repealed the act and impeached the governor for having used it.

Scores of baby-stompings, castrations, whippings and lynchings by Klansmen brought Republican demands on Governor Holden to use the militia against the Klan. But most of the victims were Black, and Holden was reluctant to crush the counterrevolution. Hundreds of freedmen formed their own militia units. Still Klan terror ruled the day, as well as the sheriff's departments and county courthouses where Klansmen held public office. More people were wounded or killed by Klan barbarism than on the fields of Gettysburg but the federal government refused to send troops to put down the KKK. Finally, Governor Holden sent in militia units made up of white mountaineers and Blacks. Hundreds of Klansmen were arrested, only to be freed by the courts. In 1870, the Democrats won a huge majority of the legislature, which promptly impeached Governor Holden for using the militia against the Klan. He thus became the first state governor ever impeached in U.S. history. During the impeachment proceedings, KKK activity reached its peak. An elderly white man who had given land to his former slaves was whipped and forced to walk home five miles naked in the cold. A white couple who had given an acre of land for a Black school were forced to burn down the building in front of a Klan audience.

The Klan was hardly made up of the stereotyped poor white "red-neck." Rather, the leaders of the Democratic Party, mill owners, leading lawyers and elected officials, and the law enforcement authorities comprised its central core and its leadership. Every newspaper in the state save two supported the wave of terror. With the ascendency to power by the Democrats, there was no longer a need for the Klan and it faded in importance.[11] The state machinery itself could now be used to protect the established order. On a national level, the Republican Rutherford B. Hayes was elected president in 1876 on a promise to the South of the withdrawal of federal troops. Northern industry, in full support of Hayes, began its movement south. Reconstruction was destroyed, wage slavery replaced chattel slavery, prison labor replaced slave labor, jim crow law replaced vigilante law.

By 1900 the poll tax and "grandfather clause" were in effect. To legalize the violent overthrow of Reconstruction, the authorities disenfranchised Black voters. The grandfather clause, a key ingredient in this witches brew of conspiracy, prevented anyone from voting whose grandfather had not, thereby keeping the state safe from democracy. Faced with the terror of the state apparatus, not one of the 18 majority-Black counties in North Carolina defeated the disenfranchisement amendment to the state constitution. In New Hanover County, which embraces Wilmington, with its 50.8 percent Black majority, only two votes were registered against disenfranchisement.[12] The new industrial ruling class, in command of the Democratic Party, was now firmly in control of the state.

Moreover, the Klan's glorification of white supremacy increased its hold on the minds of whites throughout the United States. In 1905, a North Carolinian, Thomas Dixon, published a romantic novel, *The Clansman,* which became a runaway best-seller. Ten years later, D.W. Griffith turned the book into the most popular movie of its time, *The Birth of a Nation.* Heady with the success of the movie, the Klan rose again as a national phenomenon, extending its catalogue of hatreds to include Jews, Catholics, labor unions, immigrant workers and radicals. As Klan membership reached a peak of as many as eight million,[13] President Woodrow Wilson wrote to a church editor that segregation was "distinctly to the advantage of the colored people themselves."[14]

Halfway into the twentieth century, a petition charging the United States with genocide against Black people, bearing the names of dozens of leaders of civil and human rights movements, was submitted to the United Nations in Paris and in New York by William L. Patterson and Paul Robeson. Documenting hundreds of lynchings of Blacks throughout the United States and especially in the South, the roster of mayhem in North Carolina read like that which defeated Reconstruction 50 years earlier. In the late 1940s, for example, Willie Pittman, a taxi driver, was found mutilated near Rocky Mount. His legs and arms had been cut off, his body split open, his head smashed. In Lillington, Charles Smith was killed by two whites who also shot and wounded five other Black people. A jury freed the murderers after 27 minutes of deliberation. Otis Newsom, a 25-year-old war veteran from Wilson and father of three children, was shot and killed for no apparent reason by a white gas station operator. A North Carolina A and T student died an hour after being refused admittance to Duke Hospital in Durham following an auto accident. Another veteran was shot dead near Bailey by a posse of two dozen men who swooped down on him in eight cars. He had been waiting for a bus. Still another Black vet, Paul Dorsey, was assaulted in Waynesville by 4 whites who ordered him off a bus and into their automobile. A lynch mob of 400 persons planned to murder Dorsey, until the police intervened. Dorsey was arrested however while the potential lynchers went free.[15]

The years of these attacks against Black veterans of World War Two were the years of Ben Chavis's early childhood. Twenty years later, a friend of that childhood, Henry Lee Marrow, a veteran of Vietnam, returned home to Oxford. A few months later he too was murdered by local merchants, members of the Klan. Ben Chavis had by now passed through his formative years and decided he must make his ideals a reality rather than simply upholding them. More than merely refrain from evil, he had determined that it was more honorable to fight it.

B EN had started putting things together at a very early age, by sneaking in to listen to adult conversations about one or another incident involving a white man doing a Black man wrong in Oxford. "The term 'Black,'" he now recalls, "was a bad word. I felt I was a colored person. And properly known as a Negro." When the family or friends would talk about the National Association for the Advancement of Colored People (NAACP) they would lower their voices to a whisper because it was known as a subversive organization. Many of them held NAACP membership cards but nobody dared to carry them in their wallets.

Ben was six years old when the U.S. Supreme Court ruled in 1954, in *Brown* v. *Board of Education,* that school segregation was illegal. But the law of the land wasn't applied in North Carolina, let alone Oxford, until after he'd graduated high school. So he was raised on separate libraries, a new brick building for whites, a small wooden shack for Blacks; on sitting in the balcony and paying more for movies; on water fountains painted white or black; on not being allowed to sit at eating counters even when there were empty seats.

Oxford contained one slum area called the Stronghold, where Black people were forced to live in old school buses. Young Ben couldn't understand why some kids had to live in old buses while he and others could go home to their houses. He learned that the Stronghold folks were mainly mill laborers and tobacco farmers. Mornings, he would watch the wagons heading out to the tobacco fields, working the plantations for rich white owners. They were bound to the fields by indebtedness. Year after year they would have to work the fields if they expected credit at the grocery store, if they expected to meet their medical bills. Many of Ben's schoolmates lived in shanties, trapped as "tenants" on these farms. They couldn't come to school until the late Fall, after tobacco season. Then they'd have to leave school in mid-Spring to go to the fields again. Eventually they missed too much school to continue.

Ben went to school his first years at the Colored Orphanage because it was more convenient for Mrs. Chavis, who taught there. Those like Ben who had homes to go to after school called themselves "outside kids," and the orphans "inside kids." Many of the orphans didn't have shoes, and Ben went to school barefooted so as not to accent the difference.

One of his earliest memories is of riding to Henderson, just a few miles from Oxford, with his father and his sister June's husband, Marvin Davenport. Ben was sitting in the back seat, looking out the window, and he could see men with rifles and olive-green uniforms of the National Guard. The Harriet-Henderson Cotton Mill strike was on and little Ben saw his first picket line. Broken glass covered the streets, the result of violence brought on by the company's importing of scab labor to break the strike. Ben can't remember his dad's exact conversation with Marvin, but recalls their sympathy with the workers, both Black and white.

In her autobiography, *C'nelia,* Cornelia Wallace, former wife of Governor George, offers an apologia for segregation as "a way of life": "Once the change began to be forced, the relations between Blacks and whites became strained and uneasy." But growing up in strictly segregated Oxford, for Ben Chavis Black-white relations were "strained and uneasy" as they'd ever been or ever would be. One night during his tenth-grade year at the all-Black Mary Potter High School, Ben left the school softball field to go to the corner store for a soda-pop. The store was attached to a service station and, as Ben was getting his bottle out of the machine, a carload of white men pulled into the station. Before he knew what was happening, the men jumped out of the car and were upon him, beating him bloody.

When the men left, Ben ran back to the softball game to tell his friends what happened. They all grabbed baseball bats, sticks or whatever makeshift weapons they could find and headed for the Three Way Restaurant, the white hoodlums' hangout across the street from the White Orphanage. Ben had maybe 30 friends with him as they approached the Three Way, but of course they were now in hostile territory, outside their own turf. Before they were able to find the men who had beaten him, the police were called in and Ben was brought down to the station with his father, to tell the tale of the beating. The assailants were described and identified, but the police would not let Mr. Chavis swear out an arrest warrant. "One thing I'll never forget," says Ben, now grown. "What hurt me more than the beating was the expression on my father's face when he realized that the police weren't going to do anything. I think my father still believed that the system would bring about some justice. That's why he came to the police station and gave this long statement, real detailed, for about an hour." When Mr. Chavis and Ben returned home, Mrs. Chavis was being treated for a mild heart attack, brought on by alarmist rumors about Ben being badly stabbed during the beating.

From that time on, Ben started to notice things more. Little things, like driving into a gas station with his father, the teenage attendant calling Mr. Chavis "boy," the middle-aged attendant calling his father "uncle."

As his rage built, Ben decided to act on it. The new all-white Thorton Library had just been built. Black kids used to just walk past the library. There wasn't any sign saying "whites only," but it was understood by the Black community that they weren't supposed to go there. Ben's position was, "I ain't seen no sign saying it was all white. County building, I was going in there. So I persuaded some dudes to go with me. I went up and said, 'I want a library card, I'm a student here, I pay taxes for this building, I want a card.' Sort of shocked the little old white lady behind the desk. She tried to put me off but I said I wasn't going nowhere until I got a library card." The woman called the head librarian and he gave Ben a card. Just like that. The next day, more Black students, 15 or so, went in and got library cards. The library was desegregated from then on. A week later Ben and his friends took on the local moviehouse in like fashion. Threatened with arrest when they sat in the white section, they ignored the threat and nothing ever happened. Except that never again was the theatre to have all-white seating arrangements.

One day Ben and Mrs. Chavis were downtown in the Williams Drugstore for a refreshment after completing their shopping. Mrs. Chavis had bought graduation presents for some of the students at the orphanage. Her presents were stacked in a pile while they awaited service, but the waitress, instead of serving them, was scolding a young Black boy for sitting down at the counter. As Ben recalls, "This was about the first time I saw my mother get really angry. She just threw the packages down on the floor and said she wasn't going to buy anything in a racist drugstore like this. I just said, right on."

But the Chavises were hardly militant. Ben knew of course that Martin Luther King, Jr. and Malcolm X existed, because *Ebony* reported their activities. But there were no organizations in Oxford to join. The Congress of Racial Equality (CORE) was active elsewhere, but even so it was not a membership organization. NAACP meetings were held mainly for the purpose of raising money to pay bond for people who had been arrested, or for their lawyers' fees. The Student Non-Violent Coordinating Committee (SNCC) was unheard of until much later, although it had been founded on the Shaw University campus in Raleigh in 1960. The only time Ben ever heard of Dr. King or CORE was when the radio reported some violent outburst against the sit-in movement.

But things changed in 1963 when Ben got his driver's license. He now had some mobility, some contact with things outside of Oxford. He would hear of demonstrations through a grapevine of telephone contacts in other cities, and would drive to them in his parents' car although they were never told his destination. When word came of a demonstration in

Greensboro, a rally in Durham, a picketline in Raleigh, Ben would try to get there.

In 1964, the state legislature passed the Communist speakers' ban, barring from state campuses any member of the Communist Party or anyone who had used the Fifth Amendment to the U.S. Constitution for protection against self-incrimination before head-hunting congressional committees. McCarthyism was frozen into time and color in North Carolina, like a stained-glass window. A decade after speakers' bans were imposed in other states, and years after they had already been lifted elsewhere, the burghers of Raleigh sought to outlaw anything more controversial than opposition to muscular dystrophy. About this time, Dr. Herbert Aptheker, a noted historian on the pre- and post-Civil War period and a Communist Party leader, had gained a reputation as a campus lecturer, a determined challenger to all such proscriptions against his right to speak. Now Aptheker was invited to Chapel Hill, but because of the ban, was forced to address the student body through a bull-horn from across the street from the school. Duke University, a private institution, fell outside the jurisdiction of the speakers' ban, so he was able to speak on that campus. By now Ben was caught up in the controversy. He and a group of friends went to hear the Communist who was defying the ban. Cars came from all over the state, as did the highway patrol and local cops who circled the campus at the bidding of a state government which was clearly at sea with concerns of the intellect. Ben was about to graduate from high school and his intellectual thirst was being quenched.

A decision on college had to be made. Ben's frequent trips to the state capitol city of Raleigh acquainted him with St. Augustine's College, the all-Black Episcopal school of his father and his sisters June and Helen. Upon graduation from high school, he knew, this was where he'd come to study. From the beginning however, things were wrong for Ben at "St. Aug's." A month after school started that Fall of 1965, Ben Chavis, Sr. died. Young Ben's emotional state was fragile. He was angry with himself for not spending more time with his father, always postponing to a later date the talks he wanted with the old man. It had been a long time since his father was scoutmaster to Ben's pack of boy scouts.

Ben's response was to throw himself into his studies. A chemistry major, he made the dean's list in his freshman year and was elected president of his sophomore class for the following autumn. But he felt confined by the self-containment and the strictures of homogeneity of a small, private school. He withdrew from St. Augustine's and headed for Charlotte, the largest city in North Carolina, where his sister June was now living.

It was too late in the semester to enroll at another school. So his first months in Charlotte were for Ben a series of temporary and part-time jobs—laboratory technician in a chemical plant, stockman and salesman in a shoestore, dishwasher and short-order cook in a diner. He knew he was biding his time, gathering his energies and his will, preparing for his entrance to school at the University of North Carolina at Charlotte (UNCC), one of the first Black enrollees and the first in chemistry.

Ben had never in his 18 years sat in class with a white student before UNCC. He knew he would be alone, on the fringe of campus life. Of several thousand students, only eight were Black, four of those part-time, the others freshmen except Ben. They were curiosities. The white students stared at Ben and he would stare at them. But because of his studies at St. Augustine's and reading he had done on his own, he did well in the lab and the classroom. The white students were surprised and began to approach Ben to join their study groups.

If he took the campus by surprise, the campus returned the favor to Ben. The Vietnam War had stirred students across the country as they had never been moved before and, if St. Augustine's was an exception, UNCC was not. Ben's first day on campus set the pattern for his days at the university. Leaflets were being distributed announcing an anti-war meeting that evening and he decided to go. A new organization, the Southern Students Organizing Committee, based in Tennessee, had just sent a representative to Hanoi. Lynn Wells had brought back with her a film of the Democratic Republic of Vietnam and was now making a Southern campus tour. The university would not let her speak without sponsorship of a campus organization and no existing group would sponsor her. So a new group emerged, Students for Action, for the purpose of inviting Lynn Wells to UNCC. Ben Chavis was chosen vice-president of Students for Action. If Fidel Castro had come to Charlotte, a greater commotion would not have erupted. Never had a peace symposium been held in the Queen City. Students from all the area colleges and the television newspeople came to hear this audacious display of sentiment against the Vietnam terror. Also making their presence felt were State Bureau of Investigation dicks and the men of the Charlotte police department's Red Squad, under the direction of Lt. A. T. Europa. This was Ben's introduction to the "intelligence community," the beginning of a not so beautiful relationship. In a matter of days, sleepy Charlotte awoke to find its main university campus radicalized. Students for Action decided to affiliate with the Southern Students Organizing Committee and Ben soon became president of the UNCC chapter.

While he was becoming active at UNCC, Ben made the acquaintance of some students at Charlotte's all-Black Johnson C. Smith University. Among these were T. J. Reddy, one of the South's best young poets, and Charles Parker, a high school honor student, band musician and basketball player. T.J. and C.P. were eventually to follow Ben to UNCC the next year where they would join Students for Action. But this October of 1967, T.J. and three others, including Vicky Minar, a white VISTA worker who would soon become T.J.'s wife, went horseback riding at the Lazy B Stables on the perimeter of Charlotte. Jim Crow was still the rule in North Carolina's private recreation centers and the stable manager refused to let the Black students mount his horses. That night, word of the incident got to Students for Action, which immediately called a meeting to determine what action to take. Picket signs were constructed, magic-markers applied to slogans, and transportation arranged to the stable for the next day. When T.J., Vicky, C.P. and Ben returned to the Lazy B with Students for Action, the stable manager called in the police. But the picket demonstration continued. After the news media arrived, cameras and all, the manager relented and allowed C.P. to ride for the photographers. Students for Action could claim another victory; the Lazy B was desegregated and the whole city saw it on TV or in the *Observer* or the *News*.

On campus Ben pursued public office. While heading up Students for Action, he ran for student union president and won by 14 votes. In his new post he planned all the lecture series and social activities to accompany the intellectual bread of the classroom. For the first time Black entertainers like Little Anthony and the Imperials and the Impressions performed at UNCC. The school's lecture committee invited Barry Goldwater to speak that Spring and it was Ben's responsibility to host the Air Force general and junior senator from Arizona. As president of the student union, Ben felt responsible to his appointed task and introduced Goldwater to his audience, welcomed him to UNCC, hoped his stay would be pleasant. A school reception in honor of the invited speaker followed at the Charlotte Country Club, as segregated then and today as its counterpart in Capetown. Ben Chavis, student union president, was not invited.

In Charlotte's Black community, the state's largest, folks were consciously against the war because of the high draft rate and the subsequent high casualty rate. Charlotte Citizens for Peace (CCP) was organized and marched on the local draft board. Through the CCP, Ben met Dr. James Earl Grant, a chemistry professor out of Penn State University, now a VISTA volunteer and draft counselor for the American Friends

Service Committee in Charlotte. Jim Grant convinced Ben of the need to counsel Black teenagers on how to avoid the draft. Whites knew how to avoid the draft but Blacks did not. They lacked information, didn't know they could challenge the draft boards, were unaware of the possibility of obtaining conscientious-objector status.

Meantime, Gene McCarthy and Bobby Kennedy were running for President as peace candidates that Winter and Spring of 1967–68, trying to win the Democratic nomination from Hubert Humphrey, vice-president and circuit rider in defense of the discredited war policies of President Lyndon Johnson. With characteristic abandon, Ben threw himself into the Democratic Party in Charlotte. But whereas most Young Democrats were stumping for McCarthy, Ben supported Bobby. "Most white people in Charlotte hated the Kennedys," Ben now recalls. "I remember when President Kennedy was killed, whites in Oxford and Raleigh actually held parties to celebrate his death. In retrospect I know better but at the time I figured that if the racists harbored such hostility for Jack and Bobby, they must be doing something right."

There was of course to be more to celebrate in the klaverns of the Klan that Spring, as assassins ended the lives of Rev. Martin Luther King, Jr. and Bobby Kennedy. Students for Action, under Ben's leadership, held memorial services for Dr. King. Ben addressed the service and cried throughout his remarks, but with the passing of the non-violent apostle there were to be no more tears shed by Ben Chavis. Not for a long while. As Black communities rose up in Washington, D.C. and Chicago and Detroit and a dozen other cities, so they rose in Wilmington, North Carolina. The National Guard was sent in and dropped tear gas on all the housing projects in the port city. Ben and some Students for Action headed for Wilmington but were denied entrance to the city by a highway patrol blockade. Every outlet of expression from electoral campaigning to public demonstrations were thus closed to Ben and his friends during that eventful spring of their political coming of age.

During Ben's junior year, more Black students, perhaps 25, entered UNCC. When they all joined Students for Action, Ben organized a Black caucus within the organization. And while Students for Action and its Black caucus developed on campus by day, Ben and Jim Grant moved at night to organize the Black Cultural Association (BCA) in Charlotte. They found a house at the corner of Oaklawn Street and Statesville Avenue, and the Black Cultural Association moved in. The house was painted black, and a mural created on the walls with portraits of Malcolm X, Frederick Douglass and W.E.B. Du Bois.

The police could not abide the appearance of the Black House, and a round-the-clock stakeout was imposed. The Black Cultural Association organized rent strikes, boycotts of price-gouging white merchants in the community, pickets of the housing authority, demonstrations at the school board for Black studies programs. What started with about 20 young Black activists grew in the summer months into a movement that attracted up to 3,000 citizens to its public meetings. The attraction of the Black community to the Black Cultural Association did not go unnoticed by the city and state police. As public support grew for the association, so did the dossiers on Ben Chavis and Jim Grant. Jim was relieved of his VISTA job but retained by the American Friends Service Committee.

The appearance of Ben's and Jim's activist leadership on the campuses and Black communities of Charlotte did not sit easily with the white men who controlled that center of the Southern textile industry, and the second city of the nation's trucking industry. For the men who ran Duke Power and the Wachovia Bank, the license-plate logo "First in Freedom" was demonstration enough of the good intentions of the New Southern ruling class. Chavis and Grant had other notions. They believed, with Archibald Macleish, who wrote in 1949, that, "Revolution, which was once a word spoken with pride by every American who had the right to claim it, has become a word spoken with timidity and doubt and even loathing. And freedom which, in the old days, was something you used has now become something you save—something you put away and protect like your other possessions—like a deed or a bond in a bank. The true test of freedom is in its use. It has no other test."

In those days, the Charlotte police department was still nearly all-white, and any movement in the Black community smacked of outright challenge to their notion of "lawnorder," Richard Nixon's presidential campaign credo which was gaining currency in the suburbs like beer at a fraternity party. One night the police arrested two Black Cultural Association members, took them downtown, placed pistols at their temples and demanded they confess to a bombing if they didn't want their brains drying on the wall the next morning. When the BCA was finally able to release the two men, Ben organized a press conference to let them tell their story to the city. Even the press was critical of the police action, which did little to further endear the BCA to Charlotte's finest.

That summer, a Black Vietnam veteran named Theodore Alfred Hood joined the BCA. Al Hood was the first BCA member that didn't live in the Greenville area of Charlotte. Because he was from Griertown, another Black community about 10 miles from Greenville, Hood was unknown to the BCA leaders. They were to discover later that he had a criminal record which included convictions for auto theft, assault with a deadly weapon with intent to kill, carrying a concealed weapon and assault on a police officer, not precisely qualifications for admission to the Society of Friends. But he was Black, seemingly dedicated to building the BCA and was given permission to start a Griertown chapter. Among Hood's proteges was Walter David Washington, who had recently been discharged from the Marine Corps for being a dangerous schizophrenic. Washington's career after the service was more checkered than a gingham blouse: charged with larceny, damage to property, assault, assault with a deadly weapon, and breaking and entering. Their admission to the BCA coincided with the appearance of an apparent schism in the group.

While Ben worked in the association as an extracurricular activity, he pursued his degree at UNCC. Through the Students for Action, he arranged an invitation to Stokely Carmichael, chairman of the Student Non-Violent Coordinating Committee. The Atlanta-based SNCC was then merging with the neophyte Black Panther Party of Oakland, California. Like thousands of Black students on campuses throughout the country, Ben was taken with Stokely Carmichael and his rhetoric of revolutionary nationalism. SNCC-BPP was a leading influence in developing Black student unions at many universities, and with Carmichael's appearance at UNCC, the Black caucus of Students for Action decided to become the Black Student Union, with Ben as its president. There being no Black faculty members at the university, the BSU asked Dr. Jim Grant to become its "faculty advisor."

There were now some 50 Black students at UNCC and they were determined to have a Black studies program as part of the academic curriculum. The university refused to acknowledge the demand and the BSU turned to demonstrations, marching on the administration building to register its protests. As the demonstrators approached the building, one of the Black service workers inside came out to tell the BSU that the building was evacuated, that police with billies were waiting for them to come inside. Accompanying the BSU were students from Johnson C. Smith and Livingston College, who looked to Ben and his comrades for leadership. Avoiding the police trap, they gathered outside the building to listen to T.J. Reddy read his poetry. Eventually the administration agreed to discuss the BSU demands, but the first negotiating session was held up for an hour and a half when the administration refused to allow Jim Grant in on the discussion. But that refusal, it was pointed out, would result in the breakdown of the negotiations and consequently renewed demonstrations with their implied potential for violent police retaliation. The university retreated, agreed to establish a Black studies program and a compensatory recruitment program for more Black students. Ben was beginning to learn something of the power of the state apparatus, and of the counterveiling power of mass action.

His activities at UNCC were having a felt effect in surrounding counties. At Belmont Abbey College outside of Gastonia, Black students began to organize an Afro-American Culture Association. Belmont is a typical Piedmont mill town, barren of culture or recreation, where Klansmen got their entertainment and exercise by chasing Black children coming from school. Belmont Abbey had all of 10 Black men students, to complement the 50 Black women students at Sacred Heart College across the street. Together they seized the chemistry building and demanded an end to racism in the schools and the establishment of Black history courses. They held the building for a day with the support of some sympathetic white students from the North. When the local Klan sent to Gastonia for reinforcements and for heavy artillery to make a military assault on the building, the students called Charlotte for help from the Black Panther Organization. Ben and Jim organized community support for the Belmont-Abbey students.

Ben continued to feel a special affinity for the Black community at large and worked to eliminate the artificial separation of town and gown for Blacks. He and Jim built reputations for themselves as community organizers, sort of an Avon calling for Black radicalism.

The Panther organization in Charlotte had been formed partly in response to Carmichael's visit, and partly due to the disintegration of the Black Cultural Association. The BCA's demise came after the city police stepped up their harassment of the group. The Black House remained under constant surveillance, thus intimidating the neighbors, and a narcotics trade began to develop inside the BCA. That the dope turned up about the same time as Al Hood and David Washington, who were known as dealers for the local syndicate, may well have been more than coincidental. In any case this led to further busts, then pacification and ultimately dissolution of the BCA. The more politically minded BCA members, Ben among them but not Jim Grant, moved to form the Panther organization. They insisted on calling themselves the Black Panther Organization, so as to distinguish it as independent of the Black Panther Party of Huey Newton and Stokely Carmichael. The Charlotte group subscribed to the "10-point program" of the BPP and distributed the weekly Panther newspaper published in Oakland, California, but remained organizationally independent. But as the "revolutionary nationalists" of the BCA became Panthers, the "cultural nationalists" under Al Hood set up a rival organization called US, taking its name from the California-based organization led by Ron Karenga, with headquarters in Los Angeles. (According to the testimony of police agent Louis Tackwood—*The Glass House Tapes,* Avon, New York, 1973— and secret FBI memos—New York *Post,* January 5, 1976—the FBI and the Criminal Conspiracy Section of the Los Angeles Police Department helped set up US, whose gunmen killed four Panthers in Los Angeles and San Diego alone.)

Complementing the Black Panther Organization in Charlotte was the Black Political Organization, an electoral expression of the aspirations of Black townspeople. The Reverend George Leak was running for mayor, the first time a Black person had run for public office in Charlotte in this century.[16] Although the city's population is almost one-third Black, the Board of Elections reported that whites outnumbered Blacks five to one at the polls. The BPO, announcing a platform calling for strict enforcement of the housing code and resident control of public housing, projected a slate of candidates, Leak for mayor and seven city council aspirants. Ben was selected to be one of the latter, as were three Black women. Racism hung over Charlotte like a net. Changing white attitudes seemed as easy as changing the ocean. Rev. Leak came under serious attack. Threats were telephoned to his home and to those of his running mates. Things, they were told, would get worse before they got worse. The Black community reacted. Their candidates needed protection. The "more respectable folks" rented a U-Haul van and summoned the Panthers to station themselves in the van outside Rev. Leak's home. Not much later, the Black Panther Organization was patrolling all the streets of the community.

THE old placebo that anyone can grow up to be president has unfortunately been proven several times. But Tarheel politics make a fetish of the proposition.

Joseph Branch, for example, has been a justice on the North Carolina Supreme Court since 1966. Before that he was campaign manager and then general counsel to Governor Dan K. Moore. Governor Moore also sits now on the Supreme Court. Two elections before, Judge Branch worked as general counsel to Governor Luther Hodges. In the 1960 gubernatorial election, Judge Branch campaigned for attorney I. Beverly Lake against Terry Sanford. Lake's campaign was managed by Robert Morgan, now junior U.S. senator. Morgan, like Branch, was a student of Lake at Wake Forest College. Lake was defeated by Sanford but ran again in 1964 against Moore. When Moore won and became governor, he appointed Lake to the Supreme Court, together with Branch. Moore's successor, Governor Bob Scott, whose father was also governor and senator, appointed Moore to the Supreme Court.

This Good-Old-Boy Network—Branch, Moore, Hodges, Lake, Sanford, Morgan and Scott—is entirely Democrat. Except for Lake and Morgan, all were considered "middle-of-the-road," according to Branch. Judge Lake, Branch says, "holds that the middle of the road is the best place to get run over."[17] Actually, all governors and major North Carolina politicians in this century—until 1972—have been Democrats. The pattern was set in 1898 when the Democrats and their paramilitary wing, the Redshirts, overthrew the Republicans by force and violence because of Reconstruction. Not until 1972, during the Nixon sweep of George McGovern, was another Republican elected governor. Dan K. Moore credits Luther Hodges for the rise of modern Republicanism. Although a staunch Democrat, Governor Hodges led the drive to bring Northern industry to the state and with it came Republican corporation executives.

Hodges, the son of a tenant farmer, went to work for Marshall Field, rose to become a vice-president, ran the company's textile division, and after the second world war headed up the Marshall Plan in Germany. In 1952 he was elected lieutenant governor and became governor upon the death in office of William Umstead. After being elected again in 1956 and serving a full term—North Carolina law limited the governorship to one four-year term—Hodges was named secretary of commerce in President Kennedy's cabinet. Next to the modern industrialization of North Carolina, the Hodges years in the statehouse were most notable for the massive resistence to U.S. Supreme Court school desegregation rulings. Hodges was considered a moderate—comedian Dick Gregory once described the Southern moderate as one who lynches from a low tree— by virtue of comparison with the blatant racist rhetoric of his assistant attorney general, I. Beverly Lake, who carried the state's legal burdens in the courts. Lake was accompanied in this task on the legislative level by his protege, then state Senator Robert Morgan.

With Hodges' term coming to an end in 1960, Lake started campaigning early for the governor's mansion. Under the management of Morgan, the "conservative" appeal left nothing to the imagination. Lake's campaign literature quoted from his argument before the U.S. Supreme Court: "Race consciousness is not race hatred. It is not intolerance. It is a deeply ingrained awareness of a birthright held in trust for posterity." He declared "unthinkable" North Carolina's "surrender to the NAACP." Over statewide television he argued that the NAACP's "ultimate objective is the blending of the white and Negro races into a mixed-blooded whole." Before a Lion's Club meeting in Ashboro he warned, "The mixture of our two great races in the classroom and then in the home is not inevitable and is not to be tolerated."[18]

Lake was defeated by Terry Sanford in that race, but he tried again in 1964. The Democratic primary, which had always determined the general election winner, was crowded with five candidates. Lake came in third this time, but a runoff was necessary to decide between the frontrunners, the "moderate" Richardson Preyer and the "conservative" Dan K. Moore. Moore, a Champion Paper Company executive with a personality as bland as dentist-chair music, was the beneficiary of Lake's largesse. Full-page ads in the state's major dailies carried the text of a Lake television speech endorsing Moore: "Whom do you see standing there ready to advise and direct [Preyer's] administration? . . . Kelly Alexander, head of the NAACP in North Carolina, all of those block voters who are captive pawns in the hands of Bobby Kennedy and Martin Luther King; last and least there is that small but noisy clique of professional liberals at Chapel Hill who are a *red* and festering sore upon the body of a great university."[19] (Emphasis added. The Communist speakers' ban was then in effect and was a major campaign issue of the Lake group.) Candidate Moore seconded supporter Lake's remarks: "My opponent . . . owes his lead and owes a large part of his entire vote to the block Negro vote in North Carolina." (Lake was appointed to the state supreme court by Moore in 1965 and remains on the bench today. His views have not mellowed with time. In 1969 he denied his papers to East Carolina University because, "I do not care to have anything belonging to me in the custody of an institution that finds it necessary to apologize for displaying the Confederate flag and singing Dixie." *The News and Observer,* April 10, 1969.)

The Black population in the state was only 20 percent of the whole, and the federal voting rights bill was not yet in effect at that time. No matter, race *is* politics in North Carolina. It always has been. For decades, the white-supremacy campaigns waged by the Democratic Party for the legislature and the governorship were, of course, successful. Back in 1898, accompanied by violent terrorism of the Redshirts and the Klan, the campaign had been fought on a pledge to remove Black people from politics. In 1900, Charles Brantley Aycock was elected governor. The legislature disenfranchised Blacks on the grounds of illiteracy and instituted the grandfather clause to accommodate illiterate whites.[20] Aycock, a "moderate" of his time, argued for "colored education." Writing in 1904, he said, "When the [suffrage] fight had been won, I felt that the time had come when the negro [sic] should be taught to realize that while he would not be permitted to govern the state, his rights should be held more sacred by reason of his weakness."[21]

The march of time did nothing to moderate race-baiting as an inherent part of those quadrennial rites of passage known as elections. It drove from politics Frank Porter Graham, North Carolina's most noted progressive spokeman of this century. Graham was a history professor at Chapel Hill in 1930 when he was named president of the university. Says former Governor Terry Sanford, now president of Duke University in Durham: "Frank Graham's spirit moved this state. He and UNC explain why North Carolina has a reputation for progressivism."

An early supporter of the Spanish Republic and the Committee for the Protection of the Foreign Born, Graham also became a leader of the Southern Conference on Human Rights which led the struggle for the rights of sharecroppers, tenant farmers and migrant laborers. In the days when the words "labor organizer" and "bolshevik" were synonymous, he argued for abolition of the twelve-hour day and for workmen's compensation.

For all that, Frank Graham was hardly a radical. But in the valley of blind reaction, the one-eyed liberal is considered dangerous. Dr. Graham maintained the university as an all-white institution because it was "the law" and, as he would say upon retirement, "We obeyed the law."[22] In 1949, he was appointed to fill a U.S. Senate seat left vacant by the death of J. Melville Broughton. The next year, Graham had to face the voters of North Carolina for the first time in his life. He survived the primary and came within a percent of the needed majority. But one month later he lost the run-off by 18,000 votes. Jonathan Daniels, editor of *The News and Observer* and a personal friend of Graham, described the opposition campaign strategy: "In the first primary we hit him with the Communists and the people wouldn't take it. Now, we're gonna hit him with the n----r."[23] Red-baiting and race-baiting proved to be the campaign's equivalent of assault and battery.

Two days before the elections, when newspaper subscribers unrolled their papers they found handbills headlined, "WHITE PEOPLE WAKE UP!" The flyers asked if voters wanted "Negroes using your toilet facilities?" "Negroes working beside you?" the seemingly compulsory "Negroes going to white schools and white children going to Negro schools?" etc. The leaflets asked for votes for Willis Smith, claiming "He will uphold the traditions of the South." (Smith was a former president of the American Bar Association.) Photographs were passed out at filling stations where white farmers gathered to talk; they pictured Black GIs dancing with white women in British nightclubs. Hate calls and threats were phoned into election officials favorable to Graham. The shift of votes away from Graham between the primary and the run-off was most crucial among the "well-educated, well-to-do middle class," according to one study. Especially damaging "was the insistent drumming of the fear that white and Negro children might have to attend the same schools." Samuel Lubell, who conducted the study, wrote, "Frank Graham was defeated not by a foul-mouthed Theodore Bilbo [a U.S. senator from Mississippi, remembered only for his cretinous bigotry. Author] but by a nationally honored lawyer, who was chairman of the board of trustees of Duke University. It was not only the bigots who turned against 'Dr. Frank' but many 'progressive' North Carolinians."[24]

The progressive legacy of Frank Graham has since been used as public relations foam on the mug of beery conservatism that is North Carolina politics. For a time, Governor Terry Sanford perpetuated the state's New South image outside of North Carolina. Ironically, it was just this concern with matters outside the state that brought an end to Sanford's political career. Now president of Duke University, he was roundly defeated by Tarheel Democrats in the 1972 presidential primary. Emerging as the people's choice was George Wallace. Seventy-five percent of the state's voters are Democrat, yet Wallace, running as an independent, placed second in the 1968 presidential election, outdistanced by Richard Nixon but beating out the Democrat Hubert Humphrey.

The mood of the electorate in that 1968 vote was consistent as it returned Sam J. Ervin, Jr. to the U.S. Senate for a third term. Ervin, the state's most popular politician at the time,[25] epitomized the New Southern identity of North Carolina in the minds of his fellow countrymen during the Nixon years in the White House. Adjudicator of Watergate evils, a walking Bartlett's of familiar quotations from Bard and Bible, Ervin, whose appearance has been likened to a windbag Senator Claghorn, was made into something of a folk hero in the manner that is accomplished in these contemporary times: A record of Senator Sam proverbs was produced, campus speaking tours arranged, Sam Ervin T-shirts manufactured.

A true representative of the established order in his home state, Ervin's libertarian image belied his nineteenth century politics. "Like most southerners," wrote his unofficial biographer, "Ervin believed in the separate-but-equal doctrine set forth in the year of his birth. . . . He was convinced that segregation was the natural result of people freely associating with members of their own race."[26] Ervin first entered the Senate in 1954 just weeks after the Supreme Court ruling to desegregate the schools. While his fellow Democrats Luther Hodges and I. Beverly Lake did battle on the home front, Ervin joined the fray in Washington. Together with Richard Russell of Georgia and John Stennis of Mississippi, Ervin wrote the "Southern Manifesto" in 1956, a blood oath encouraging states to resist the law of the land. Syndicated columnist Tom Wicker, himself a North Carolinian, chides the man who came to be known as the Senate's foremost defender of the Constitution: "He did not find anything in the Constitution about a Black man's right to eat a toasted-cheese sandwich or a Moon Pie at a dime-store lunch counter, and he did not even see any language that expanded to fit the case."[27]

Ervin employed all his country-lawyer folksiness in the Senate in behalf of his favorite causes: against the 1964 Civil Rights Act, the 1965 Voting Rights Act, the 1966 Mine Safety Act. He led the filibuster against the repeal of the law preventing closed union shops and became a favorite speaker of the National Association of Manufacturers. Ervin received a perfect rating of 100 from the American Security Council, a collection of retired Pentagon brass and munitions industry executives, for his votes favoring the space shuttle, military aid to the Greek junta, the Trident submarine, B-1 supersonic bomber and C-5A transport plane, and continuation of the draft. Ervin in turn called the Joint Chiefs of Staff a group of "fine Christian gentlemen" and declared his unwavering support of the Vietnam War by explaining, "If we pull out, Old Glory will be turned into a white flag."

Welfare for the Pentagon was scarcely matched by a concern for the powerless. Ervin opposed the Equal Rights Amendment for women, day care for children, highway funds for mass transit, a Fair Employment Practices Commission for North Carolina, federal relief for nutrition and health care in his own home state, legal services for the poor, unemployment compensation for migrant workers, medicare for the sick, and the Occupational Health and Safety Act to protect 55 million production workers on the job. In 1971, Ervin co-sponsored legislation to prohibit food stamps to families engaged in labor strikes.[28]

Senator Sam also led the opposition in the Senate in defeating ratification of the United Nations Convention against genocide. An outgrowth of the Nazi slaughter of European Jews, the convention has been subscribed to by 78 countries over the last quarter-century. North Carolina's senior senator helped assure that at least while he was in office, the United States would not officially stand against genocide.[29]

In his classic study, *Southern Politics,* V.O. Key found that those North Carolina counties that had had the fewest slaves came out of the Civil War with the strongest Republican leanings. Most of these were located in the Blue Ridge, "the great spine of Republicanism which runs down the back of the South." When Key made his findings in 1944, 81 percent of the state's Republican votes came from those western counties. Three decades later, the pattern hasn't changed much. The first Republican governor in this century, James Holshouser, who served from 1972 to 1976, comes from the mountain town of Boone.

Not that the party label makes a difference. James E. Broyhill, for more than 20 years Republican national committeeman and a member of the national Republican finance committee, was, not incidentally, owner of Broyhill Furniture, one of the nation's giant wood furniture manufacturers. North Carolina is the leading furniture producer in the United States and Broyhill's Lenoir is one of the state's main manufacturing centers. A former director of the National Association of Manufacturers, and a personal friend of such Republican leaders as Herbert Hoover, Robert Taft, Dwight Eisenhower and Richard Nixon, Broyhill was, to use Nixonian lingo, the Big Enchilada of North Carolina Republicanism.[30] One of Broyhill's son's, James T., has been a Republican congressman since 1962. A son-in-law and vice-president of Broyhill Furniture, William Stevens, was the GOP opponent in the 1974 U.S. Senate race against Robert Morgan.

Republican U.S. Senator Jesse Helms, who hails from the eastern part of the state, was a Democrat until 1970. For years the editorial voice of Raleigh's ABC television affiliate, Helms describes himself as "the sorriest politician that ever came down the pike." But in 1972 he benefited from the Nixon sweep and claims to have received more than 90 percent of the George Wallace vote as well. Indeed, gas stations and diners throughout rural North Carolina still feature Wallace wall posters and "Give 'em Helms, Jesse" bumper stickers alongside one another.

The only way Helms could have won, in fact, was to obtain even more Democratic votes than Republican, which led him to conclude that his and the country's future lay in a realignment of parties and the creation of a third, ultra-right party. In February 1974 he was chosen chairman of the Committee on Conservative Alternatives to study the possibilities of building such a party.[31] A collection of reactionary politicians who feel that the Democrats and Republicans are moving too fast and too far to the left, the committee believes that what America needs more than a good five-cents cigar is an outspokenly right-wing political center. In 1976, when Ronald Reagan declared himself for the presidency, Helms gave up his third-party notions for the time being to chair Reagan's primary campaign in North Carolina. That primary gave Reagan his first victory over Gerald Ford and paved the way for him to the Republican convention. (Such were the politics of the 1976 primaries that Henry Jackson, surely the Democratic candidate furthest to the right, save George Wallace, was forced to pull out of North Carolina two weeks before the election when his campaign manager and half the campaign staff dropped Jackson for stating opposition to Section 14b of the Taft-Hartley Act, which allows states to enact "right-to-work" laws. The Greensboro *Daily News* pointed out to Jackson that in North Carolina Section 14b "is cherished rather like one of the crown jewels.")

Helms has been likened to South Carolina's Strom Thurmond, who led a Dixiecrat third-party effort in 1948 and eventually left the Democrats for the Republicans. Like Thurmond, Helms is full of country bromides: "Prayer is, after all, a Constitutional right and a moral duty"; "We must reverse the trend that says that women must be liberated from the dignity of motherhood and from the femininity of her natural development," etc.[32]

During the Watergate scandal, and the movement to impeach Richard Nixon, Helms rose to the defense of his president. Claiming that the disgraced Nixon was falling victim to "the major media," Helms said the press "serves the same function in today's naked power struggle as the manipulated mobs of the past brought pressure for the removal of kings."[33] Many are the sows' ears made silken by the prose of Jesse Helms. His concern for and praise of kings made for a natural bond with the Czar-gazing exiled writer Alexander Solzhenitsyn, whom Helms befriended and sponsored in the Senate for honorary U.S. citizenship. In 1974, Helms' concern for freedom throughout the world brought him to Taiwan to address the annual Freedom Day Rally at the invitation of the late Generalissimo Chiang Kai-shek. A like speaking engagement was fulfilled in Santiago de Chile at the bidding of General Pinochet.

That the Democrat Senator Robert Morgan—who rose to power as a segregationist state legislator and as the attorney general who led the persecution of the Wilmington 10—and the Republican Senator Helms are simultaneously visited upon the people of North Carolina capsulizes the myth of this state as in the van of a progressive New South. The General Assembly building in Raleigh may be the only thing modern about Tarheel politics. In the legislature there are no roll calls in committees, no fiscal control of government, no ethics legislation, no conflict-of-interest legislation. Ralph Nader's Citizen's Conference on State Legislatures rated North Carolina's 47th in the country on the basis of functioning, accountability, representation and handling of information.

In 1971 the average state legislature spent two dollars per constituent; North Carolina's spent twelve cents, perhaps the most obvious indication of its domination by what have come to be known euphemistically as special interests. Raleigh's *News and Observer* editor Claude Sitton spells out those interests: "The banks, power companies, real estate, trucking, developers, textile interests; but mainly the banks."[34] The General Assembly meets only two months of the year and North Carolina is the only state in the union in which the governor has no power of vèto. Clearly the politicians are only in the basement of the power structure.

That race is still *the* political issue, no matter how masqueraded, speaks volumes about the nature of that structure. In 1974, Alabama had 15 Black representatives in its state legislature, 13 in the House and 2 in the Senate. That year, South Carolina voters elected 9 Black state legislators; in Georgia, the number of seats held by Black representatives went from 16 to 22. North Carolina had 3 out of a total 170 members of the General Assembly.

Until the early 1960s, North Carolina led the South in voter registration. By 1970, after a decade of the biggest civil-rights upsurge in history, the state was at the bottom of the ladder in Black registration. The state's ruling class preferred to manipulate voting procedures rather than deny Black registration outright, as occurred in much of the Deep South during those years. Between 1955 and 1969, most counties and cities switched from the ward system of electoral representation to the council-manager form, whereby representatives are elected at-large. There being no large Black majority in any single county, white supremacy was assured. Meanwhile, the tidy image of moderation was preserved. Again, this splendid method of excluding Black representation was instituted in the name of reform. Blacks became convinced that the only way to win any election was by "bullet" voting; that is, casting the ballot for a single candidate in a large field where more than one office is open, thereby increasing the worth of the "single-shot" vote. The powers that be responded by outlawing "single-shot" votes. Other laws were passed to force run-offs between the two highest vote-getters in elections where no one received a majority. Hence, a Black candidate could receive more votes than any of his eight white opponents, but if he did not receive 50 percent plus, he faced a run-off against a single white candidate, and near-certain defeat. The at-large elections and anti-"bullet" laws help explain why in 1972 only 3 of 468 county commissioners were Black; and only 12 of more than 600 school-board members were Black.[35]

One

E VEN as he directed the Black Student Union, helped the Panthers and ran for Charlotte City Council, Ben, together with Jim Grant, became the organizers for Western North Carolina for the late Dr. King's Southern Christian Leadership Conference (SCLC). Jim had already set up shop in Shelby at the foot of the mountains in the West. A young Shelby Black man, Robert Roseboro, had been sent to death row over the killing of a white woman. Jim organized a march in that conservative mill town demanding clemency for Roseboro and jobs for Blacks in downtown Shelby. More than 500 people participated in the march and courthouse rally, the first in the history of the town.

A year earlier, Marie Hill, a 15-year-old Black junior high school student and tobacco hand, was arrested and charged with the murder of a white grocer in Rocky Mount, in eastern Carolina. She was picked up in South Carolina while on a family visit. Coerced into signing a confession without benefit of legal counsel, she would later repudiate the confession. After a hasty extradition, and without being informed of her right to remain silent, she waived any preliminary hearing. Thus it took less than a week for the authorities to lay the basis for her certain prosecution and conviction, before they allowed her to speak with her parents or confer with a lawyer. A few weeks later, Marie Hill was tried for murder, the state's case being only her forced confession, convicted and sentenced to die in the gas chamber.

Now, after the Shelby demonstrations for Robert Roseboro, Jim and Ben, together with SCLC statewide coordinator Golden Frinks, developed plans for a "Mountaintop to the Valley" march to save Marie Hill. Starting in Thomas Wolfe's Asheville in the heart of the Great Smokies, they set off for the state capitol in Raleigh, appealing for help along the way. The march took 25 days and perhaps 250 people went the entire distance. But in each village they would pick up 10 here, 20 there, until they arrived at the next town. Their appeal was to those whom Paul Robeson used to sing of as "the etceteras and the and-so-forths that do the work." Thousands participated in the hundred or so towns along the 300-mile route. The marchers arrived in Charlotte at the peak of the city election campaign. City Council candidate Chavis told the city that they would sit in the main intersection unless food was provided for the marchers. The city fathers asked Johnson C. Smith University to feed the good people; in their haste to accommodate the demonstrators and get them on their way again, rubber mattresses were provided for their comfort. (The only woman in the country on death row at the time,

39

Marie Hill remained in isolation at Womens' Prison in Raleigh for nearly three years, until May 1972. Her sentence was reduced to life imprisonment after the U.S. Supreme Court ruled against arbitrary methods of applying the death penalty. Since being imprisoned, she contracted gangrene in her foot and a toe was amputated. She also developed ulcers. Still imprisoned, Marie Hill became 25 in 1977.)

The only trade union in Charlotte to support the Black Political Organization candidates was the American Federation of State, County and Municipal Employees (AFSCME) local. Jim Pierce, then regional director for AFSCME, put Ben and Jim Grant on staff as the union launched a drive to organize the city's sanitation workers. Ben had to share his time with UNCC where he was now in his senior year. Still SCLC coordinator for western North Carolina, Ben was attracted to the idea of working for AFSCME, in part because his ideological mentor, Dr. King, had given his life in the effort to organize sanitation workers in Memphis. In the few months he and Jim worked for the union, AFSCME organized a strike. Their responsibility was to put together the picket lines and demonstrations, to march the workers downtown to city hall and win a contract that included dues checkoff. The garbage strike proved to be the first successful one in the history of Charlotte. That elite did not take kindly to the kind of organizing being carried out by Messrs. Chavis and Grant.

Ben's first arrest came that year on trespass charges. He and a friend, Jerome Johnson, were invited by students at Charlotte's Second Ward High School to come speak on racism in the school system. In 1969, the federal district court ruled that Mecklenburg County's schools were segregated and ordered busing to desegregate the schools. This was the first busing order by the courts in the country and the racist outroar that followed throughout North Carolina foreshadowed later events from Pontiac, Michigan, to Boston, Massachussetts. The Charlotte school board decided to close down Second Ward, the most prestigious and only inner-city Black high school in town. The students wanted to save the school, so they called in Ben and Jerome Johnson. As Ben started to address the assembled students, city police rushed the stage and carried him off. They threw him into the back of a black-and-white and began to drive off, but the students surrounded the car and refused to let it move. Out of spite, Jerome was arrested by the frustrated police. After some negotiations, the police finally got Ben and Jerome to the jail and into a cell. Curiously, an hour later, Al Hood was put into the same cell. He said that he too was busted for trying to speak at Second Ward, after Ben and Jerome were taken away.

Shortly after Ben's release—the charges were eventually thrown out of court—Treasury Department special agent Stanley Noel of the Alcohol, Tobacco and Firearms Bureau burst into Ben's apartment, armed with a shotgun, on the pretext of "looking for suspects." In the next few months, Ben would be arrested twice more for "trespass," and his home and SCLC office busted into a few more times. Presumably, his Treasury agent nemesis was hard at work. Neither a graduate of charm school nor of law school—the U.S. Constitution protects the right of persons to be "secure in their persons, houses, papers and effects against unreasonable search and seizure"—Stanley Noel had not even been paying attention to local police and FBI directives urging the community not to open its doors to strangers. Perhaps the G-man was aware that his shotgun would have a dampening effect on the free flow of ideas.

It was time for Ben to leave Charlotte.

Hacking his way through a bush of decision-making about his future, Ben finally arrived back home in Oxford. His father had been dead for almost five years, during most of which time he had been away from his mother and the family home. He was uncertain of what might come. Oxford was just a small tobacco town, exuding all the Babbitry of a Shriners' convention. There was a sense for Ben, after the pace of 200,000-strong metropolitan Charlotte, of stepping back into a time capsule, and of being rapidly reduced, Alice-like, tumbling down into this teeny wonderland.

First things coming, as they do, first, Ben had to find a job. His family, traditionally teachers, encouraged him to apply to Mary Potter High School as a teacher. The school board had already announced that this, 1970, was to be Mary Potter's last year as the town's all-Black high school, that next year it would become a desegregated junior high.

No more full-time teaching slots were available but Ben was able to hook on as a substitute. Every time a teacher would call in sick, Ben would fill in. Whatever was needed, Ben would teach—English, journalism, physics, chemistry, even home economics one time. In the course of these itinerant wanderings from class to class, he was able to meet most of the student body. Some of the students already knew of Ben through the newspapers, or from his sister Francine, who graduated the previous year as class valedictorian.

If there is no such thing as a natural-born organizer, there are at least those who catch a terminal dose of the bug and Ben was one such. Organizing coursed through his veins, set his heart to pumping, shot through his body as sure as adrenalin. The kids at Mary Potter, in fact the entire Black population in Oxford, had no recreational facilities. The county had a swimming pool, but only for whites. Not a single public basketball court was available for Blacks. So the students got together with Ben Chavis, at age 21 their adult advisor, to form the Granville County Steering Committee for Black Progress. The Steering Committee met with the city council to demand playgrounds, courts, swimming pools, but the council responded with a hand as heavy as a bucket of wet sand. Black Oxfordians could look forward to another very long, hot summer.

They got an early start that year. On May 11, Jimmy Chavis, Ben's cousin, and Henry Marrow, a former classmate who had just come back from Vietnam, and some other young men were standing in front of Robert Teel's business enterprise. Teel was the local Klan leader, a fact well known throughout Granville County. A week earlier, Teel had beaten up a Black teacher in Oxford who had accused Teel of cheating him out of some gasoline. The teacher had sworn out a warrant against Teel but the police refused to serve it. Now, this Tuesday afternoon, one of the youngsters whistled at Teel's wife. The Klan leader ran into his store, came back out with his son and stepson, armed with shotguns, and started firing into the crowd of 20 Black youths. The young men ran, but pellets hit Henry Marrow and Jimmy Chavis. Jimmy was able to crawl into a nearby patch of grass and hide but Henry wasn't so lucky. He fell to the ground, bleeding from the back and the knee. One of the Teel men got an axe handle and beat in Henry Marrow's head. Then Robert Teel ordered his son Larry to shoot Henry dead. Larry placed his Owen under-410-gauge shotgun with a .22 on top against the dying man's temple and blew his head off.

The kids who had witnessed the shooting rushed over to the Soul Kitchen, Ben's family-owned Ridley Drive-in, with its name and decor changed to attract young people. Ben was working the Soul Kitchen when the youngsters came in to tell their story. He listened a moment, and decided to go directly to the Teels to investigate. Finding the grocery open as usual for business, he went to the police station, where the chief said that he hadn't arrested the Teels because he still lacked full information.

The next day was one of Ben's teaching days, but rather than hold class, he met with the entire student body in front of the school. Nobody went to class that day. All 450 students joined Ben to march on the courthouse to demand justice. The principal threatened expulsions but still the students marched. At the courthouse, they learned that the State Bureau of Investigation had arrested the Teels and brought them to Raleigh for safekeeping. Ben announced a meeting that night in the field in back of the Soul Kitchen. He appealed to the students to bring their parents when they came home from the tobacco fields and the mills. Nearly a thousand folks gathered that night to declare the next day Black Thursday.

Nobody would go to school; they were going to march again. They met at the First Baptist Church in early morning. This time more than just the kids showed up. From 8 to 80, they came to march. Ben appealed to the crowd to exhibit solemnity. This was not to be a jovial march. He recalls, "We weren't going to have a whole lot of laughing, because white people in town were used to seeing Black folks as hee-hawing happy-go-lucky peons. None of that this time. We wouldn't give the white structure a chance to deceive itself this time." All you could hear that morning from the church to the courthouse and back was the pat-pat-pat of marching feet.

The Steering Committee for Black Progress became a community organization, holding regular meetings at the First Baptist Church. Through his activities in Oxford, Ben came to the attention of Reverend Leon White of nearby Henderson. White was director of the United Church of Christ's Commission for Racial Justice for North Carolina and Virginia. He was looking to hire an organizer who could tap the growing Black resistance in the state. Ben was obviously the man for the job.

When the state held a bond hearing for the Teels, to which the president of one of Oxford's banks and other Chamber of Commerce elders testified as to the good character of the defendants, Ben and the Steering Committee set into motion two actions. They called a consumer's boycott of Oxford's downtown stores. And they decided to hold a funeral march for Henry Marrow, from Oxford to Raleigh, 34 miles away. Setting out with a wagon, a mule and a casket, the Oxford folks began the three-day trek with the intention of gaining an audience with Governor Bob Scott to appeal for justice. Henry Marrow's pregnant widow joined them for the duration. Along the way they held local rallies in churches in Creedmor and Raleigh. Starting out from Oxford with 200 marchers, they arrived at the governor's office with a thousand. They had made an appointment with the governor but he refused to see them. The angry marchers returned to Oxford. Their anger was matched by that of the people who remained in Oxford. When word came of the governor's lack of good faith, Oxford went up in flames. Warehouses caught fire, burning a million dollars worth of tobacco sold to the U.S. government. Now Governor Scott became more responsive. He ordered Oxford under curfew and sent in the state riot squad, under the aegis of the highway patrol. Everybody was to be off the city streets by 6 P.M. for the next 10 days.

The Steering Committee began to meet at the Soul Kitchen again, because it was outside the Oxford town limits. Committee members would stay all night or sneak back home through highway patrol lines. As many as 200 came to these nightly meetings. Earlier, Jim Grant and Joe Goins, another friend from Charlotte, had come up to Raleigh to join the march on the governor's office and had returned to Oxford with the disappointed demonstrators. Jim was now on the staff of the Southern Conference Education Fund (SCEF), based in Louisville, Kentucky. He remained in Oxford on behalf of SCEF and its newspaper, the *Southern Patriot.*

During one of the Steering Committee's afternoon meetings, a strange car drove into the Soul Kitchen parking lot. Al Hood and David Washington had also arrived from Charlotte. Came to help, they said. But the meeting was in progress, so Ben and Jim told them to come back later that night if they wanted to talk. Joe Goins took off with Hood and Washington, and they were never seen again in Oxford. The next day, Ben and Jim heard that they had been busted. Seems they had driven up to a highway patrol roadblock with a car full of dynamite.

Things cooled down in Oxford for a short while. But the Teel murder trial was scheduled for the summer, and the Klan began to hold statewide rallies in Oxford to raise money for the defense. Advertisements calling upon all white people to "stand up" in Oxford appeared in the local press. The trial was presided over by Judge Robert Martin of High Point, one of a dozen circuit-riding judges in the state superior court. An all-white jury was selected to render the verdict. The Steering Committee hired attorney James Ferguson of Charlotte to serve as private prosecutor, which was allowed under one of North Carolina's more peculiar ancient statutes. The trial had about as much quiet reserve as a Legionaire smoker. Robert Teel announced in court that he was going to dynamite the Soul Kitchen. During a court recess following this remarkable testimony, Teel picked up a chair and tried to attack attorney Ferguson. Judge Martin sat with his head down, refusing to acknowledge the incident. The jury, for its part, acquitted the Teels.

The Steering Committee for Black Progress moved into action again. Pickets marched every day to build the boycott of downtown merchants. Car pools were organized to take shoppers to Henderson, 11 miles away. A number of businesses were forced to close down. The Steering Committee upped its ante. It was no longer protesting the murder of Henry Marrow only, but was demanding Black salespeople in the stores and Blacks in local law enforcement agencies. The Chamber of Commerce finally agreed. Blacks were hired in the stores for the first time, the one Black policeman was made a lieutenant, several others were hired, and Granville County got its first Black sheriff's deputy. On behalf of the Commission for Racial Justice, Ben organized a statewide Black Solidarity Day on August 22, 1970, and 4,000 people came to celebrate.

In September, the federal explosives-possession trial of Al Hood, David Washington and Joe Goins was set to be held in Raleigh. One morning before the trial, Hood and Washington came to the Soul Kitchen and asked Ben to cash a $100 check they received from Jim Grant. The money was to help pay for the trial, they explained. On the morning the trial was scheduled to open, Ben and Jim went to Raleigh. When the bailiff called out the names of the defendants, Joe Goins was there but Hood and Washington were not. Federal fugitive warrants were issued and the judge called the FBI into the case.

Three months later, just before Christmas, Ben read in the Charlotte *Observer* that Hood and Washington had turned themselves in to the government, after returning from Canada.

Curiouser and curiouser.

Two

In Harrisburg, Pa., it was disclosed that Col. Oran K. Henderson, the highest-ranking officer charged in the My Lai massacre . . . has gone to work, for the Pennsylvania Bicentennial Commission. . . . Colonel Henderson, in his $16,900-a-year job, would coordinate the Congress of World Unity, a meeting of philosophers from all over the world, to draft a 'declaration of human rights.'

The New York Times, September 18, 1974

L
UTHER Hodges became governor back in 1955, just six months after the U.S. Supreme Court ruled in *Brown* v. *Topeka Board of Education* that segregation in the schools was unconstitutional. Hodges' autobiography, *Businessman in the Statehouse,*[1] reads like he discovered in office that there is no Tooth Fairy and he is disturbed with this newfound knowledge. Part of his inheritance from his predecessor was the report to the General Assembly by former Governor Umstead's Special Advisory Committee on Education. Its objectives were "the preservation of public education and the preservation of the peace" in the state. The report concluded, according to Hodges, that "the mixing of the races forthwith in the public schools could not be accomplished and should not be attempted"; attempts to fill the Court's requirements "without materially altering or abandoning the existing school system" should be made;[2] and another committee should be set up to make further recommendations.

Hodges grabbed the third recommendation first and named former North Carolina House speaker Thomas Pearsall to head up a new panel. Pearsall came with experience to the task, for he also chaired the Umstead advisory committee that made the initial recommendations. The first panel had nineteen members, three of whom were Black. "Unfortunately," wrote Gov. Hodges, "these particular Negro representatives were on the state payroll and were 'suspect' by the state's Negro citizenship." They were "high-grade, honest representatives" but were in "a tough situation" because they "were under great pressure from their fellow-Negroes, many of whom felt strongly that there should be immediate integration." The governor and Pearsall discussed "carefully and prayerfully" the racial composition of the new seven-member committee. They finally decided not to "include a Negro because a Negro member of such a small group" would be under impossibly difficult "outside pressure." The new Pearsall panel avoided this problem; all seven members were white.[3]

Meanwhile, carrying the legal burden for North Carolina was Assistant Attorney General I. Beverly Lake, of whom it can be said as it was of Churchill, "There but for the grace of God, goes God." In an *amicus curiae* brief for the state before the U.S. Supreme Court in 1955, Dr. Lake argued that "an attempt to compel the intermixture of the races in the public schools of North Carolina would result in such violent opposition as to endanger the continued existence of the schools." Over statewide television, Lake—now a State Supreme Court Justice—proclaimed, "The NAACP's objective is not better schools for the Negro children. Its ultimate objective is the blending of the white and Negro races into a mixed-blooded whole." And, also from Mr. Justice Lake: "The mixture of our two great races in the classroom and then in the home is not inevitable and is not to be tolerated." Lake, "speaking as a private citizen or at least attempting to do so," according to Hodges, "advised communities to close their schools rather than submit" to the decision of the high court. The North Carolina branch of the NAACP called on the governor to dismiss Lake. After all, here was the assistant attorney general, the second highest law enforcement official in the state, urging the citizenry to break the law of the land *en masse*. Governor Hodges was incensed at the demand. He immediately issued a statement: "I am amazed that this private organization, whose policies are determined in its national office in New York and are obviously designed to split North Carolina citizens into racial camps, and which I am convinced does not actually represent any substantial portion of our Negro citizens, should have the effrontery to make such a request." He would not accede to the demand: "On the contrary, it is my intention to use every means at my command to retain for the state the services of this distinguished lawyer." One is reminded of the reply of a segregationist lawyer to Robert Penn Warren who asked if Autherine Lucy, the first Black woman to enter the University of Alabama, wasn't acting under law. "Yes, yes," said the lawyer, "but it was just the Federal Court ruled it."

Hodges went on television to present a plan for "voluntary separation of the races." Speaking "directly to the Negro citizens," he appealed: "Any stigma you may have felt because of laws requiring segregation in our public schools has now been removed by the courts. No right-thinking man resents your desire for equality under the law. At the same time, no right-thinking man would advise you to destroy the hopes of your race and the white race by superficial and 'show-off' actions to demonstrate this equality. Only the person who feels he is inferior must resort to demonstrations to prove that he is not. . . ." And finally: "A race which can achieve equality has no need to lose itself in another race."[4]

I. Beverly Lake drafted a counter plan to abolish the constitutional requirements for public schools. It would have had the General Assembly provide grants to parents of children enrolled in private schools. The bill was introduced into the state senate by Lake's protege, then state senator Robert Morgan of Harnett. In the end the Pearsall-Hodges plan won, and the governor was exuberant. (Morgan lived in Lake's house for three years while a student of Lake's at Wake Forest Law School. When Lake later went onto the Supreme Court, "Morgan is generally regarded as having assumed the mantle of leadership to the Lake political faction." (*News and Observer,* April 10, 1969.) Morgan served as state's Attorney General in the late 1960s and 1970s, during the period of court-ordered school desegregation by busing. In that office he supervised the arrests and imprisonment of the militant leadership of the Black student movement. While Morgan was making his successful run for the U.S. Senate in 1974, Lake was still considered the Godfather of the Morgan wing of the Democratic Party, according to Mason Thomas of the University of North Carolina's Institute of Government. Such were Democratic Party politics and consequently North Carolina state politics, that these two racist options, were presented to the voting public as "moderate" versus "conservative."

By 1966, a dozen years after desegregation was declared the law of the land, only 6 percent of North Carolina's Black children were enrolled in school with whites. The relationship between racist school systems and quality education, for Blacks *and* whites, can be seen in a study by the North Carolina Fund of that year. One of six state residents over 24 years old had not achieved a 5th grade education. Less than half the number of those entering first grade completed the twelfth grade, a full one-quarter below than the national average. More than half the armed forces draftees from the state failed their pre-induction mental tests. Less than 8 percent of the population was employed as professional or technical workers, the lowest rate in the United States.

Eighteen years after the Brown decision, North Carolina officials still felt that the federal courts were raining on their parade. Asked in 1972 to cite the state's number one problem, Senator Sam Ervin, Jr., answered, "Busing." Just as his Senate career began with his staunch opposition to the Supreme Court's 1954 ruling, Ervin finished out his career on the same note. When, in *Swann* v. *Charlotte-Mecklenburg Board of Education,* the federal district court ordered busing to desegregate the schools of North Carolina's biggest city and subsequently the whole state, Ervin went before the U.S. Supreme Court as attorney for the Charlotte-Mecklenburg Classroom Teachers Association to fight the court's ruling.

For a quarter of a century the main racist thrust in North Carolina was on the issue of school desegregation. After the Swann decision, violence broke out in dozens of cities and hamlets throughout the state. For a period the Ku Klux Klan was revived and new paramilitary groupings came together, such as the Rights of White People organization in eastern North Carolina. Several hundred Black schoolchildren and students were jailed and their leaders imprisoned for long sentences. The usually outspoken Sam Ervin maintained a curious silence about the repression of the Black student movement. But in the Senate he pressed for a law to end the "horrible tyranny" of school busing.[5]

Despite his elucidating such a dubious, though popular, proposition, Ervin lost favor with his electoral base. The Watergate investigation proved to be his last hurrah. Richard Nixon had, after all, won the 1972 presidential election in North Carolina as nearly everywhere else; and Nixon too was a staunch opponent of busing. Ironically school desegregation, long the Dixiecrats' favorite issue, played a great role in breaking up the solid South, including solid North Carolina. The Nixon "Southern Strategy" was based, in the first place, on a not very subtle appeal to racist fears. The strategy, despite its public moniker, was national in scope—designed to appeal to the voters of the Detroit suburbs and to those of Greenville, Mississippi. North Carolina was a testing ground for its appeal. Most political observers in the state agree that the Nixon appeal, combined with the "pro-busing" sentiments of the national Democratic Party, brought about the reemergence of the Republican Party in North Carolina. For the first time in this century, a Republican, James Holshouser, was elected to sit in the governor's mansion in Raleigh, and another, Jesse Helms, to represent the state in the U.S. Senate. Sim A. Delapp, a former state GOP chairman, remarked, "The leadership hasn't brought this party to where it is now. I can tell you what's brought it—and any man that knows politics knows. The race question brought it."[6]

W̲HAT you felt mostly was scared if you were young and Black in those first couple of years following the federal busing order in Mecklenburg County. North Carolina became a focus of racist terror, of mass jailings of Black students, and finally of numerous political trials and the long imprisonment of scores of key activists and leaders—Black and white.

From hundreds of cases in those years, consider only the following: Charles Lee Parker of Roanoke Rapids was sentenced to life imprisonment on a burglary charge, although the federal district court in Raleigh held that he was indicted by an illegal grand jury. Parker, whose mother was for years active in the Black community, was 15 years old at time of sentencing.

In Greenville, a white youth and a young Black man were charged with raping a white woman. Both defendants denied the charges. They were given separate trials. The white boy was freed, the Black sent to prison for life.

Nathan Shoffner, an elderly Black man in Greensboro, was shot to death by state patrolman R.A. Clark, after a highway accident. Shoffner was alleged to have threatened the patrolman with a knife, before he was shot in the leg and allowed to bleed to death on the highway. Clark was cleared of any criminal intent. A month before, an unarmed 20-year-old, Michael Riggins, was shot in the back by a Greensboro policeman who claimed Riggins was running from the scene of a crime. The death was ruled justifiable homicide.

Another young Black man, Lawrence Covington, returned home to the rural town of Laurinburg after receiving an engineering degree in the North. Hired by a poverty program, he became a defender of the Black community against police brutality, and joined a local school boycott. He was then accused of raping a 16-year-old white woman on Thanksgiving eve, 1970. The alleged victim, whose husband was in the service, said that she had come to Covington for food stamps for Thanksgiving; that after they had talked about her returning to school to get a high school diploma, he turned out the light and had sexual relations with her. The young woman was involved in a similar incident some months earlier with two Black men, a case in which the charges were dropped. Three months after being jailed, Covington was granted bail of $15,000. But it was more than he had and he remained in jail. His trial by an all-white jury was halted pending a psychiatric examination. The long period of confinement had had an adverse effect on Covington's nerves.

In Charlotte, Roy and Leroy Miller, 21-year-old twins, were stopped by police for questioning about a car theft. Roy Miller was shot at point-blank range by patrolman J.S. Swain. He was left on the pavement for almost an hour and a half while he bled to death, although two ambulances arrived immediately. Leroy Miller was arrested and beaten at police headquarters until he pleaded guilty to 14 counts of housebreaking and 3 of resisting arrest. He was sentenced to 8 to 10 years in prison. The Miller twins are Black, the police white. Also in Charlotte, patrolman J.D. Ensminger killed 18-year-old Frankie Dunlap after Dunlap allegedly attacked the officer with an "Afro" comb. The police chief would not suspend Ensminger; the grand jury refused to bring an indictment against him.

Police in High Point conducted an early morning raid against the Black Community Information Center, in what law enforcement officials said was an effort to evict the occupants. The building was owned by a district court judge who, when told who the tenants were, ordered the eviction. No reason was given for the action and none need be under North Carolina law. The eviction party included 75 city, county and state police, armed with tear gas, bullet-proof vests and automatic shotguns. Clearly this was a landlord with a vengeance. The cops sealed off the Black community at 6 A.M., an unusual precaution for serving an eviction notice. The assault on the office was led by High Point police chief Laurie Pritchett, who came to national notice as chief of police in Albany, Georgia, in the early 1960s. He was known there to lock up every man, woman and child who dared protest racial injustice in that town. Many were beaten in the Albany jail and police even threatened one young girl with rape by a police dog.

In Charlotte, the law offices of Chambers, Stein, Ferguson and Lanning, the firm which won the school-busing suit, were burned to the ground. Soon afterwards, a business in Montgomery County, 50 miles away, owned by the father of Julius Chambers, head of the law firm, was also set afire. A few years earlier, Chambers had escaped assassination when his house was dynamited. The FBI and police made no arrests in any of the incidents.

Since the court had ordered desegregation of the Charlotte schools, the state's high schools had become the scenes of regular clashes between Black students and white students inflamed by racist propaganda or police. The Blacks without exception came up short. Over 200 persons were arrested in Edenton, for example, growing out of protests over the firing of a Black band director in a local high school. Most of those jailed were booked on charges of parading without a permit or blocking traffic as they marched downtown. Six were arrested for burning a Confederate flag, charged with "mutilating, defacing and defiling the flag." Presumably the authorities considered the Stars and Bars as the legal symbol to which they owed allegiance.

In Wilson, 6 teenage boys and girls were imprisoned after a Black-white high school clash in which 16 Blacks and one white were arrested. On pronouncing sentence the judge allowed as how, "We're tired of all this protesting. We've got the guns, we've got the money, and we've got you outnumbered. We're going to stop you in this way or people are going to take things into their own hands."

The Statesville high school closed for a few days and several students were hospitalized after a free-for-all over a white bus driver's refusal to let a Black student board the bus. There were 711 whites and 171 Blacks at the school. Mayor Francis R. Quis urged parents of the white students who were hospitalized to swear out warrants against Black students, whom he described as "criminals." He said that "justice would be swift and sure." Police serving papers on one sixteen-year-old Black student, beat him, his mother and younger sister, and brought them down to the jail, leaving behind a one-year-old child alone.

School was also closed and several students sent to the hospital in the mill town of Kings Mountain, when a group of Black teenagers was attacked by a larger group of whites armed with sticks. Two Black students, but no whites, were suspended in the wake of the beatings. The principal at Kings Mountain, who referred to Black students as "n-----s," took no action against white students who brought guns to school.

About 200 Black students walked out of school in South Mecklenburg after a fight between Black and white students. Several carloads of county police arrested some of the students leaving the school, on grounds of disorderly conduct. The next day more Black students stayed home as 17 county police in riot gear patrolled the school. Both West Mecklenburg and Myers Park high schools were closed after fights between whites and Blacks. The white racist "Concerned Parents Association" had sent their children to West Mecklenburg in the 1960s to escape court-ordered desegregation; subsequently, Black students who transferred there in the 1970s were called "n-----s" and "boys" by their teachers. A school coach publicly announced that if he were 20 years younger, he would "go out and kill me some n-----s."

Teachers in Pender County openly boasted of membership in the Ku Klux Klan or in the Rights of White People, another terrorist organization. But a Black student was expelled from school on grounds of "suspicion" of belonging to the Black Panther Party.

Numerous incidents occurred around the efforts of Black students to observe the birthday of the Rev. Martin Luther King, Jr. At Charlotte's Garinger High, fire drills were started by whites during Dr. King's birthday memorial, and white non-students appeared on campus with machetes, trying to provoke fights with Black pupils. At Harding High School, Black students were refused permission to hold a memorial for Dr. King, and those who attended services at nearby Johnson C. Smith University were suspended. Yet school officials sanctioned country-and-western music shows and religious programs for white students.

Sixty-nine Black high-school students were arrested on felony charges of rioting, after fights with whites at Myers Park, South Mecklenburg and Olympic high schools in Charlotte. Although evidence indicated that whites started the fights in each case, only two whites were apprehended, and they were set free after a preliminary hearing. The Black students remained in jail for weeks.

The village of Ayden was torn apart by months of turmoil initially sparked by the killing of William Murphy, a Black farm laborer, by white patrolman Billy Day. Murphy was shot to death while in handcuffs. Day said he arrested Murphy for drunkenness, but Murphy's employer said the man was "not noticeably intoxicated" when he saw him five minutes before the arrest. The Ayden hospital refused to perform an autopsy, but an examination at a Chapel Hill funeral parlor found that Murphy was shot in the back. The coroner's jury held that patrolman Day shot the man in self-defense. Day was promoted to the highway patrol's personnel department.

Protests of the killing came immediately from the American Civil Liberties Union, the NAACP, the Black Panther Party, the Southern Christian Leadership Conference, the Black Pastors' Conference of Pitt County and the Commission for Racial Justice. In response, Ayden authorities declared a curfew to prevent picket demonstrations and hundreds of demonstrators were arrested. The Rights of White People offered to send 300 men to Ayden "to keep order."

The Klan threatened to bomb the Ayden-Grifton High School rather than permit desegregation. Shortly thereafter a bomb exploded in a rest room in the school. Nobody was nearby, so no one was hurt. No fingerprints were found, no eye-witnesses located, no evidence of any kind discovered. Still, deputy sheriffs arrested a 13-year-old Black student and threatened him with death if he didn't "name others." The boy said police held a gun to his head at the time. He finally gave names of several other boys who were active in the Pitt County movement. One of those named, Donald Smith, 17, son of a factory worker, confessed to the bombing after being denied the right to see a lawyer and being threatened by police if he didn't confess. His forced confession was the only evidence against him.

Donald's trial was a startling example of New Southern justice. During the proceedings the judge indicated to the jury his belief in the guilt of the defendant. The prosecuting attorney took the members of the jury to dinner just before they returned their verdict. When the guilty verdict was announced, the prosecutor and the sheriff's deputy who had obtained Donald Smith's confession laughed loudly and jumped with glee. The deputy has since been named police chief in Ayden.

The teenager was sentenced to 40 years in prison. Notice of appeal was filed but later withdrawn when the defense attorney received a sentence of 20 years for the youth in return for agreement never to again appeal. On the day that Donald's appeal was withdrawn, 10 other teenage boys also pleaded guilty. With no evidence against them except forced confessions, the Ayden 11, teenagers all, were sentenced to a total of 133 years in North Carolina prisons.

Such were the circumstances in which Ben Chavis emerged as the leader of North Carolina's Black youth and their families in the quest for equal education.

B Y September of 1970, Ben was really into his work as the commission for Racial Justice's field organizer. Requests for help from Black communities all over the state came into the Commission office and Ben tried to respond. Even after his Charlotte and Oxford experiences, he was to retain "unbelievable" and "incredible" in his lexicon, testimony to the American Dream. He would be going into town after town to organize with his eyes wide shut, as it were.

Black parents would call upon the Commission to help, and the Commission would call upon Ben. Now he was asked to come to the Nutbush community, a Black section of Vance County, four miles north of Henderson, the county seat, about 20 minutes drive from Oxford. Again, schools were the issue: The county schools had just been desegregated, resulting in the busing of some children from the all-Black Nutbush elementary school to the formerly all-white Middleburg school, crowding the classrooms beyond capacity. The board of education refused to provide enough mobile units to hold the students, using the resultant overcrowding as an excuse to send most of the Black students back to Nutbush. Black parents felt this was unfair: Nutbush's facilities were terribly inadequate, and if students were going to be moved out of Middleburg and back to Nutbush, they should be Black and white alike. Hot lunches were prepared only at Middleburg, then driven several miles to Nutbush where they were cold upon arrival.

Ben's first act, together with the Rev. Leon White, was to call the parents together at Oak Level United Church of Christ Church, and set up a rudimentary organizational structure—elect a president and secretary, have minutes taken at meetings, develop a program, in this case how to close down the Nutbush school and get all the kids back over to Middleburg. Obviously Nutbush did not exist in a vacuum. Ben went into Henderson, the scene of his childhood memories of the National Guard violently crushing the cotton-mill workers' strike. Black students in the Henderson schools also had problems and, with Ben's help, joined the Nutbush community in organizing a Vance County United Student Association. The association drew up its demands for equal education and presented them to the school board. When no response was forthcoming, they decided to march.

The march was to begin at the all-Black Kittrell College and continue eight miles into Henderson. The police chief and city manager said they would march only "through their own blood" but not through Vance County and Henderson. The association asked the governor for protection; its members were determined to march, despite threats from on high. Four hundred students started out from Kittrell and were joined by others along the way. Some folks came up from Granville County, and by the time they approached the city line their numbers had swelled to 2,500. They marched along a state highway, and when the highway patrol showed up they assumed their petition to the governor had been answered. But the patrolmen were asking them to call off the march, to get off the highway. On the other side of the city line, the Henderson police had gathered, reinforced by the cops of Oxford, Franklinton, Warrenton and surrounding communities. They blocked the highway with firetrucks. All the businesses in downtown Henderson were boarded up. Car dealers took their automobiles off the lots and hid them out of fear of broken windows, as the schoolchildren and clergy approached the town. Police, firetrucks and blockaded highways notwithstanding, the Vance County United Student Association was going to march. They had already gone eight miles and were not going to stop now. The highway patrol, seeing their determination, pulled rank on the locals and persuaded the Henderson police to allow the march to continue. Numbers told that day, thousands of marchers and only scores of police.

With the success of the march, the association organized an economic boycott of downtown Henderson. If it could work in Oxford, why not here. The protest movement had grown from tiny rural Nutbush to a county-wide movement, and Henderson became the center. Association meetings moved to the Davis Chapel in town. One night they met to plan a march on the courthouse where a number of Black students were on trial for fighting whites in the schools. The association decided to fill the courtroom. When the judge arrived in court the next day to face a room full of Black people, he called Ben back to his chambers and wanted an explanation. "We want to see justice done," said the young organizer. "I know you're going to turn the brothers loose 'cause they didn't do anything and we all wanted to witness this justice." The judge said he wasn't going to be intimidated, but would let the students go if they marched back to the Black community, and didn't cause a disturbance downtown. Ben agreed they'd march back home real orderly. But the police chief argued that there would be no march in his town, not after there had just been one against his firm determination and best judgment. The judge decided there had to be order in the court, and the order he issued the police chief obeyed. The students were allowed to march back home, another victory in hand.

As the protests gathered, so did the resistance. State police tailed Ben wherever he went in Vance County. One evening a patrol car pulled up behind Ben and stopped him. The cops told him it was a routine check, they just wanted to see his license and registration and to search the car. Ben said they couldn't search his car without a warrant. The police pulled out their billies and drew their revolvers—warrants enough in Henderson—and asked Ben to put his lights on. One of his signal lights was faulty. They arrested him, took his car keys, searched his car, took him downtown, booked him for driving with only one signal light, and set bond for $200. Ben refused to post bond, arguing he was arrested without cause. The association began to demonstrate at the jail, and a Human Relations Division man from the U.S. Justice Department, aware of the tension accumulating in Henderson, decided to post bond for Ben. When the case was brought before the judge, he dismissed the charge after the police testified they were searching the car for weapons but found none.

The association planned another march on the school board. Autumn was turning to winter and the first frost had come and gone. It was growing cold and marches in comfort were a thing for a season past. Demonstrations were organized without permits from the city, which denied each request. On the morning of a march on the school board, the town newspaper reported that the county had acquired a pepper-fog machine for riot control. The march to the board took place without incident, but as the students headed back home, a line of police with gasmasks on approached them. They were towing a strange machine, billowing white smoke. The marchers panicked and ran back to the Black community, making their way into a church. Ben began to lead them in singing spirituals, certain in their knowledge that their holy surroundings would be off-limits to the pepper-gas. But the police were relentless; tear-gas canisters were thrown through the windows of the church. Outside the pepper-fog machine was cranking out its toxic smoke. Inside the church, the demonstrators lay on the floor, gasping for breath.

The community reacted with anger. A struggle ensued to wrest the gas machine away from the police. The police drew their guns and fired some warning rounds. Folks in the neighborhood headed home for their own protection. In the melee, an 88-year-old Black woman who lived across the street from the church, choked to death from the tear-gas. A fireman was found dead, fatally wounded by his own pistol according to the next day's paper. A tobacco warehouse across the street from the Davis Chapel went up in smoke, destroying several thousands of dollars worth of Bright leaf. Governor Scott, with a nose for property rights, sent in the National Guard.

It took a few days for the air to clear and the Guard to clear out and by that time the school board had come to terms with the demands of the association. Save one: The Nutbush school was still open and Black kids in that community were still coming up short. The superintendent of public education was holding firm on that, the problem that initially brought Ben to Vance County. It was marching time again, this time with a warning from the association that the marchers were going into the school board building, that Nutbush would be closed and the kids there sent back to Middleburg, or hell would be paid before the demonstrators left the building.

Agents from the State Bureau of Investigation warned of arrests if they entered the school board building. Ben's reply was that they'd been struggling for over a month to close Nutbush and the struggle had been just, they'd take their chances with arrests. One SBI man asked the demonstrators to give him a few minutes alone with the school board chief, and entered the building. Before the hour was up, the school superintendent came outside and announced that Nutbush school was closed from that day on.

U<small>NTIL</small> the Nutbush student protest came along, Henderson had been a pretty quiet town for nearly a decade. But back in November 1958, over a thousand members of the Textile Workers Union of America walked out of the two Harriet-Henderson Cotton Mills, the start of what was to become one of the longest—and among the most violent—industrial strikes in U.S. labor history. Adopting more positions than the Kama Sutra, then Governor Luther Hodges called the Henderson strike, "a blot on North Carolina," "the most difficult single problem I faced," "one strike in which just about everybody was at fault."[7]

In fact the Henderson strike, which lasted nearly three years, saw the entire repressive state apparatus used to break the union. One fifth of the state's police forces were used against the strike. A virtual police state was established by injunction and enforced by the highway patrol and National Guard, with fixed bayonets and with authority to arrest arbitrarily, given to them by a special act of the state legislature. A superior court judge ordered in the Guard to prevent mass picketing. Soon a military police platoon from Greensboro came to Henderson, followed by other units, all of the 2nd Battle Group of the 119th Infantry of the 30th Division.[8]

In the course of the strike, nearly $300,000 in bail bonds were exacted from almost 200 union members, arrested on at best flimsy pretexts. In addition, the state sent a special judge and special prosecutor to hold a special court in which union members and their sympathizers were, in almost every case, sentenced to hard labor on road-gangs and given heavy fines.

The company had been unionized for 14 years; union recognition was not at issue. Rather this was an attempt by the company to break the contract and destroy the union. At contract negotiations, the company tried to rewrite and void every clause in previously held union contracts. When the union voted to walk out, Governor Hodges ordered 150 highway patrolmen to Henderson. The town and the whole of Vance County quickly became "an armed camp," in the view of Boyd Payton, Carolinas director of the union.[9] Payton, who became a central figure in the strike, was beaten in his Henderson motel room the day after he arrived in town to help out. Some 40 instances of bombings or dynamitings of workers' homes and neighborhoods were on record when Governor Hodges sent in the National Guard—against the strikers. Madness enveloped the company's agents; one assistant foreman broke his leg when he plunged from an upper-story window of the mills, screaming, "They're after me," and pointing at the mill where only other supervisors and strike-breakers remained. A striker's son, home on leave from the army, reached the injured foreman and obtained medical help for the man. A few hours later, that same striker's son was wounded by a shotgun blast directed by another supervisor.

The strike quickly became a lockout, with union members barred from the plant, strike-breakers brought in in their place, the first real test of the "right to work" law in North Carolina's huge textile industry. Between February 16 and May 1, 1959, to take at random ten weeks of the strike, 90 cases came before the special court dealing with the strike. These included 7 strike-breakers with a total of 12 charges, 2 company foremen with 4 charges, and 29 union members with a total of 74 charges. The 7 strike-breakers were found "not guilty" on 8 of the 12 counts, 2 other charges were declared "non-suited," one was found "guilty" for speeding, and the other was disposed of with a notation, "pending further action." Of the two foremen, one was found guilty of disorderly conduct, the other of assault with a deadly weapon, but the records for both show, "Sentence to be given later." Of the 29 union members, 2 received "not guilty" verdicts, the rest were sentenced to numerous fines and prison sentences of as much as 21 months "on the roads."

Not one strike-breaker or company supervisor in the course of the three-year strike was ever fined or given a jail sentence.[10] Eight top union officers, including Boyd Payton, were sentenced to 9 and 10 years in prison on charges of "conspiracy" to dynamite a textile plant and a Carolina Power and Light sub-station. Special Judge Raymond Mallard kept his pledge when he declared in court, "If you want to be sons of bitches, I can be a bigger son of a bitch than all of you put together." The case against Payton and the other union leaders—a conspiracy of the oddest sort, some of the "conspirators" never having met nor talked to one another until the trial—rested on the testimony of a tormented, alcoholic informer with a record of a dozen arrests for hit-and-run, auto theft, impersonating a policeman, drunk-driving, assault, and such. This petty criminal, Harold Aaron, in league with the State Bureau of Investigation which held a handful of prosecutions over his head, was called "the bravest man I know," by the state's special prosecutor. The solicitor compared Aaron ("a brave man with real guts") to the defendants ("low-bellied cowards") and concluded that Aaron was an "honest and trustworthy citizen of the state who believed in preserving law and order and was willing to expose himself to great danger in order to protect the good people of North Carolina."[11] The sum of Aaron's testimony was that, while in the employ of the SBI, he had talked on the telephone with the defendants and that he discerned a conspiracy.

When Boyd Payton and his co-defendants were well into their prison terms for a "dynamiting" that even the state never alleged took place, it was revealed that Aaron received at least $1,100 for his testimony. The evidence came to light when Aaron was arrested in Martinsville, Virginia, where he was sharing a motel room with a 17-year-old high school girl, and where he shot another man who refused to leave the room. Indicted and brought to trial, Aaron was found guilty and fined only $100 for this aggravated assault and attempted murder. The sentencing came after secret conferences between North Carolina and Virginia "criminal justice" officials.[12]

The combination of company manipulation and government coercion left the Henderson Cotton Mill workers without a union, unprotected against future abuses. Given the amount of resources garnered on both sides, the outcome of so many months of sharpened class warfare ending in the workers' defeat had an anaesthetic effect on textile organizing in North Carolina which has not yet worked off completely.

VICTORY day for the students in Henderson in 1970 was so different from the weeks that preceded it. The demonstrators marched back to the Davis Chapel—no teargas on this march—to celebrate. But first they met and agreed to establish a permanent community organization, the Vance County Improvement Association, which still carries on its work. Later that evening a public celebration was held to hail the latest victory and the new organization.

In the audience were some high school students who had driven over from Warrenton in the next county. They said that they too were having problems in the schools and that they needed help. A man with a mission by now, Ben Chavis never went home that night, but left the celebration and headed directly for Warrenton to meet with the students. Their grievances were similar to those of the students in Henderson and every other town in North Carolina. Black students had to sit in the back of the classrooms; white teachers constantly abused them with racist epithets; Black girls were not allowed to become majorettes with the school band.

The protest movement in Warrenton was patterned on that of Henderson. Marches on the school board met with no results in the beginning. A school boycott was called and the school-bus drivers, in some cases parents of students, refused to drive. The highway patrol was called out; police cars followed Ben, even when he went home to Oxford. Black high school seniors were expelled, but Ben helped set up a mechanism to enroll them in a General Education Degree program at Kittrell College, where they finished high school and many continued on to also complete college studies. The Henderson police sent their pepper-fog machine to Warrenton, as a symbol of fraternity in malice. Frank Ballance, a Black attorney and community leader in the town and a friend of Ben's, was beaten up in the street by some Warrenton cops.

(At the age of 16, Alfreda Jordan, president of the Warren County Student Association, was sent, along with 30 other Black female students, to Women's Prison in Raleigh for two days as punishment for their movement activities. When she finished high school at Kittrell College, she entered Shaw University and later graduated from the North Carolina Central University Law School in Durham. Had it been left to the

Warren County school officials Alfreda Jordan might have remained at Women's Prison.)

What was happening in Warrenton was happening throughout North Carolina. Ben left Warrenton in the midst of its struggle, which would be protracted, and headed for Bladen County in the southeast part of the state. The Warrenton students were already organized and leading themselves, and those in Bladen County were asking for his help.

By now the problems were familiar—racism in the schools growing out of the court-ordered desegregation. The rural east of North Carolina, which engulfed the towns Ben was organizing, is part of the original Black Belt of the U.S. South. Industrialization was still unfamiliar for the most part. Folks here were farmers, some in tobacco, some in peanuts, but farmers all. Forty miles from the Bladen County seat of Elizabethtown is East Arcadia, a virtually all-Black community. The authorities had closed down the elementary and junior high schools in East Arcadia, compelling the students to go to school in Elizabethtown. That meant an 80-mile round trip every day. The highway was particularly dangerous because it was used by oil tankers supplying the state from Wilmington.

The day after Ben arrived in Bladen County, he took some of the East Arcadia students and parents with him to meet with the school board in Elizabethtown. The delegation wanted to know why it was necessary to close down the East Arcadia schools, and asked that there at least be parity, with some white students being bused there instead of the planned one-way busing. The board refused as expected, and the demonstrations began. It has been said that violence is as American as frozen foods, and if that be the case, Elizabethtown is an All-American city. One evening, in response to the student demonstrations, a group of racist thugs drove out to a Black youth club on the outskirts of town and shot eight people. Four of them died. One of the killers was a department-store owner whose enterprise was destroyed by fire the next day.

Out in East Arcadia, the high school continued in operation. Only the smaller children from the grammar school and junior high were bused to Elizabethtown. In the weeks of the demonstrations for equity in busing, the Bladen County sheriffs received a bomb threat at the high school. A helicopter with demolition experts from Fort Bragg was flown to the school; some sticks of dymanite were found in the cellar, although they were not wired to explode. Nevertheless, the authorities were concerned enough to reopen the elementary and junior high schools for integrated classes in time for the New Year, 1971.

While Ben was working in East Arcadia, nearby Wilmington was beginning a long, hot winter. Fights were breaking out in the high schools as Black students moved to celebrate Martin Luther King's birthday, January 15, in the schools. Rev. Eugene Templeton, the white pastor of Gregory Congregational Church, a United Church of Christ affiliate in Wilmington's Black community, asked the Commission for Racial Justice to send Ben to the port city.

No town in North Carolina summons up images of the mint-julip-and-magnolia anti-bellum days as does Wilmington. Here it was that the state militia fired 100 guns to salute the withdrawal of South Carolina from the Union in December 1860. Wilmington soon became the center of the state's secessionist movement. The Red Shirt counterrevolution of 1898, which brought the violent overthrow of the democratic Reconstructionist city government and the massacre of scores of Black Wilmingtonians, is recorded for posterity as the town's glory days. Once named an "All-American City" by the now defunct *Look* magazine, Wilmington's main parks, schools and historical sites are named for the Red Shirt leadership. Historical markers abound in this city of azalea festivals and weeping-willow gardens. Recorded here are such precious historical trivia as the fact that Mary Baker Eddy lived in a house in town for part of the year 1844.

The city fathers are not totally immersed in the distant past, however. Once the state's largest city, Wilmington is still its major port. Its importance to the state's economy can be ascertained from the fact that each year it handles nearly a quarter of a billion pounds of leaf tobacco, worth more than $250 million for a single commodity. In recent years major industries like DuPont Chemical, General Electric and Hercules Power have built plants with total investments reaching hundreds of millions of dollars.

Social change however has come to Wilmington at a slower pace than economic change. In 1968, following the murder of Martin Luther King, passions surfaced in Wilmington as elsewhere. Several businesses were destroyed by fire and the National Guard was sent in. Still, the power structure remained unresponsive to the needs of the Black community. Blacks occupied nearly all of the city's public housing, but when a vacancy opened on the housing authority in 1968, another white was appointed to the post. A few weeks later, the city reopened the municipal incinerator, located in the heart of the ghetto, which had been closed as a fire and health hazard. Some voices of opposition were raised but it was clear that individual protests could be absorbed like rain on an ocean.

In 1970, the housing authority refused to consider the request of Black residents that a new project be named for Dr. King. That same year, a career marine at Camp Lejeune named Leroy Gibson left the corps, after

65

putting in his 20 years, to form the Rights of White People organization (ROWP). The ROWP was composed primarily of ex-Marines and some active-duty soldiers as a paramilitary unit which would "do the job the Klan was afraid to do," according to Gibson. Based in nearby Jacksonville, off base from Lejeune, the ROWP made frequent forays into Wilmington, at first to protest the hiring of Black stevedores on the docks.

Gibson, who is considered clinically sane, has discussed the formation of ROWP: "The marines were going downhill. They started giving Blacks permission to use the Black-Power salute in the Corps. This is a Communist salute to start with . . . Blacks were on a rampage throughout America and nobody was saying anything about it. So I said, 'What we need is an organization to meet these people head on' . . . You can no longer give in to these revolutionaries and ever expect to get anything done. You've got to stop them . . . Stop all this rape, robbery and demands, is what it amounts to . . . We [ROWP] strive for leadership, for people that know a lot about firearms. . . . Now we've put together sort of a leadership council of 12 organizations—the Klan, the Renaissance party, the Minutemen, you name it . . . The newspapers don't bother me. As long as they don't attack us openly, I can live with it. That's their business, that's the free enterprise system. But if they printed an article that I didn't like, and it wasn't proven, then I'd shoot them." (Interview with author, February 23, 1974.)

As usual the schools were central to the racial tension that gripped Wilmington. That semester, city police beat and arrested Black students who were protesting the barring of Black cheerleaders at the newly desegregated Hoggard High. At New Hanover High, a similarly peaceful protest by Blacks was broken up by white students shouting racial slurs. Again, city police armed with mace entered the school and beat Black students with blackjacks while letting go free the whites who provoked the clash.

Ben Chavis was still organizing in Bladen County late that fall when fights again broke out in the Wilmington schools. Just before Christmas vacation, 17 Black students at New Hanover High were suspended indefinitely for fighting with whites, but no whites were suspended. In response, 500 of the school's 700 Black students walked out of school. The boycott continued past the Christmas vacation into January. Then, in late January, a white boy assaulted a young Black girl with a knife. The New Hanover principal suspended the victim but did not punish the white boy.

Black students called a meeting at the Gregory Congregational United

Church of Christ, pastored by the Rev. Eugene Templeton, to draw up a list of grievances to present to the board of education. The list included demands for no suspension of students without stated cause; establishment of a Black studies program; celebration of Martin Luther King's birthday as a day of mourning; agreement of the New Hanover High principal to hear the Black side as well as the white in Black-white disputes; agreement of the principal to investigate the knife-assault on the Black woman student by the white student. When the board of education chose to ignore the demands, the students decided to call a boycott and Rev. Templeton decided to ask the United Church of Christ Commission for Racial Justice for help. The commission sent Ben Chavis to Wilmington.

WILLIAM Faulkner once said of the continuum of history, "The past is never dead; it is not even past." So it is (and was) with the New South of Wilmington—of 1898.

Speaking before the New England Society of New York in 1886, Henry Grady, editor of the Atlanta *Constitution,* uttered words "that subsequent generations of Southern schoolboys would be required to commit to memory."[13] Those words pronounced the end of the Old South of slavery and the beginning of a New South of freedom. New South visionaries pinned their hopes on the industrial revolution moving in a southerly direction, leaving towns in its wake where there had previously been mere villages. With the white whale of finance capital and industry inside smelling distance, the New South mariners pursued their prey without relent.

For more than a century the New South myth has been perpetrated at various moments, and in each case North Carolina has been put forth as the prime example of progressivism. Most often this image of North Carolina results from its heavy industrialization in the midst of traditional rural backwardness. During the Civil War, North Carolina was the only state in the Confederacy to clothe its own troops, for example. And after the Southern defeat, Northern capital moved into the state in a big way. In 1880, Northern capital investments in North Carolina industry amounted to $13 million; by the turn of the century they reached $76.5 million. Between the end of the war and 1900, the state's industry saw its capitalization increase six-fold, its industrial workforce, four-fold. The bulk of this influx of Northern investment came after the violent overthrow of Reconstruction. In the 20-year period between 1880 and 1900, capitalization of the state's textile industry increased on an average per factory from less than $60,000 to $186,000. According to Burlington Industries, "The textile industry before 1900 was based predominantly on local enterprise, local capital, local management and local labor. In the 1890s however, there was a notable movement of Northern capital into the state's textile interests and a small beginning of the exodus of Northern mills to the south." Small wonder: Annual wages then averaged $216 for men, $157 for women and $103 for children, the latter used extensively.[14]

The story of Buck Duke and his tobacco discovery is as much a part of North Carolina folklore, and is told to children at least as often, as Ben Franklin's kite-flying and Davey Crockett's death at the Alamo.[15] Seems that when the first shot of the Civil War was fired at Fort Sumter, a workable method of curing Bright leaf tobacco had been perfected in Caswell County, North Carolina. With Richmond on the front lines and its plants cut off from new supplies, the demand for good southern tobacco caused a number of manufacturers to set up shop in the Old Bright Belt of the Tarheel state. When the war was over, 45-year-old Washington Duke, captured at Richmond, imprisoned and freed after Appomattox, came home to his farm outside of Durham with all of 50 cents in his pocket. War had stripped his 300 acres bare, save for a little Bright tobacco leaf. Hitching his wagon to two blind mules, Duke and his sons hauled their tobacco to market, where the tobacco was readily sold.

Old Wash Duke discovered that, while he had been languishing in prison, some 80,000 Confederate and Union troops under Joe Johnson and Sherman were awaiting peace terms near Durham. They discovered Caswell County Bright leaf, bought it out, loved it so much they yearned for more. When the soldiers were discharged at war's end, they returned to their 80,000 homes, walking advertisements for what was soon to be known as Bull Durham.

Sales multiplied, the Dukes moved to Durham, and the youngest son, James Buchanan "Buck" Duke took over the manufacturing end of the business. Using machines from Virginia and leaf from North Carolina, Buck went to market in New York. By 1889, Duke was selling more than 800 million cigarettes annually, nearly 40 percent of all U.S. sales. He formed the American Tobacco Company in 1890, and by the turn of the century had a capitalization of $25 million. Duke followed the premise of his contemporary, Southern Pacific railroad magnate Collis P. Huntington, who held that, "Everything that isn't nailed down is mine, and anything I can pry loose isn't nailed down." He bought up Lorillard, Liggett and Meyers of St. Louis, Reynolds and several lesser companies.

"America has many merchant princes and captains of industry," wrote *Leslie's Weekly* in 1906, "but only three industrial kings: John D. Rockefeller in oil, Andrew Carnegie in steel, and James B. Duke in tobacco."

Buck Duke said to himself, "If John D. Rockefeller can do what he is doing for oil, why should not I do it in tobacco."[16] Textile and tobacco towns grew up throughout the Carolina Piedmont. Greensboro, populated by only 497 persons in 1870, had more than 10,000 at the turn of the century. Winston rose from 443 to 10,000 in the same period; and Charlotte from 4,473 to 18,091. Durham, unlisted in the 1870 census, had 6,679 by 1900.[17] By 1880, most of the state's 126 tobacco factories were located in Durham or Winston. Tobacco was regarded as a strictly private enterprise or a family affair. And though the families were named Duke and Reynolds, the labor force was almost exclusively Black, with an average per capita annual wage of $136 at the opening of the twentieth century. As Nelson Rockefeller was to remark more than half-way into that century, "The chief problem of the low-income farmers is poverty."

Northern investors found they could pick up a nice piece of change in the South, especially in North Carolina. The Arkwright Club of New England, under the direction of textile manufacturers, issued a report in 1897 which delineated the South's obvious virtues: cheap labor, longer hours of labor, legislation restricting the organization of trade unions but not corporate plunder. The report estimated that Southern labor cost 40 percent less than in New England; the North Carolina work-day was 24 percent longer than that of Massachussets.[18] In 1906 the average work week for a mill hand was 69 hours. Tied to their machines day and night and housed in mill-owned shanty villages, the developing North Carolina working class lived an existence out of a Dickens nightmare.

The year 1900 saw the Carolina Piedmont shaken by labor strikes and lockouts in at least 30 separate mills. Caesar Cone, whose Cone Mills are today the country's leading manufacturer of denim, closed his factory and announced he would tear down his mill before submitting to a union. He soon reopened the plant with non-union labor under a "yellow-dog" contract. In the state's textile center, Alamance County, which had also been the site of the Klan's most violent crusade, 17 mills combined to resist a strike by firing every union member and evicting them from the mill villages.[19]

That the initial industrial growth of North Carolina took place in tandem with the Ku Klux salad days was no mere coincidence. The Klan was led after all by the bankers and textile barons and by the politicians and clergy that did their bidding. The absolute control of labor depended on the establishment of white supremacy. If white workers saw their interests in common with white industrialists instead of with Black workers, their fidelity to capitalism was secured. Meantime, those whites who resisted felt the same lash wielded against Blacks. [20] In the years 1889–1899, nearly a third of the lynch victims were white. The Charlotte *Observer,* which has been through the years a sort of house organ for the textile industry, hailed on June 27, 1900, "the struggle of the white people of North Carolina to rid themselves of the dangers of the rule of Negroes and the lower class of whites."[21]

The consolidation of democratic gains under Reconstruction had to be blocked, the new political realignment subverted, the new constitutional amendments countermanded. At "the peak and crown" of Reconstruction, in W.J. Cash's words, 62 Blacks held public office in North Carolina's Craven County. In more than 50 counties in the state, Black magistrates "sat in judgment on white men—and, as the orators did not fail to note, white women." Blacks debated in the state legislature, and one Black man was a member of the Tarheel congressional delegation in Washington.[22]

To reverse this situation required the violent overthrow of the democratically-elected government, the first in the state's history. A climate of fear and hatred was created. Racism was combined with sadism in defense of the old order to produce the same kinds of results that in the next century became commonplace under the Third Reich. Cash wrote,

> From the 1880's on . . . there appears a waning inclination to abandon such relatively mild and decent ways of dispatching the mob's victim as hanging and shooting in favor of burning, often of roasting over slow fires, after preliminary mutilations and tortures—a disposition to revel in the infliction of the most devilish and prolonged agonies. . . .
>
> The growing lads of the country, reflecting prevailing sentiment in naked simplicity, and quick to see that the man who was pointed out as having slain five or eight or 13 Negroes . . . still walked about free, quick to penetrate the expressions of disapproval which might accompany the recital of his deeds, to evaluate the chuckles with which such recitals were too often larded, to detect the hidden note of pride and admiration—these lads inevitably tended to see such a scoundrel very much as he saw himself: as a gorgeous *beau sabreur,* hardly less splendid than the most magnificent cavalry captain.[23]

The overthrow of Reconstruction was completed with the violent counterrevolution in Wilmington, the largest city in North Carolina at the end of the nineteenth century. Wilmington had been the most important Confederate seaport in the upper South. Here an elaborate system of forts had been constructed by Black slaves and the forced labor of Indian workers, kidnapped and taken from nearby Robeson County by the Confederate Home Guards to work and die in the pest holes of New Hanover County.[24] With the post-war industrial development, the port city became vital to the state's burgeoning economy as a shipping outlet.

From 1870 to the present, the Democratic Party has had majority representation in the North Carolina legislature with one brief, exceptional interlude—the years 1895–1901, commonly known as the Fusion period. The Fusionists were those who combined the Republican Party with the Populists to defeat the Democrats. The Fusionist effort finally met defeat with the forceful overthrow of the government by the Democrats. That putsch was centered in Wilmington.[25] The virtual dictatorship of the Democrats came into power using the false issue of "Negro domination," not alone to establish a one-party system in North Carolina, but to do so on behalf of the emerging industrial and commercial forces in the state.

"The industrial growth of North Carolina in the 1880's and 1890's," wrote a leading scholar of the period, "was reflected in the growth of the Democratic party into whose ranks came many lawyers, textile mill owners and railroad magnates. While the leadership of the party was not captured by the industrial or capitalistic element until the 1890's, its presence gave the party in the 1880's a 'pro-corporation' attitude which was further enhanced by 'machine politics.'"[26] In the 1890s, North Carolina was in the midst of tremendous industrial growth. Invested capital in manufacturing had increased from $13 million in 1880 to $76.5 million in 1900; the value of manufactured goods from $20 million to $95 million. The furniture industry, for example, increased from 6 factories making $159,000 worth of products to 44 factories making $1.5 million in the 1890s alone. Textile mills increased four times over, invested capital twelvefold, value of products elevenfold, and number of workers nine times over between 1880 and 1900. "The industrial magnates and railroad financiers who managed these aggregate capitalistic enterprises were members and beneficiaries of the Democratic party."[27]

Capitalist industry is by its nature undemocratic: Owners set goals, managers and their foremen drive the workforce to produce those goals, the workers themselves are not consulted. If the workers should protest, they are fired. This set of power relations held even more true in the milltowns of North Carolina than elsewhere, as the mills owned the towns and the houses in which the workers lived. That "dictatorship of the bourgeoisie" which characterized North Carolina industry, also characterized North Carolina government when the bourgeoisie took state power.

In Wilmington today tribute is still paid in varied forms to the "founding father of modern Wilmington," Hugh McRae. McRae became president of the Wilmington Cotton Mills in 1895. Five years later, with the destruction of the Fusion effort, he was named president of the Wilmington Gas Light Company, in which position he was able to consolidate the railways, mills and light and power facilities of the coastal capital. The Tide Water Power Company, a forerunner of today's Carolina Power and Light, was formed a few years later under McRae, in cooperation with representatives of all the major banks in the area.[28] Such rapid consolidation of financial and industrial power and its consequential control over government was enabled to take hold, in large measure because of the demolition of the democratic features of Reconstruction, most especially the voting rights of Black people. The brutal events in Wilmington at the turn of the century were the culmination of that demolition. Not that disenfranchisement would be limited to Blacks. One of McRae's contemporaries, Charles Aycock, who became governor of North Carolina in the years after the defeat of the Fusionists, led the statewide campaign for disenfranchisement. Although Aycock repeatedly assured whites that they would retain the vote, it soon became apparent that leaders of the movement "saw in it an opportunity to establish in power 'the intelligence and wealth of the South,' which would of course 'govern in the interest of all classes.'"[29]

The disenfranchisement campaign centered around an appeal to racist fears of "Negro domination." The campaign's success rested on its ability to awaken that particular sleeping dog. Actually only one member of North Carolina's congressional delegation to Washington in those years, George H. White, was Black, hardly a "dominating" ratio. In addition to Rep. White, the customs collector in Wilmington's port, John C. Dancy, was Black. A Black postmaster, S. H. Vick, served in Wilson, and a Black deputy revenue collector, Dr. James E. Shepard, worked in Raleigh. In addition to these federal posts occupied by Black men, there were four Black representatives in the state legislature and several in county positions—registrars of deeds, deputy sheriffs, coroners and justices of the peace—primarily in the Black Belt areas. Dozens of city aldermen across the state were Black. In the Wilmington of 1897, three Black aldermen served on the city board, representing the Fusion ticket.[30]

Nevertheless, in May 1898, the state Democratic convention adopted a platform which pledged the abolition of "Negro domination," and promised "rule by the white men of the state."[31] As the Democrats charted the path to white supremacy, their press marched to the beat of a crazed drummer. *The News and Observer* of Raleigh carried stories during the Fall election campaign under the following headlines: "Negro Control in Wilmington," "Unbridled Lawlessness on the Streets," "Greenville Negroized," "The Negro in Power in New Hanover," "Flagman Caught Negro Convict," "Tried to Register an Idiot," "Chicken Under His Arm," "Black Radical Convention Wants to Send Delegate to Congress," "Arrested by a Negro: He Was Making No Resistance," "A Negro Insulted the Post Mistress Because He Did Not Get a Letter," "Negroism in Lenoir County," "Negro on Train With Big Feet Behind White," "Is a Race Clash Unavoidable?" and on and on and on. The paper's cartoons followed the same dubious star. The Black legislator, James H. Young, was depicted inspecting the living quarters of frightened white women. Other cartoons showed a big black foot with a white man pinned underneath, with the caption, "How Long Will This Last?"; a Black man hit on the arm by a sledge marked "Honest White Man," captioned "Get Back, We Will Not Stand It"; a body drowning at sea with a hand inscribed "North Carolina" reaching out of the water, captioned "White Man to Rescue"; a Black road overseer ordering whites to work on the chain gangs; a bat with claws and "Negro rule" written on its wings, with white men and women under the claws, captioned "The Vampire that Hovers Over North Carolina."[32]

The Democrat Aycock's gubernatorial campaign managers held "White Supremacy Jubilees," in which paraded hundreds of red-shirted men bearing arms. Sympathizers in Virginia shipped 50,000 rounds of ammunition and a carload of firearms in the week preceding the election.[33] The gun-toting Red Shirts performed much the same tasks as the Klan—intimidation of whites and Blacks and, on more than a few occasions, murder of Blacks—and had a similar composition. One historian of the period described the Red Shirts as made up "in the main of respectable and well-to-do farmers, bankers, school teachers and merchants—in many cases the best men in the community."[34] These pillars of community virtue, bearing arms, broke up political meetings, fired on citizens in their homes, kidnapped and whipped political opponents as they carried out God's work in the coastal plains of North Carolina.

Days before the election, the Democrats held their final campaign rally at Goldsboro to which all who wanted to attend were granted free transportation by the state's railroads. They issued a proclamation on that October 28, declaring that the sanctity of white womanhood was endangered and property rendered less valuable, and that white men would rule North Carolina because they must. The Charlotte *Observer,* a newspaper partisan to the Democrats, later wrote: " . . . the businessmen of the State are largely responsible for the victory. Not before in years have the bank men, the millmen and the businessmen in general—the backbone of the property interests of the State—taken such sincere interest. They worked from start to finish and furthermore they spent large bits of money in behalf of the cause. . . . When Democratic rallies were held, mills and shops were shut down so that the operatives could attend the speakings. Indeed North Carolina is fast changing from an agricultural to a manufacturing state."³⁵

The Democratic campaign was aimed at Wilmington in the first place, with its Fusion government including three Black aldermen out of ten, a Black county treasurer in New Hanover, a Black assistant sheriff, a Black coroner and a Black port collector. One of the city fathers and chairman of the city Democratic Party, a racist out of central casting named Alfred M. Waddell, had declared during the campaign, "We in Wilmington extend a Macedonian call to you to come over and help us. We will not live under these intolerable conditions. No society can stand it. We intend to change it, if we have to choke the current of Cape Fear River with Negro carcasses."³⁶ Waddell was a member of a Democratic committee known as the "Secret Nine," which drafted the "Declaration of White Independence" charting the course of Wilmington after the Democratic victory. Among its proclamations were that the undersigned would no longer be ruled by Blacks, "an inferior race, not anticipated by the U.S. Constitution"; that whites in Wilmington would no longer pay taxes levied by Blacks and Republicans; that whites were the most advanced group in society. Viewing Reconstruction democracy as a prospect about as pleasant to contemplate as hemophilia, the Secret Nine gave the Black Fusionist newspaper, *The Wilmington Record,* 24 hours to cease publication and its editor the same time to get out of town.

On November 10, exactly half an hour after the warning time had expired, Waddell led bands of Red Shirts in a raid on the Wilmington Light Infantry Armory. The vigilantes armed themselves, proceeded to the office of the *Record* and burned it to the ground. From there they set out for Wilmington's Black community where they conducted a virtual pogrom. The most complete study of the Wilmington massacre summarized the events thusly:

> Streets were dotted with dead bodies, some of which were lying in the street until the day following the riot, others of which were discovered later under houses by their stench; colored men who passed through the streets had either to be guarded by one of the crowd or have a written permit giving them the

right to pass; little white boys searched Negroes and took from them every means of defense, and, if the Negroes resisted, they were shot down by armed white males who looked on with shotguns; rioters went from house to house looking for Negroes whom they considered offensive and killed them, and poured volleys into fleeing Negroes like sportsmen firing at rabbits in an open field; Negro churches were entered at the point of a cannon and searched for ammunition; and white ministers carried guns.[37]

When the carnage was over, the Cape Fear, true to Waddell's pledge, was choked with hundreds of Black bodies. Not one white man was arrested of course. Quite the contrary: Waddell and other Democratic leaders marched to the city hall in the wake of the riot, forced the Fusionists to resign, and appointed themselves to office. *The News and Observer* hailed the massacre as imperative to save the city from degradation. The Wilmington *Messenger* praised the coup d'etat as an heroic act in liberating whites from Black tyranny.

Few survivors of the Wilmington massacre were able to record their accounts of the brutality. One, the Rev. Charles S. Morris, left the city and moved to Boston. Still a refugee in 1899, he told a Boston audience:

> . . . One man, brave enough to fight against such odds would be hailed as a hero anywhere else, was given the privilege of running the gauntlet up a broad street, where he sank ankle deep in the sand, while crowds of men lined the sidewalks and riddled him with a pint of bullets as he ran bleeding past their doors; another Negro shot 20 times in the back as he scrambled empty-handed over a fence; thousands of women and children fleeing in terror from their humble homes in the darkness of the night, out under a gray and angry sky, from which falls a cold and bone-chilling rain, out to the dark and tangled ooze of the swamp amid the crawling things of night, fearing to light a fire, startled at every footstep, cowering, shivering, shuddering, trembling, braving in gloom and terror: half-clad and bare-footed mothers, with their babies wrapped only in a shawl, whimpering with cold and hunger at their icy breasts, crouched in terror from the vengeance of those who, in the name of civilization, and with the benediction of the ministers of the Prince of Peace, inaugurated the reformation of the city of Wilmington. . . . All this happened, not in Turkey, nor in Russia, nor in Spain, not in the gardens of Nero, nor in the dungeons of Torquemada, but within 300 miles of the White House, in the best state in the South, within a year of the 20th century, while the nation was on its knees thanking God for having enabled it to break the Spanish yoke from the neck of Cuba. This is our civilization. . . .[38]

The Wilmington massacre closed out the nineteenth century and set the tone for twentieth century life in North Carolina.

BEN arrived in Wilmington on the morning of February 1, 1971. He had just gone home for a family visit in Oxford from Elizabethtown when Rev. Templeton's call came. Events were pressing and he had to come down to Wilmington, Ben was told. He arrived in the port city a little after midnight and went directly to Rev. Templeton's home, next door to the Gregory Congregational Church. The minister explained to his guest that he had opened up the church to the students for their meetings because their cause was just, he felt, but being white, he really couldn't provide leadership to them in the struggle. He would be supportive but thought it best not to be in the forefront. Rev. Templeton wanted to know how long Ben could stay in Wilmington. Based on his recent experiences in Henderson, Warrenton and East Arcadia, Ben was convinced it wouldn't be necessary to stay for very long. He would meet with the students in the morning, ascertain the problem, try to head them in the right direction, and return to Oxford, to remain on call if new difficulties emerged.

Early the next day, a few of the students came to Rev. Templeton's house. There had been no student organization, but an informal leadership had developed out of the student protests. Steve Mitchell, a high school senior, seemed to be the most articulate of this budding leadership, and he convened the meeting that morning. They decided to generalize their demands, to embrace all the Wilmington schools. The new demands included: a cessation of physical attacks by white teachers against Black students; recognition of Martin Luther King's birthday as a school holiday; establishment of Black studies programs; an end to the practice in some classes of making Black students sit in the back of the room; agreement that Blacks be allowed the same equipment in business courses as whites (white teachers expressed fear that Blacks would break the IBM typewriters or were unable to type correctly because "their fingers are too big.")

The students at Rev. Templeton's house constituted themselves a committee to deliver the demands to the school board that same afternoon. They gave the board until noon the next day, Wednesday, to chew over that particular bone. To back up their demands, the students agreed that they would walk out of school at the sound of the lunch bells on Wednesday and head for the Gregory Congregational Church. Students from all of the city schools were notified of the plan, including those at J.T. Hoggart High School in the suburbs. Drivers at the Black bus company in Wilmington volunteered to pick up the Hoggart students and take them to the church to pray for the school board.

Exactly at noon, 400 Black students at New Hanover High walked off the school grounds and headed for the church. Over 300 of their mates at Williston Junior High joined in. Little first graders at the grammar schools put away their books and trooped into the streets. Folks on the street scratched their heads in wonderment. It appeared to be a fire drill, nice and orderly, but this wasn't possible, not a simultaneous drill for all the schools. About that time busloads of Hoggart students from out in the county began to arrive at the church. After the church rally, more than a thousand students marched on the board of education to press their demands. Police were there with riot equipment and paddy wagons but the school board was gone. The students agreed to continue their boycott of school until they received some satisfaction.

A meeting was called for that night at Gregory Congregational. By now Holy War had been declared against Ben Chavis and Rev. Templeton. Ben was dubbed an "outside agitator," an apparent miracle worker who had disrupted the schools within 36 hours of his arrival in Wilmington. City officials called Templeton to say he shouldn't allow the meeting. Less official callers bearing essentially the same message let the white minister know that his church would be blown up, his wife killed and himself run out of town if he continued to let the church serve as the boycott center. Rev. Leon White, state director of the Commission for Racial Justice, ordered Ben to return to Oxford.

But the next morning Ben was awakened in Oxford by another phone call from Rev. White saying things had changed, fires had been set the night before in Wilmington, and the North Carolina Good Neighbor Council—statewide racial trouble shooters appointed by the governor— had asked White to let Ben return to the port city because he seemed to be the only one who could control the students. Wilmington is about 160 miles southeast of Oxford, and Ben now drove the distance for the fourth time in less than two days.

Wilmington had changed in the few hours of his absence. The Klan had brought in members from enclaves in Burgaw and Whiteville. Rev. Templeton was still receiving bomb threats and even the Good Neighbor Council was saying the threats were for real. The council welcomed Ben back to town, saying they hoped he would be able to keep things orderly. But the burden was on the school board to grant the students' demands, and on the authorities to keep the peace.

Another meeting was called for the church that night, Thursday. Again the bomb threats came. The students decided that they would protect the church with their bodies by remaining inside, hostages to the potential violence of racist fanatics. Pickup trucks filled with whites wearing cowboy hats and packing guns arrived in town from Pender County and from across the South Carolina state line.

Shortly after the meeting started at the church a volley of shots came through the window. The students crouched on the floor and the lights were cut. Ben asked that the lights be turned back on. He said that he was going to stay in the church that night and invited the students and their supporters to join him if they wished. The students decided to stay. Rev. Templeton went home to join his wife. By now Jim Grant had come in from Charlotte to offer assistance to Ben. Again Jim was to play the familiar role of "faculty advisor."

Shots rang out in the community all night. For the most part they missed the church, fired as they were from speeding trucks. Some bullets went into nearby homes. Two people were wounded and were tended to by Mrs. Templeton, a registered nurse who had been fired by the city hospital earlier that day because of her husband's activities at the church.

When dawn arrived Friday, Ben and the students learned that there had been sporadic gunfire that night in other parts of Wilmington. Every indication promised worse to come if the city did not act. Ben and the students went through the neighborhood organizing an impromptu march on City Hall to demand a curfew before madness completely engulfed Wilmington. Mayor Crowmonty, a direct descendant of the attorney general of the Confederacy, refused to meet with the students. The requested curfew was denied.

As night approached so did the nightriders. Carloads of armed whites cruised Wilmington's Black community, testing its defenses. When its defenselessness became apparent, the whites became bolder, shooting at folks on the street from their speeding cars. A block away from the church, one man was felled by shots in the legs. After that the students set up roadblocks. Trash cans, benches, anything to block the streets, even pews from the church, were used to build barricades. By this time the community was moved to act in self-defense. Old hunting rifles were brought out of musty closets and cleaned. Inside the church the Black students were joined by some of their sympathetic white classmates. Other adults joined in, including Ann Sheppard, a white volunteer from the Good Neighbor Council and mother of three, and Molly Hicks, the Black chairperson of the parents' support group for the student boycott.

A command post was set up and foot patrols with walkie-talkies cased the neighborhood around the church. More rounds of fire were shot, but what had been shotgun pellets the night before were more often now high caliber bullets. Some "brothers" from Fort Bragg came down to Wilmington to help defend the community. Ben sent word from the church that everybody was to use the utmost caution and care that the community not be harmed. When someone argued for burning, Ben challenged the provocation of the suggestion. These were Black homes surrounding this Black church; even if a business was white-owned, fire knew no discretion when it spread.

Night fell, and with it any hesitation of the Klan to fire on the Black community. Nearly 5,000 rounds of ammunition were fired that Friday evening. Seventy people in and around the Gregory Church were hit, among them Marvin Patrick, one of the leading student activists. The receiving hospital treated and released whites that evening, but any Black who showed up with a gunshot wound was arrested for rioting.

Ben recalled later, "I was really shocked to see people battling like that. At that point, I just didn't understand the depths of feelings involved. I didn't know much about the history of Wilmington. I had heard something about 1898 but I didn't know it was as deeply ingrained as it apparently was. You had some folks that actually thought that just because the Black students marched and because they were having some meetings, that they were going to pay back the white people for what happened in 1898. And so to keep the Blacks from paying them back, they were going to wipe out the Black community again. And even with all this shooting the mayor refused to set a curfew. People could still go downtown, buy a gun and ammunition, come shooting into the community, and go back downtown again."

Meanwhile, huddled inside the church, were a couple of hundred students, mainly teenagers, dozens only 10 or 11 years old. Two of the influential elders of the church hastily called a meeting of the church board to evict the students and ask for police protection of the church. That such protection had previously been denied failed to impress the two men. The young people left the church, but other adults in the congregation, especially those from the neighborhood, prevailed upon the trustees for a reconsideration of their decision. They were concerned about Rev. Templeton, now without protection, as well as the students and the church itself. The students were invited back.

This was now Saturday night. Jim Grant later reported for the *Southern Patriot*: "Early that evening, six carloads of whites, with guns prominently displayed, drove through the police barricades and headed toward the church. The first truck stopped right in front of the guards' barricade and started shooting. A Black minister who was a little slow about taking cover was hit, but he managed to crawl out of the line of fire. The [community] guards [of the church] returned the fire and the motorcade sped off. The minister was able to drive for medical help and has since recovered. Later that night the police tried to lay down a cover of fire behind which the Klansmen would rush the church." Inside Gregory Congregational, Ben was taking care of the students when he was hit in the back by three shotgun pellets.

All regular television programming in Wilmington was canceled for live newscasts about the "Holy Wilmington Insurrection" interspersed by calls for "law and order" by the city authorities. The grass was clearly getting ahead of the gardener.

While Ben was resting in Rev. Templeton's living room and Jim was in the church basement checking on remaining supplies, someone ran into the church to announce that Mike's Grocery was on fire. Mike's Grocery was a white-owned store in the neighborhood which had caught on fire the past two nights in a row. Rumor among the neighbors had it that Mike was taking advantage of the gunfire to collect insurance money on a store that was sure to be put out of business by a boycott anyway.

Next door to the grocery on either side were family houses. Some of the people were still asleep that night, unaware of the fire next door and their imminent danger. Others, still awake, were determined not to leave their homes for fear of being hit by vigilante bullets. Ben asked for volunteers from among those inside the church and let them out into the street to bring the neighbors back to the church for their protection and, if possible, to save their furniture from the fire. One of Ben's volunteers, Steve Mitchell, moved up the street to pull a nearby fire alarm. Police, waiting across the street in darkness, shot him down and dragged him 50 feet to a police car. Later word came that Steve was dead, although witnesses state that he was alive before being dragged into the car.

When the community heard the television announcement of Steve Mitchell's death, hell just broke loose. The distinction between the Klan and the police was thereafter eliminated in the minds of the Black community surrounding Gregory Congregational Church. When some police were shot at, the television reported the authorities downtown deputized white "volunteers." Everybody was now the law, including the Klan and the Rights of White People. Still the city refused to impose a curfew.

By now Governor Bob Scott ordered the elite riot squad of the North Carolina Highway Patrol into Wilmington. In the wee morning hours, Rev. Templeton was awakened by a call from the highway patrol commander of the riot squad, William Guy, who asked to speak with Ben. Guy said that the patrol was in Wilmington to protect the citizenry, that he understood that "you people" were complaining about some folks shooting at the church, that the government had sent in the patrol to stop the violence, that he was sending his men into the church to protect the young people inside, that he wanted Ben to order his men not to fire at the patrolmen.

Ben explained that he had no men, that he was lying on the floor along with everyone else, that he had no control over what was breaking outside, that he would step outside the church to talk with Guy. When Ben opened the door of Rev. Templeton's house, a .357 magnum bullet, pride of the highway patrol, whizzed past his head and tore a plank off the minister's house. With splendid protection like this, negotiations broke off.

Sunday morning came in with church bells ringing and the staccato of gunfire providing counterpoint. Ben remained inside the Templeton home. About 10 o'clock, a white man in a pickup truck drove up to the barricades outside the church, pulled out his gun and started to fire into the building. He never made it. One of Templeton's neighbors came in the house to tell Ben and the minister and his wife that this white man was laying outside in the gutter, his blood running down the sidewalk. Again, Ben left the church area to call for an ambulance, explaining that this time it was a white man that was dying. The ambulance never came but eventually two Wilmington police pulled up, took the man, later identified as a Harvey Cumber, and placed him in the back seat of their squad car. The police reported that Cumber had a gun with a spent shell in his hand at the time he was shot. But when the news was announced on television 90 minutes later, it was reported that the second fatality of the Wilmington race riots started by Blacks was a white motorist on his way to church, murdered by Black snipers.

News of Cumber's death brought dozens of cars and trucks with armed whites into Wilmington ghettos. The Gregory Church was no longer the target. Any house inhabited by Blacks was fired on indiscriminately. Any Black person on the streets of Wilmington was fair game. Chief Williamson of the Wilmington police acknowledged that he had lost control of the situation. His orders by now had proved useless. Williamson called upon Governor Scott to send in the National Guard.

It took some time for the Guard's artillery division to get its tanks into Wilmington. Some guardsmen came by dusk but the main contingents didn't arrive until after midnight, Monday morning. The Adjutant General of the Guard provided a press bus for CBS and NBC, *Time, Newsweek* and the rest of the national press coming in from Washington and Atlanta. A huge searchlight and infrared gun-scopes were provided to the newsmen to watch the Guard's operation. Live television cameras showed North Carolina viewers the National Guard sporting M16s creeping up the sidewalks toward the church, while armored personnel carriers and tanks bearing .50 caliber machine-guns rolled up to the doors. The assault troops pulled out their grenades, readied their tear gas cannisters, and kicked down the doors of a little Black church in Wilmington. Inside they found—nobody.

Ben Chavis and the students watched the scene on television in Raleigh. They of course also heard that the Guard was coming to town and, based on the treatment they had received from the Wilmington police and the highway patrol, knew they might be killed. Especially after a white man had been killed. So under cover of darkness, they had evacuated the church, Rev. Templeton's house, and the homes of 30 families in the area and left Wilmington, passing the Guard as it rolled into the city.

The National Guard and Governor Scott were incensed, having staged a million-dollar live television show, with the national press on hand, all for naught. They responded by breaking down the doors of Black homes, without search warrants. The community was sealed off, highways were blocked, cars stopped and searched, and Black housing projects searched door to door. For the next week Wilmington's Black community lived under virtual martial law.

NORTH Carolina has respect for the soldier boy," says a former military reporter for the Raleigh *News and Observer*. "This is a whole 'nother country. With more volunteers in the Civil War than any other southern state, it suffered a military defeat a hundred years ago. But if you go out with the national guard today it seems like going out with old Joe Johnson's troops a century ago. All these good old country boys spitting tobacco and shooting the whiskers off a cat."[39]

This is one state that better have respect for the "soldier boy." There are 600,000 veterans in a total population of 5 million. Of those, 142,000 are Vietnam vets. Veterans and their dependants are 2.5 million North Carolinians, fully half of the state.[40]

North Carolina is far from the top of the list in "defense industries," but is just about number one in direct military presence. It contains the largest military base in the United States at Fort Bragg; the largest coast guard base in the world at Elizabeth City, with 10,000 coast guardsmen and civilian employees; and nearly one third of all U.S. marines are based at Camp Lejeune, the Cherry Point marine air station and the New River marine air station. Pope and Johnson air force bases add another 11,000 men in uniform. On the northern shore of Albermarle Sound sits the Harvey Point Defense Testing Activity, a CIA facility for training in sabotage and demolition. According to *The News and Observer* (August 3, 1975) there are no published figures for the number of CIA "soldiers" on this secret base. What can be counted adds up to nearly 90,000 servicemen and another 200,000 civilian personnel, military dependents and retirees gathered together in the eastern third of the state. That's more people than the combined populations of Winston-Salem and Raleigh. Over $1.4 billion spent each year by military personnel and their families in the shops and country stores of eastern North Carolina has a powerful impact.[41] If they ain't just whistlin' Dixie, it's because the Marine Corps Hymn is higher on the charts these days.

Camp Lejeune, brags Commanding General R.D. Bohn, is "one of the largest 'industries'" in the state and the "greatest single contributor" to the economy of eastern North Carolina.[42] Built in 1941, the reservation covers 170 square miles, and contains two golf courses, some 6,000 buildings and facilities for a city of 60,000 people. Lejeune's population alone spends about $23 million a year on North Carolina goods and services.

The political influence of the marines in this part of the state is at least as important as the economic clout. This was the launching base for the 1958 invasion of Lebanon, ordered by President Eisenhower; the 1962 Cuban missile crisis, directed by President Kennedy; the "incursion" into Santo Domingo, under President Johnson. During 1971 and 1972, according to the official base history, "units were engaged in training exercises in the Mojave Desert, across the Appalachian ranges, along cold rocky Maine beaches as well as in the Caribbean."

From the halls of Montezuma to the shores of Jacksonville, N.C., the marines of Camp Lejeune make their presence known. Jacksonville, the town adjacent to the base, is said to have been a favorite hideout of buccaneers like Henry Morgan and Blackbeard. Now, "The City on the Go," as the Greater Jacksonville Chamber of Commerce would have it, is the favorite hangout of the 2nd Marine Division. The town did well by the Vietnam War: in the decade 1963–72 Jacksonville grew 240 percent.[43] In the last five of those years, more than 3,000 marines retired in the county.

Of the marines on base, more than 3,000 are originally from in-state. As one marine officer says, "Camp Lejeune *is* North Carolina."[44] A civilian-military council has been organized to bind more tightly the ties between town and base. The council includes generals and Onslow County Chamber of Commerce leaders, the mayor of Jacksonville and assorted gentry of civic mind. Off-duty marines volunteer for community activities—putting roofs on nursing homes, plastering shacks, and such, under names like Operation Concern. A Lejeune spokesman claims that the marines, subject as they are to federal law, are a force for civil rights in backwater North Carolina. "Seventy-nine-year-old Aunt Janie won't change, but the New South will," he argues. But the same officer recalls the summer of 1969 when Black and Chicano marines fought white marines off base. Two were killed.

At that point a career marine named Leroy Gibson became fed up and left the corps to form the Rights of White People organization (ROWP). The ROWP was nothing if not active. A Jacksonville anti-war bookstore called United We Stand was bombed by ROWP terrorists. Marines were recruited by Gibson to break strikes. Civil rights demonstrations were broken up by force, synagogues and newspapers bombed, Black leaders shot at and threatened. The ROWP organized armed patrols of Black and white communities. Leroy Gibson, who lights up any room he leaves, claimed the existence of seven or eight cells at Camp Lejeune in the early 1970s. A Lejeune spokesman acknowledged that after 20 years in the corps, "there are officers who served with him and who still maintain their friendship."[45]

If North Carolina is New South, Fort Bragg is New Army. Public relations plumage covers the old basics and masks the new. Officers are trained to deal with the public. Community services, human relations, equal opportunity, civic action—these are the new tasks of Fort Bragg, to read the publicity brochures. The base, whose population makes it the second largest city in the state after Charlotte, was named for Braxton Bragg, a North Carolina general in the Confederate Army. Here is housed the XVIII Airborne Corps with its attached units, including the 82nd Airborne. Bragg is also home base for the Green Berets, and the Psychological Warfare Center, renamed the JFK Center for Military Assistance by some enterprising huckster.

The 82nd Airborne, nicknamed the "All Americans," not only had successful engagements in Santo Domingo and Saigon, according to official army propaganda, but "on several occasions . . . sent forces on Civil Disturbance missions to various cities within the United States." Division training programs take place in "an adventure-filled atmosphere"—deployments to Puerto Rico, Panama, Texas, Kentucky, Georgia and Alabama; also in "Greece, Turkey, Korea and on the North Carolina coast."[46]

The 503rd Military Police Battalion, based at Bragg, "continues to serve in the same tradition established in such places as the beaches of

Normandy, the Dominican Republic and, more recently, our nation's capital and Miami Beach." Truly All Americans, the 16th Military Police Group is stationed near corps headquarters but one never needs travel far: "A look in your rear-view mirror will usually reveal the presence of one or two of the finest military policemen anywhere."[47]

John D. Granger, commander of the 503rd MPs, is a man of vision, believing as he does that a concerted military effort could make an anachronism of social work agencies. The Pentagon "can make a more rapid and profound impact on our society than any other single institution," Granger argues. "If each member of the department were to spend an hour a month on a socially productive project, this would exceed the total efforts that all volunteer welfare agencies provide in a year."[48] Just such thinking prompted Lt. Gen. John J. Tolson, then CO at Bragg, to pioneer the Domestic Action programs in 1970. Tolson, a man with an ear for current trends, called the programs "Nation-building."

Hoke County, adjoining the base on the west, is one of the 100 poorest counties in the United States, with severe economic and medical problems. So Ft. Bragg Domestic Action Teams updated county medical records, conducted tests for tuberculosis and provided medical corpsmen to help operate the county clinic. Temporary water mains were installed, children's playgrounds constructed. At the same time, Green Berets were sent to Anson County "to improve the ability of military assistance personnel to work with civilians" in clearing brush, learning first aid, training in "public safety," and otherwise meeting public needs. An athletic field was built for East Bladen High School in Elizabethtown. At the Western Correctional Center, a high-rise prison, Special Forces troops came to train select groups of inmates. Apparently the soldiers made an impression. According to Granger, "Most of the prisoners now spit-shine their shoes to emulate a glittering Green Beret look. Some have even converted prison-brown to Army-black."

The North Carolina Department of Human Resources has thrown its weight behind Domestic Action. Together with local corporations to help foot the bill, the state now organizes week-long encampments at Fort Bragg for North Carolina children to experience the hidden joys and spiritual rewards of military life. Domestic Action programs have proven so successful to their designers that they have now been effected in Salinas, California, Orangeburg, South Carolina, and a score of other communities from sea to shining sea. No ghosts of George Custer past are these soldiers as they check teeth on Montana's Northern Cheyenne Reservation or instruct Florida Seminoles in methods of law enforcement.

Domestic Action was to become the army's answer to the war on poverty. Who better to conduct a war, no matter the enemy, the army might argue. Besides, the soldier, subject to military discipline, is a far more dependable representative of Old Glory to the poor and powerless photos of soldiers stoned on heroin with garlands of human ears strung than a civilian VISTA volunteer who, likely as not, was a peace-creep trying to avoid military service in the first place.

Domestic Action was an idea whose time had come at just the right moment for the Nixon Administration, which had set about the task of dismantling the Office of Economic Opportunity. With its vaccination programs and building playgrounds for impoverished children, Domestic Action would have important residual effects. It could win the hearts and minds of those who may have become disaffected at the daily news of Vietnamese being thrown to their deaths from helicopters, and news photos of soldiers stoned on heroin with garlands of human ears strung on their jeeps.

North Carolina is hardly unique in its hiring of retired military personnel—a colonel to be Charlotte city engineer, another to head up a branch of the state corrections department, for example. But the state may have set a precedent when it hired General Tolson, the commander of Fort Bragg and resident genius of Domestic Action, to become secretary of the North Carolina Department of Military and Veterans Affairs (DMVA). General Tolson, a bear of a man with the sort of enthusiasm one associates with the chairman of a save-our-parks committee, says, "We make no distinction between the military and the community at large. You can't separate the two."[49]

One of the general's responsibilities in his new position was that most direct of military-civilian ties, the National Guard. In North Carolina, the Guard has 12,000 troops. General Tolson, bearing a disarming personality and grim statistics, boosted the Black and Indian composition of the Guard to more than 6 percent. Five years before, 99 percent of the Guard was white. These were the troops that were sent in to quell "civic disturbances" that grew out of racist attacks on Black communities in the early 1970s. Judge John Walker of Wilmington, which saw the state's worst violence of those years, says he received letters from Guardsmen in nearby Blyden and Pender counties. "They have organized armed citizens' committees, patrolling against the few known criminal revolutionists. I don't blame them," says Judge Walker. "The Guardsmen are ordinary American citizens—farmboys, workers, lawyers. They are supposed to defend their families."[50] (During Governor Robert Scott's administration, 1969–73, the Guard was called to state service 28 times; nine times for "civil disorders"; once for a student demonstration; 12 for missing person searches, and six times for ice storms and hurricanes. In those same years, the number of Black Guardsmen increased from 76 to 233 out of 12,000, or from half of one percent to almost two percent.)

General Tolson's DMVA also included Veterans Administration, the Civil Air Patrol, the Adjutant General's office, and the Division of Civil Preparedness. This latter aspect of the general's work used to be called "civil defense" but was switched "to change the public image." The division prepares plans for nuclear attack or other man-made and natural disasters. DMVA's office is located in the sub-basement of the state administration building. This was the governor's "nerve center" in times of disaster, complete with its own power plant, water supply, sleeping and cooking facilities, and emergency food supply. Called the Emergency Operating Center, General Tolson occupied the space in lieu of thermonuclear fall-out over Raleigh. The DMVA still has its shelters and fall-out testing. The North Carolina Department of Transportation offers a 40-hour course of instruction for radiological treatment. In local communities, county governments bring students to the fairgrounds to simulate bombing casualties. Fort Bragg lends its helping hand in this effort.

The state legislature gave General Tolson's DMVA new powers in early 1974 when it added to his domain the implementation of state energy politics. With coordination of the National Guard, civil defense, and energy policy under his command, General Tolson was the quintessence of his own view that there is no distinction between soldier and civilian. Two months before the legislature acted, the 82nd Airborne at Fort Bragg was put on riot control training and alert, planning for martial law. Operation Garden Plot was in effect as a caution against gasoline riots during the weeks of the international fuel crisis.

Operation Garden Plot was nurtured in 1967 as a Department of Army contingency plan for imposing martial law. It called for centralized army coordination with local and state government and police authorities in case of civil disorders. While the Pentagon denies that Garden Plot contained provisions for rounding up dissident civilians, one officer said that "it would be unlikely that such plans would have been committed to writing." Garden Plot exercises are known to have been carried out in part at Kent State University in 1971, resulting in at least four student deaths, and at Wounded Knee on the Pine Ridge Oglala Sioux Reservation in 1973. Apparently other Garden Plot exercises were held in the late 1960s somewhere in California. For at a planning conference in anticipation of the action, Governor Ronald Reagan hailed the operation: "Garden Plot is in line with the 6,000-year history of man pushing the jungle back, creating a clearing where men can live in peace and go about their business with some measure of safety. Of late, the jungle has been creeping in again a little closer to our boundaries." Inasmuch as "civil rights movements" head the list of "dissident elements" that Garden Plot seeks to quell, Reagan's references to the jungle leave little room for misinterpretation. Those in his audience included 500 military men, police officials and corporate executives from Boeing, Sylvania, Bank of America, Pacific Telephone and Telegraph, Pacific Gas and Electric, and Standard Oil of California. The governor jocularly said that if his enemies saw him there they would see it as proof he "was planning a military takeover."[51]

In 1974 Garden Plot was being implemented for North Carolina motorists, under the gaze of fatherly General Tolson.

WHEN the 600 flak-jacketed National Guardsmen took the Gregory Congregational Church on that Sabbath in February 1971 and finally imposed a curfew, Reverend and Mrs. Templeton were forced to flee Wilmington. Later at a meeting of the state civil rights commission the minister would testify that over 50 shots were fired into his house and church in the four days of "rebellion." The local authorities claimed they could find no evidence of such shots, despite the obvious bullet holes that pockmarked the church walls. One evening during the siege, a white man shot into the Templeton home after the minister refused to open the door at 3:30 A.M. "so they could talk." When Rev. Templeton asked the police to come they refused. They showed up instead four hours later because, as one policeman explained, "We heard that Rev. Templeton had been killed and we came over to identify the body." Finding the minister alive, the cops photographed and fingerprinted him in order "to be able to identify the body" at a future date. Police made no effort to locate the nightriders nor protect this house of worship and this man of the cloth. The handwriting was clearly stained on the broken glass windows of Gregory Church.

The following Thursday was designated Black Thursday by Ben Chavis at a Raleigh press conference. High school students from throughout North Carolina were asked to come to Wilmington that day for the funeral of Steve Mitchell. City officials obtained an injunction to prevent the funeral from being held at the Gregory Church. As nearly

3,000 mourners gathered for the funeral march, another nearby church opened its doors for the ceremony. The violence and horror of the past week had frightened most of the city's God-fearing church community. But the young Black people were determined that Steve Mitchell's death not be in vain.

They asked Ben to remain on in Wilmington and he agreed. They formed an organization to continue the struggle, Black Youth Builds a Black Community (BYBBC), and elected a president, Roderick Kirby. The New Hanover Board of Education responded by initiating a federal injunction, naming as defendants Rev. Templeton, the Commission for Racial Justice, and the Southern Christian Leadership Conference, to prohibit them helping to organize the school boycott.

By now Ben had become the Reverend Benjamin F. Chavis, Jr. After completing an 18-month In-Service Ministerial Training Program under the sponsorship of the Commission for Racial Justice, he was ordained a Christian minister of the Black Christian Pan Africanist Church at a ceremony conducted by clergy of the United Church of Christ in New York. The church was part of a denomination founded in 1967 by the UCC's Rev. Albert Cleage, Jr. of Detroit. The ordination was part of a logical development for Ben. His father had been lay reader and senior warden in an Episcopal church in Oxford. Frequently without a minister, the church often asked Ben Sr. to serve as its pastor. Every Sunday for 20 years, Ben Jr. carried the cross and lighted the candles. During his student years in Charlotte, when he became a part-time organizer for the Southern Christian Leadership Conference, Ben found himself every evening speaking on civil rights issues in rural churches, large and small, througout the state. Years later, Ben would write to a friend, "It was in, through, and by the Church, that I was learning how to organize on the community grass-roots level. At this time, I became a devoted follower of Dr. Martin L. King, Jr. The effective and creative non-violent role the church was playing to bring about social change impressed me to the point that I knew that sooner or later I would devote my life to the church and struggle for justice and humanity." After the Oxford struggle when he became field organizer for the Commission for Racial Justice and entered its In-Service Ministerial Training Program, Ben joined the Oak Level United Church of Christ in Henderson. The Oak Level Church was pastored by Leon White, Ben's co-worker, who gave his church over to serve as a center for organizing the Henderson students and parents movement. Now, having survived the assault on the Gregory Congregational Church in Wilmington, Ben felt that Black Christian nationalism was at its peak in terms of new directed goals for the church in the Black community. While the Black Christian Pan Africanist Church did not meet every traditional requirement of the more orthodox, Black communities had their own traditions which harkened back to slavery, in which they recognized their spiritual leadership in a style different from the seminary training imported from Europe, to which whites had access and Black slaves did not. In an article for the magazine *Christianity and Crisis*, Robert Maurer would write about Ben's father serving as minister in the Oxford church although not actually ordained to do so: "The requirements of the Spirit took precedent over the strictures of the Law. In his son's case as well, the requirements of the Spirit have been paramount and, at times, because of his keen sense of justice, set squarely against the law."

Now back in North Carolina after his ordination ceremony, the Reverend Chavis had no church of his own. To supplement his income from the Commission, Ben reopened the Soul Kitchen in Oxford and commuted the 160 miles back and forth to Wilmington. One night in March, a month after the siege of the Gregory Church, Ben was working in the Kitchen when he received a call from Leon White of the Commission for Racial Justice. Rev. White explained that he had just been called by Molly Hicks, one of the key adult supporters of the Wilmington school boycott. A shooting had just occurred at her house. There was a rumor that a white man came up to the Hicks home, knocked at the door, and when Clifton Eugene Wright, a teenage friend of Molly's daughter Leatrice, opened the door, the man blew young Wright's head off with a shotgun. Ben agreed to go to Wilmington in the morning. But Molly Hicks called him and said she was being grilled by the police and needed legal help immediately. Ben called attorney James Ferguson in Charlotte who agreed to advise Mrs. Hicks. For the next year Molly and Leatrice Hicks were targeted by the Wilmington police for harassment.

The assault on the Gregory Church and the shooting of Clifton Wright were only the beginning of a year of bloodletting in Wilmington. Violence wracked the schools and in March both high schools were closed down. Armed bands from the Rights of White People began to patrol the streets in cars again. The reigning mood of racist revanchism was expressed by District Court Judge John Walker who, referring to Black Wilmington students, declared, "We should have sent in Lieutenant Calley to clean them up." In May a Black woman, Carrie Lee Johnson, was shot in both legs by whites in a moving car. A Black soldier on leave, A. D. Wright, was shot from ambush that same month. Two white policemen beat up a Black man, Willie Powell, on the street, sending him to a hospital with eye damage and a concussion. Powell was sentenced to four months imprisonment for resisting arrest; the police were found not guilty of assault.

Another young Black man on his way home from school was shot in the back by a policeman, causing him to be paralyzed from the waist down. The cop had been called to the scene by a middle-aged white woman who reported a "white peeping Tom." Nevertheless the policeman shot the first Black man he saw. The victim, who was on probation from prison, was sent back to prison for violating parole, even though no indictment was ever handed down against him. The policeman was not even subjected to departmental discipline.

At a fund-raising party to finance a drug-abuse program, the middle-aged Black hostess was grabbed and hit by police several times for protesting harassment of departing guests. As the woman was dragged to a police van, her clothes were partially torn off. Two young people at the party protested the beating and they in turn were maced, beaten and arrested. The two youths and the hostess were charged with disturbing the peace, resisting arrest, and assault on police.

A Commission for Racial Justice hearing on Wilmington also reported the following incident: "While attending a football game, a Black youth leader observed an eight-year-old being chased by a group of 15–18 white youths. After he had successfully intervened in this fray to prevent physical harm to the youth, two police officers grabbed the eight-year-old. While grabbing the eight-year-old, the Black youth leader was knocked aside. When the youth leader protested this treatment, he was shoved by one of the police officers. During this time, six other officers arrived. Upon their arrival they joined the first policeman who had continued to beat on the youth leader. The youth leader was arrested and convicted of 'assault on a policeman' despite testimony from eight witnesses that the youth leader was only attempting to defend himself. The youth leader was found guilty in District Court and sentenced to 12 months."

Meanwhile Ben and the BYBBC found a building on Castle Street in the center of the Black community and moved in, with some help from the Commission for Racial Justice. They painted the building black. Ben formed a church, the African Congregation of the Black Messiah, which was affiliated to other Temples of the Black Messiah in Detroit, New York and Washington, D.C. Wilmington's Temple of the Black Messiah also occupied the Black House. Roderick Kirby, the leader of the BYBBC, changed his name to Kojo Natambu and became Ben's assistant pastor at the Temple.

The Rights of White People announced that it was going to seek a military victory over the Black community. ROWP kingfish Leroy Gibson challenged Rev. Chavis to meet him in a field outside of Wilmington to "fight to the death." Gibson, a sort of permanent loose part, declared: "If necessary, we'll eliminate the Black race. What are we supposed to do while these animals run loose in the streets? They'll either abide by the law or we'll wipe them out." Such a declaration was the equivalent of shouting "fire" in a crowded ghetto.

Gibson's next step was to move ROWP headquarters into the Black community on the same block as the Temple of the Black Messiah, set up military command posts in front and on top of his building, raise the Confederate flag, and conduct martial exercises with loaded weapons in the street. While the ROWP infested the block, members of the Temple were being busted for jaywalking and loitering. Legal costs sapped the church of its meager funds. On Sundays church members were harassed by ROWP "soldiers" and on two occasions shots were fired into the Temple during services.

One morning after conducting services, Rev. Chavis left the Temple in his mother's car. He was riding in the back seat with two companions; three others were in the front seat. As they headed down the street a station wagon full of white men pulled up beside Ben's car. One of the men in the back seat drew out a snub-nosed pistol and aimed it at Ben. All of his security men hit the floor, leaving him exposed. "I jumped out of the car," Ben remembers. "I wanted to knock the gun out of the guy's hand. I wasn't going to let him shoot me just like that. But when I jumped out of the car they drove off. We gave chase, and although we couldn't catch them we got close enough to get their license number. We went downtown to the police department and reported the incident and the license number but no arrests were ever made." (A year later during the trial of the Wilmington 10 the same station wagon was parked each day at the Burgaw courthouse in Pender County.)

On August 31 a delegation of whites, led by G.D. Gross, Grand Cyclops of the Ku Klux Klan, met with Wilmington school superintendent Heywood Bellamy in a last-minute effort to postpone the federal court decision to desegregate the city schools. Bellamy received them with cordiality but explained that his hands were tied, nothing more could be done. That night 19 school buses were destroyed by fire. Two hours later the Klan burned a cross in the yard of the Temple of the Black Messiah.

Police repression of the Temple and the BYBBC continued in concert with the vigilante assaults. In October, Kojo Natambu was arrested in one of the local schools when he tried to prevent 6 policemen from beating up a 10-year-old Black student. The police turned their attack on Kojo and fractured his skull. Kojo was arrested for assaulting the officers, convicted and sentenced to 4–6 months in prison.

Leroy Gibson addressed a ROWP rally of 400 armed men in Hugh McRae Park on October 3. On display were numerous sawed-off shotguns, pump-guns and rifles. He declared that the ROWP was going after Ben and Kojo and their followers and would "hunt them down like rabbits." After the rally, 50 ROWP members approached the police department to volunteer their services. When the police told them to go home, the vigilantes went into the Black community and started shooting into homes. Police Chief H. E. Williamson was also offered 500 Klan members by Grand Cyclops Gross but Williamson said their help was not needed at present. The following day, county officials put through an emergency order banning citizens from moving about with firearms for the next week.

The evening of October 6 Rev. Chavis was driving to the Hillcrest Apartments where Kojo lived. The building had recently been sprayed with bullet holes by the ROWP and a police blockade was still posted outside. When Ben pulled up, a policeman stepped forward with his riot shotgun. The officer knew it was Ben whom he had stopped and asked him for his license. Ben showed his wallet but when the policeman asked for his car registration, he was told it was in the trunk. The cop ordered Ben to stay in the car and called downtown for instructions. Over the radio came the order, "Bring him in." Ben was arrested for operating an unregistered vehicle.

On the ride downtown Ben sat handcuffed in the back of the police car. The officer in front clicked his shotgun, put a shell in the chamber and leaned it in Ben's direction in back. During one sharp turn the gun fell to the floor but failed to discharge. At the stationhouse Ben was booked and allowed to call attorney James Ferguson in Charlotte. Bail was set at $350. Ben could have gone the $35 bond but refused and stayed in jail instead. That night and the next demonstrators outside the jailhouse protested. After three days Ben was brought before the court. He told the judge about his registration card in the trunk of the car, but the judge refused to listen and found Ben guilty. His car was impounded and he had to go to Raleigh to retrieve it. When he picked up his car the trunk was empty. While in Raleigh Ben went to the Department of Motor Vehicles for a duplicate registration card. He returned to Wilmington, card in hand, and the judge reversed the verdict to "not guilty."

Wilmington fell quiet for the next month but on November 10, the anniversary of the 1898 massacre, a 17-year-old Black girl at Hoggard

High suffered head injuries when she was hit with a chair thrown by a white student. A melee of 200 students ensued. The Hoggard principal called sheriff's deputies who moved in and beat and maced the Black students. Several were arrested but no whites were apprehended.

The ROWP called another meeting at Hugh McRae Park for November 12 but the county declared another state of emergency, banning transportation of firearms into the city and preventing use of public parks during evening hours. The ROWP moved its rally to a city park to elude the county ruling. Leroy Gibson led an armed motorcade to police headquarters to demand Chief Williamson's resignation for being "too soft" on Ben Chavis. Three days later the ROWP violated the parks curfew. Forty ROWP "soldiers" were arrested but most were released on their own recognizance. ROWP supporters held a demonstration at city jail protesting the arrests. Cars with armed whites continued to patrol the Black community, unhindered by the police. (Only 10 days before, two young Black men standing watch in front of the Temple of the Black Messiah were arrested for "armed terror of the populace," a law on the North Carolina statute books for nearly a century.) Gibson and the ROWP continued to pressure Williamson to jail Ben Chavis or else they would make a "citizen's arrest."

On December 17, 1971, the police issued warrants for the arrest of Ben Chavis, Molly Hicks, her daughter Leatrice, and a young friend Jerome McClain. They were charged with "accessory after the fact of murder," in connection with the shooting of Clifton Eugene Wright at the Hicks home nine months earlier.

Three

What's a tough guy? A guy with an edge—a bankroll in his pocket, a stripe on his sleeve, a rock in his hand, a badge on his shirt—that's an edge.
Orson Welles in *Lady from Shanghai*

There are people in our society who should be separated and discarded.
Spiro Agnew

F OUR decades ago, in 1936, the famed defense attorney Clarence Darrow wrote about the art of picking a jury:

> When court opens, the bailiff intones some voodoo singsong words in ominous voice that carries fear and respect at the opening of the rite. The courtroom is full of staring men and women shut within closed doors, guarded by officials wearing uniforms to confound the simple inside the sacred precinct. This dispels all hope of mercy to the unlettered, the poor and helpless, who scarcely dare express themselves above a whisper in any such forbidding place. . . . Never take a wealthy man on a jury. He will convict, unless the defendant is accused of violating the anti-trust law, selling worthless stocks or bonds, or something of that kind. Next to the Board of Trade, for him, the Penitentiary is the most important of all public buildings. These imposing structures stand for Capitalism. Civilization could not possibly exist without them. Don't take a man because he is a "good" man; this means nothing. You should find out what he is good *for*.[1]

Darrow's warning of the class nature of justice in the United States is as precise as the crosshairs on a rifle-sight as every courtroom docket shows. At a homecoming party after his Watergate indictment, H. R. Haldeman and his wife were described by Los Angeles civic leader Z. Wayne Griffin as "an example of what a good American family can be—well-motivated, well-mannered, well-disciplined. Good people." Good for what, asks Mr. Darrow from his grave of the other guests at the party, including the chancellor of UCLA, the president of the Times-Mirror Publishing Company, and former HEW Secretary Robert Finch.[2]

Three weeks after those festivities, several hundred judges including six justices of the state Supreme Court, politicians including Mayor-elect Abe Beame, clergymen, businessmen, news executives and lawyers gathered at New York's Biltmore Hotel to honor attorney Roy Cohn's 25 years as a member of the New York Bar, during which he was indicted on three separate occasions for conspiracy, bribery and fraud. Even as the ball was held, Mr. Cohn was evading back tax payments to the city. Praise for the honored guest's years as counsel to Senator Joseph McCarthy and as prosecutor of Julius and Ethel Rosenberg on the road to later corporate wealth was further evidence of the by-now axiomatic theory that those with flag-pins in their lapels have stickum on their fingers.[3] Mr. Cohn had just taken a kindred spirit, Spiro Agnew, to task, in the pages of *The New York Times,* for making "a dumb mistake . . . in quitting [the Vice-Presidency] and accepting a criminal conviction."[4]

Cohn may have been right, knowing as he does the legal lay of the land. Richard Kleindienst, former U.S. Attorney General, for example, was fined a hundred bucks for perjuring himself regarding an anti-trust suit against ITT. The U.S. district judge in the case said that Kleindienst's offense demonstrated "a heart too loyal and considerate of others." For Kleindienst, the system works marvelously: "There isn't another country in the world," he said, "where persons situated in the highest seats of power would have had the application of justice as occurred here."[5] Meanwhile, Richard Nixon, Godfather to Kleindienst's *consigliere,* lives in peace with dishonor at San Clemente, not San Quentin. And a Nixon enforcer named William Calley was confined to a Columbus, Georgia, rent-free apartment complete with lady-love, a Mercedes Benz sports car and $17-an-hour flying lessons, for having been found guilty of murdering 22 women and children by a jury of his military peers. Support for the mass murder in his home state was headed by the then Governor and Latter Day Human Rights Saint Jimmy Carter. In a domestic My Lai, 39 prisoners and prison guards were shot down by state police at Attica Correctional Facility in upstate New York. Sixty other prisoners were indicted on hundreds of charges with potential sentences of 600 years or 37 life terms each, while the Lord High Executioner went on to become Vice President of the United States in charge of domestic planning

Crime in the streets, the fear of which has been so perfectly orchestrated by the corporate media, is actually miniscule when compared to crime eminating from the board rooms and government suites. Watergates, FBI conspiracies, and the more spectacular crimes in high places aside, the run-of-the-mill white-collar crime wave dwarfs street crime. In the 18 months between January 1973 and June 1974, for example, white-collar crime by businessmen and government officials cost over $4 billion. In the fiscal year 1973, fraud and embezzlement took six times more money from people than did hold-ups and burglaries. Even FBI statistics show that that $4 billion loss was four times the national loss from larceny, burglary and theft, including auto theft.[6]

The toughest penalties, however, were dealt to defendants without means. Ralph Nader cites the sentence of Spiro Agnew to three years unsupervised probation and a $10,000 fine for failing to pay taxes on the $13,551 given to him as bribes, and compares this to the sentencing a day later of a California man to 70 days in jail for fishing without a license and possessing seven striped bass under the legal size.[7]

In the land of the free enterpriser, no one really expects that the ruling class would establish a system of justice more likely to penalize or imprison its peers than its antagonists. It goes without saying that the prisons are filled with the poor, while the criminals with wealth are, if caught, made to go stand in a corner and keep quiet. In recent years, so-called country-club prisons have been built to lodge the influence peddlers, stock manipulators and price fixers who overextend their prerogatives. The Allenwood (Pa.) federal facility, which housed second-string Watergate criminals, is surrounded by 4,250 acres of verdant, rolling hills on the southern fringe of the Allegheny Mountains. No walls, fences, gates, cells and bars do these prisoners face. There are two tennis courts—one indoors and one outside, a baseball diamond, basketball courts, patios, verandas with umbrella tables, a well-stocked commissary, telephones, grassy courtyards, liberal visiting and furlough privileges. Jeb Stuart Magruder could keep his tennis rackets, sneakers and can of balls alongside his bed, ready to get to the courts for a game or two upon waking.[8]

Nowhere is the class nature of the criminal justice system felt so sharply as in North Carolina, for nowhere are class distinctions seen in such bold relief with an all-powerful ruling group and its working class and poor without organization. And nowhere in the United States has punishment of the poor been so harsh as it has historically been in the Tarheel state. In times past, crimes were considered the work of the Devil. The North Carolina Supreme Court declared in 1862, "To know the right and still the wrong pursue proceeds from a perverse will brought about by the seductions of the Evil One."[9] The Old Testament appeal of an eye for an eye has always brought a quicker response than the New Testament call for forgiveness. Raleigh *News and Observer* editor Claude Sitton suggested that "the amount of violence in North Carolina has a religious connotation. Folks here believe in stern punishment, a reflection of their Baptist and Presbyterian Protestantism."[10] The case has been made more than once that the same ersatz Christianity of the Klan pervades official state criminal justice policy. Bogus Christians see those of different color or persuasion as "less than Christian." In the

"Christian" order of things, those who seek change are spurred on by "outside agitators," messengers for Old Nick.

THREE days after Ben Chavis was indicted on the accessory charge, one man of the church, the Rev. Norman Vincent Peale, demonstrating his power of positive thinking, hosted Richard Nixon on the president's 1971 New York Christmas shopping visit. In his pastoral prayer entitled "When Christmas Comes," Dr. Peale said, "O Lord, we ask thy great blessing upon thy servant, the beloved President of the United States. Undergird him, we beseech thee, in all the vast problems which he must consider. What a responsibility laid upon him, the future well-being of the mass of human beings. We thank thee that he has become one of the truly great peacemakers in history. Seldom if ever has a world statesman, O Lord, fought for peace on so wide a scale with so dramatic purposes. Just surround him with your love, guide and help him every day in all ways." Mr. Nixon, in his practiced Rotary Club luncheon manner, was reportedly shyly pleased with the sermon.

A year earlier, while Ben Chavis was organizing the Black community of Granville County to protest the Klan murder of Henry Marrow, Attorney General John N. Mitchell and his wife, Martha, were hosts at a swinging 100th birthday celebration for the usually staid Justice Department. "This is repression?" asked one department official as he drank some of the 3,100 gallons of free draught beer that was served along with 4,000 sandwiches, 4,000 chocolate brownies and several big birthday cakes. Mitchell, who had once described himself as "foremost, a police officer," was a kindred spirit to Nixon. "Not merely a chip off the old block," as Edmund Burke said of the younger Pitt, "but the old block itself."

In the years Ben Chavis and Jim Grant were organizing their people for equal education, for better working conditions, for protection against police violence, Vice President Spiro Agnew was flying back and forth across the land calling for law and order, returning home to Washington and Baltimore in time each month to receive his bag-men with their bundles of cash. When, later, Agnew precipitately retired from the second highest office in the country and pleaded no contest to the same charges that sent Al Capone to Alcatraz, he received a three-year probation, a $10,000 fine, a "Dear Ted" letter from his benefactor in the White House, permission to keep the house he furnished with criminal money, and freedom to pursue his business interests in Greece and his six-figure publisher's advance, and to play tennis with one of his favorite partners, George Bush, then Republican Party national chairman, later director of the Central Intelligence Agency. Agnew's pursuit of happiness was considerably more than was allowed to the dead or mangled Kent State students he called "bums."

While Ben was in Wilmington preventing the slaughter of innocents at the Gregory Congregational Church, Messrs. Maurice Stans, Jeb Stuart Magruder and Charles Colson were building up the campaign treasure chest for the Committee to Re-Elect the President (CREEP). Later, when their illegal $2 million gifts from the dairy monopolies came to light, an administration apologist, Treasury secretary George Shultz, explained that they took the money to prevent lobbying payoffs to Congress for higher milk prices. Preventive corruption could now take its rightful place alongside preventive detention and preemptive first strike in the Nixonian lexicon.

Among the preventive corruptors of these years of Ben Chavis' coming of political age were Orin Atkins, chairman of Ashland Oil; Harding L. Lawrence, chairman of Braniff International; H. Everett Olson, chairman of Carnation Dairy Corporation; Russell De Young of Goodyear Tire & Rubber; and Thomas V. Jones, chief executive of Northrup. All were convicted for illegal campaign contributions, a felony crime. All were fined a thousand bucks, except Jones who was fined $5,000. All retained their same positions at yearly salaries ranging from $212,500 for Olson to De Young's $350,000.

Herbert Kalmbach, Nixon's attorney and keeper of the $1.9 million purse that paid for the president's private police force in the years when Ben Chavis and Jim Grant were walking on the "Mountaintop to the Valley" march to prevent execution of sixteen-year-old Marie Hill, was sentenced to six months for his Watergate crimes. Six months is less than hundreds of thousands of poor people spend in jail awaiting trial on minor charges of which they are presumed innocent. Kalmbach told a press conference he had "renewed appreciation and confidence in the essential fairness of America's justice."

Still bitter is G. Gordon Liddy, who headed the Nixon secret police team. Liddy, a former prosecutor and federal narcotics agent, believes that Nixon's error lay in being "insufficiently ruthless," a remarkable charge against a man who ordered the deaths and permanent maiming of two million Vietnamese, Cambodians and Laotians. Speaking of the Watergate conspiracies, this member of the New York Bar argued, "If one is engaged in a war, one deploys troops, one seeks to know the capability and intentions of the enemy."

These were the men who called each other code names like Fat Jack and Sedan Chair and Ruby II while they played their deadly games during the time Ben Chavis was organizing garbage workers in Charlotte. They were not bad men; none of them ever burned down a convent.

In the years 1967-1971, when Ben emerged as the leader of North Carolina's Black youth and their parents, U.S. Department of Defense Intelligence agents carried out illegal surveillance actions against an "estimated 100,000 individuals" and a "similarly large" number of domestic organizations, according to the Senate Select Committee on Intelligence Activities. Their targets included the 1968 Poor People's March on Washington, every organization opposed to the Vietnam War, the Southern Christian Leadership Conference, New York University, Dr. King, singers Arlo Guthrie and Joan Baez, Georgia legislator Julian Bond, Dr. Benjamin Spock and Illinois Senator Adlai Stevenson III. In those same years, Army intelligence cooperated with local police intelligence units, as in Chicago, to finance and direct right-wing terrorist organizations like the Legion of Justice, which was unleashed against the pacifist Quaker organization, the American Friends Service Committee. Few in North Carolina, one of the most militaristic of states and the one with the biggest Department of Defense (DOD) installations, would wager that the Pentagon targets in those years did not include Ben Chavis and Jim Grant, both associated with anti-war activities, with the Southern Christian Leadership Conference and the American Friends Service Committee.

While the DOD carried out its illegal domestic activities, its kin in cloaks-and-daggers at the CIA were similarly engaged. Under Presidents Johnson and Nixon and the direct supervision of agency director Richard Helms, the CIA implemented Operation Chaos from 1967 to 1974. This plan which Helms later admitted exceeded even the agency's own security interests, included the infiltration of spies and disrupters into "radical groups around the country, particularly on the campuses," as well as into "such groups as the Women Strike for Peace, the Washington Peace Center, the Congress of Racial Equality and the Student Nonviolent Coordinating Committee." As the CIA went about its pursuit of "national security" by staging simulated chemical-warfare attacks on the New York subway system, feeding LSD to unsuspecting bar patrons, developing and hoarding exotic poison gases from shellfish for future mass extermination plans, using newsmen, teachers and clerics as spies, overthrowing the democratically elected government of Chile, and meshing operations with organized crime syndicates to assassinate foreign leaders and perhaps domestic ones, Operation Chaos gathered information on 300,000 U.S. citizens. As SNCC and CORE were targets of the CIA's Chaos, undoubtedly Ben Chavis and Jim Grant were among its victims.

The 30 million television viewers who watched "The FBI" each week in those years never saw portrayed any of J. Edgar Hoover's poison pen mail aimed at getting schoolteachers fired and pitting wives against husbands. ABC-TV's "FBI" never showed the compilation of lists of millions of citizens, with a priority list of 15,000 to be rounded up for concentration camps in "a national emergency." Nor was there dramatized the story of FBI informer Gary Thomas Rowe, Jr. who told the Senate Select Committee on Intelligence that the FBI condoned his participation in acts of violence as a member of the Klan in the 1960s.

The FBI's acceptance of Klan violence was of a piece with the entire thrust of the Cointelpro operations directed against the Black leadership of the United States. The FBI's Cointelpro (Counterintelligence Program) found its legs in provocations directed against the Communist Party, like Operation Hoodwink, designed to incite organized crime syndicates to violently attack the Party. Cointelpro operations expanded to include disruptions and provocations against the Socialist Workers Party and the "New Left" and anti-war movements. But the main Cointelpro efforts were aimed at the Black communities, what J. Edgar Hoover called in his secret memos, "Black Nationalist-Hate Groups." Hoover, in his Cointelpro directive, wrote that, "The purpose of this new counterintelligence endeavor is to expose, disrupt, misdirect, discredit or otherwise neutralize the activities of Black nationalist, hate-type organizations and groupings, their leadership, spokesmen, membership and supporters, and to counter their propensity for violence and civil disorder. . . No opportunity should be missed to exploit through counterintelligence techniques the organizational and personal conflicts of the leadership of the groups and where possible an effort should be made to capitalize upon existing conflicts between competing Black nationalist organizations."

At the top of Hoover's list of apparent "Black Nationalist-Hate Groups" was the Rev. King, the Nobel Peace Prize winner. After Hoover's death, the FBI admitted to at least 25 separate incidents of bureau harassment of Rev. King during a six-year campaign to discredit the civil rights leader. The acknowledged incidents do not include the at least 16 illegal wiretaps of King's home, offices and hotel rooms, although they do include attempts, through poison pen letters, to induce Dr. King to commit suicide. This "vicious vendetta"—the words are those of the Senate Select Committee on Intelligence—did not end with Dr. King's murder, but continued with attempts to smear his memory and harass his widow.

The Hoover memo was signed in August 1967 and the FBI admits that Cointelpro activities against the Black communities and their organizations continued until at least mid-1971. Those were the years Ben Chavis came to leadership of Black students in Charlotte, Raleigh, Oxford, Warrenton, Henderson, Elizabethtown and Wilmington, North Carolina. (Special Cointelpro directives aimed against SCLC, SNCC and the Black Panthers came out of Hoover's office in the years Ben was associated with those organizations.)

To the Nixon White House—as subsequent investigations demonstrated—every longhair football player, liberal news columnist and Hollywood peacenik had become enemies. But the Nixon Justice Department and State Department singled out certain "enemies" for havoc. The muscle for these operations was provided by the Justice Department's Internal Security Division (ISD), which had been abeyant since the height of the Cold War. In 1970 the ISD was revived under Assistant Attorney General Robert Mardian, Southwest campaign manager for Barry Goldwater's 1964 presidential quest and Nixon's emissary to the right-wing yahoos of Arizona and the Southwest. Before coming to the Justice Department, Mardian served as chief counsel to Nixon's Department of Health, Education and Welfare, where he supervised the Southern strategy and anti-busing policies of the Administration.

Mardian brought to the ISD a hard-nosed and heavy-handed prosecutorial bent, going after pacifist Catholic priests, draft resisters, Daniel Ellsberg and Tony Russo, Irish Republican supporters, and all other manner of White House "enemies." Mardian is said to have told an FBI agent that the way he intended to proceed was "to set up a list of key leaders and we target them for prosecution, and we go after them with blanket coverage 24 hours a day until we get them." Through prosecutions, grand jury inquisitions and through cooperation with the FBI, Mardian's ISD relentlessly went about its nasty business.

A special feature of the Mardian method was the use of the *agent provocateur*: The FBI informer Robert Hardy who provided the skills, supplies and logistics for the draft board raid by the Catholic pacifists of the "Camden, N.J. 28"; the FBI informer Larry Grathwol, the most experienced bomb-maker for the Weather Underground; the FBI informer William Lemmer, advocate of bombing the 1972 Democratic and Republican conventions in Miami and chief witness against the eight Vietnam Veterans Against the War in Gainesville, Fla. Mardian organized through similar personnel and tactics the prosecution of the

Harrisburg 8, Chicago 7, the Pentagon Papers defendants, and the Wounded Knee cases.

Mardian and his boss at the Justice Department, John Mitchell, were of course themselves convicted as leaders of the Watergate conspiracy. But while in authority Mardian, through his ISD, was a key element of the White House police apparatus, giving intelligence information on political opponents to H. R. Haldeman and John Erlichman, or to their counterparts at the Committee to Re-Elect the President. James McCord, Jr., CIA agent and convicted Watergate burglar in charge of CREEP security, received "almost daily" reports from Mardian's ISD.

Mardian seemed to view civil liberties as a memorable phenomenon but happily a thing of the past, like goldfish swallowing or Cro-Magnon man. His aggressiveness at ISD was rewarded by Nixon when the administration decided to "reactivate the moribund Intelligence Evaluation Committee (IEC) of the Department of Justice," according to the report of the Rockefeller Commission, "On CIA Activities Within the United States." The Rockefeller report concludes: "The initial meeting of the reconstituted IEC occurred on December 3, 1970 in John Dean's office in the Old Executive Office Building. . . . The Committee was composed of representatives from the Department of Justice, the FBI, the CIA, the Department of Defense, the Secret Service and the National Security Agency. A representative of the Treasury Department was invited to participate in the last two IEC meetings. The Chief of Counterintelligence was the CIA representative on the IEC, and the Chief of Operation Chaos was his alternate." Mardian was chairman of the IEC, what one critic dubbed, "a sort of domestic war room," which met weekly on such matters as "The Inter-Relationship of Black Power Organizations in the Western Hemisphere."

The Rockefeller Commission reported: "The IEC was not established by Executive Order. In fact, according to minutes of the IEC meeting on February 1, 1971, Dean said he favored avoiding any written directive concerning the IEC because a directive 'might create problems of Congressional oversight and disclosure.' Several attempts were nevertheless made to draft a charter for the committee, although none appears to have been accepted by all of the IEC members. The last draft which could be located, dated February 10, 1971, specified the 'authority' for the IEC as 'the Interdepartmental Action Plan for Civil Disturbances,' something which had been issued in April 1969 as the result of an agreement between the Attorney General and the Secretary of Defense. Dean thought it was sufficient just to say that the IEC existed 'by authority of the President'. . . . [CIA Director Richard] Helms testified that he understood that the

IEC had been organized to focus and coordinate intelligence on domestic dissidence."

Nobody in the IEC has ever divulged what its files contained or where the information it obtained came from. Only one known outsider, from the Senate Subcommittee on Constitutional Rights, ever saw the files and he reported that they included detailed dossiers on leaders and memberships of "movement" organizations. One student of criminal justice under Nixon, Mitchell and Mardian suggests that the way the IEC was set up, without charter and without checks, indicates that it may have been a front or intelligence-laundering operation for the CIA, which is forbidden by law to spy domestically. That James Angleton, with Mardian; it seems Huston was more interested in spying, Mardian of revelations of CIA domestic illegalities, was the CIA representative on the IEC, lends credence to this hypothesis.

In 1970 while the ISD was still going full-force under Mardian, White House aide Tom Charles Huston devised his now infamous plan for wire tapping, burglary, mail covers and other illegal activities under Oval Office authority. But J. Edgar Hoover, pleased as Punch with his own Cointelpro, refused to go along with the Huston Plan, and Nixon was forced to abandon it. After Hoover's veto, Mardian asked Huston to become his assistant. Huston declined the offer because of differences with Mardian; it seems Huston was more interested in spying, Mardian with jailing. Three months later Mardian set up the IEC.

Students taught to believe the words chiseled into marble courthouses might question Mardian's fist-in-the-velvet-glove approach to criminal justice. What right, they might ask, has the government to infiltrate, spy on and disrupt the lives of citizens and their organizations if that government is democratic. Regrettably, the answer would appear to be that government in these United States is not of the people but in opposition to the people. It is one thing to protect against crime, another to protect against political opposition. Marxists of course hold that any government is a superstructure built upon and representative of the economic system in which it operates. In the United States, the most fully developed capitalist system in history, a "dictatorship" of the capitalist class prevails. That is, all the basic decisions of the society—foreign policy, whether or not to go to war, expansion or restriction of the public sector, austerity or spending, repression or relaxation—are determined by the interests of the dominant class and its political representatives. Particularly in the last 40 years of U.S. history has the role of government as arbiter in favor of capital become clear, first to save the system from economic crisis and organized mass insurgency in the 1930s, then to transform the economy to a permanent wartime footing during the 1940s, the subsequent maintenance of a worldwide army and police force, and the development of the biggest police and prison establishment in the world since then. If the economic structure is based on "private enterprise" dominated by monopolies, where decisions are made for and in the interests of the few, and the many—the workers— are excluded from decision-making, then the government that is built on that structure will reflect those tendencies. Only sustained, organized and united popular movements are able to force alterations in the decisions by those in power.

Democratic gains, expansions of civil rights and civil liberties came only after mass demands and mass struggle, often at great sacrifice, including the sacrifice of lives. This was true in the revolution to found the United States, in the wave of slave revolts and the Civil War, in the struggle for democracy and Reconstruction, in the fight for economic justice in the 1930s, for civil liberties in the McCarthy period and for civil rights in the years that followed. Each of these attempts to expand democracy were seen as threats to, and treated as such by, the economic dictatorship that prevails.

In the North Carolina of Duke Power and Wachovia Bank and J.P. Stevens and R.J.Reynolds, the civil rights movement of the late 1960s and early 1970s, led in large part by Ben Chavis, was perceived in much the same way as earlier labor struggles in Gastonia and Winston-Salem and Henderson. That movement was seen by mill owner and banker, by the "special interests" that control the state government, by their surrogates in power intent on attracting still more industry to the state, as a threat to their power. They were determined to kill that movement by decapitation.

When Richard Nixon was elected president in 1968, using his "Southern Strategy," the idea was to create a "New Majority," to shatter the traditional Democratic Party base from the New Deal days with organized labor and the Black population at its core. The formerly "solid South" of the Democrats was to be broken up; the idea being that the Democratic Party on a national level was "too liberal" on the question of racism, so Southern Democrats were asked to vote Republican in national elections. In fact, this practice had been in effect for a number of years and the Democrats remained as ardent in the pursuit of Southern racist votes as the Republicans. But in 1968, George Wallace as a presidential candidate was a new factor on the national scene. Nixon and his campaign manager, John Mitchell, struck a number of bargains with Southern politicians, promises to be kept after the election.

Primary among these deals was the vow to maintain segregated schools. The busing question was before the federal courts, and Southern racists backed by the White House had agreed to block busing at all costs. The FBI was conducting its Cointelpro operations, in coordination with other federal, state and local police agencies, with the stated goal of beheading any militant Black liberation movement. Black Panthers were being killed, the Rev. King had just been murdered, local Black leaders were being sent to long prison terms in virtually every state. When, during the first Nixon term, with Mitchell in charge of Justice and Mardian his assistant, Federal District Judge James MacMillan ruled that the Charlotte-Mecklenburg school system must desegregate, by busing if necessary, the implications were clear for all of North Carolina's schools. Fifteen years after the U.S. Supreme Court ruled that school segregation was illegal, North Carolina, through its largest school district, was becoming the test case on busing. White parents were organized into the Klan and the Rights of White People to defy the law and to create hysteria among whites and fear among Blacks.

The movement among Black students and parents for equal education grew spontaneously in city after city, village after village. That movement needed organizers. Ben Chavis and Jim Grant became the best known and the most talented of these. As such, they became targets number one for the repressive authorities of the state, acting in league with the Nixon administration. In North Carolina, whites in government used to wear Confederate flag pins in their lapels. Under the Nixon presidency, they changed to the stars and stripes. They had come to the belief that the rest of the country had changed its mind.

In the eighteenth century, racist fears of Black people were somewhat allayed by the enactment of laws in North Carolina permitting castration as punishment for sexual offenses by Blacks, for striking a white or running away. In 200 years the laws have changed but the fears remain. New Southern whites holding the reins of power deny their racism. Individually, they are capable of kind acts and go to great lengths to publicly display their charity and good works, but they are also capable of barbarism; kind acts because they are human, barbarism because they are racist. The great fear of "Black power," when push finally came to shove, was "because if they get power they may do to us what we have been doing to them," as one white man admitted in a moment of candor.

Writing of another time in another place, James Baldwin might well have been thinking of North Carolina in 1967-72: "The population becomes more hostile, the situation more tense, and the police force is increased. One day, to everyone's astonishment, someone drops a match in the powder keg and everything blows up. Before the dust has settled or the blood congealed, editorials, speeches and civil rights commissions are loud in the land, demanding to know what happened. What happened is that Negroes want to be treated like men.

"Negroes want to be treated like men: a perfectly straightforward statement, containing only seven words. People who have mastered Kant, Hegel, Shakespeare, Marx, Freud, and the Bible find this statement utterly impenetrable. The idea seems to threaten profound, barely conscious assumptions. A kind of panic paralyzed their features, as though they found themselves trapped on the edge of a steep place."[11]

Ben Chavis' "problem" apparently was that he was out of sync with the times. For most of the South, the civil rights movement had come and gone, and was now something of a political hoolahoop. Civil rights were viewed by most whites as a once-pressing moment, now long forgotten, like last year's World Series. Yet the civil rights movement had for the most part passed North Carolina by, opting for the more retrograde states of the Deep South. The Tarheel state was, after all, the New South. But now, in 1971 and 1972, as Blacks entered state legislatures and sheriff's departments, albeit in small numbers, in Alabama and Georgia, they were still left waiting in North Carolina. Little gray "Johnny Reb" caps still filled the curio shops of North Carolina, and "Dixie" was still standard fare at stockcar races and high-school assemblies.

During the days of McCarthyism following World War Two, Communists and other leftists of the 1930s were referred to as "premature antifascists" for their support of the Spanish Republic against the onslaught of Hitler, Mussolini and Franco before it was the current thing to do. Perhaps Ben Chavis and Jim Grant would some day be called "deferred freedom-fighters" for taking up the civil rights fight in the South after most of the North was running for cover as the struggle for justice moved closer to home. "Civil rights" had again become unmentionable in polite society; this year ecology was preferable.

Only one week before he was indicted on December 17, 1971, with Molly and Leatrice Hicks on the "accessory after the fact of murder" charge in Wilmington, Rev. Chavis was indicted along with Jim Grant on federal charges of conspiracy to aid Al Hood and David Washington flee the country to avoid prosecution on the dynamite-possession rap in Oxford the year before. Bail for Ben and Jim was set at $20,000 each. When the "Wilmington Three" indictments came down seven days later,

Ben had to post an additional $10,000 bail. One month after that, on January 30, 1972, Jim Grant, T. J. Reddy and Charles Parker were indicted for arson conspiracy in Charlotte around the Lazy B stable fire four years earlier.

Ben was in Portsmouth, Virginia, when the news came of the federal indictment. Still working as field organizer for the N.C.-Virginia office of the Commission for Racial Justice, Ben was asked to come to Portsmouth by Black parents and students trying to save the I.C. Norcum High School from being closed down. In the course of the school struggle, other problems in Portsmouth were exposed—police brutality, discriminatory hiring practices, and such. On Thanksgiving, the Black community, through Ben, called for a school and merchants boycott for the rest of the year.

Black students went to school every morning but not to classes. Instead they held a peaceful picketline, joined by their parents. But the police soon tired of the daily demonstrations and on December 10, brought their canine squad to the school and turned the dogs loose on the students. That night the Portsmouth radio announced that the police were searching for Ben Chavis, wanted in North Carolina for committing a federal crime. Chavis, said the news, was a criminal fugitive hiding in Portsmouth.

Ben asked attorney Ferguson in Charlotte to meet him in Raleigh where he would turn himself in. He would travel to Raleigh unannounced, to avoid being shot down by the Portsmouth police, North Carolina Highway Patrol or vigilante bounty-hunters along the way. He went first to Norfolk, grabbed a Trailways bus to Raleigh and walked across town to his sister Helen's home. Helen was then teaching at St. Augustine's.

In the morning, Ben turned himself in to the Alcohol, Tobacco and Firearms people of the Treasury Department who were in charge of the case. Placed in handcuffs and rushed before the magistrate, he was charged with aiding the federal fugitives Hood and Washington, and with possession of the illegal dynamite which Hood and Washington drove into the Oxford roadblock 18 months earlier. Bail was set at $20,000 and the Commission for Racial Justice posted the $2,000 security bond.

Ben went to New York to discuss the case with the Commission's national office and its executive director, Dr. Charles Cobb. While there, the Wilmington Three charges were announced on the radio. Chavis was wanted for murder, the news said, for the shooting at Mrs. Hicks' home in March. Ben flew back to Wilmington with a Commission attorney and co-worker Irv Joyner, who had prearranged with the local authorities that Ben would turn himself in. At the airport, Kojo and other members of the Temple of the Black Messiah were on hand to meet Rev. Chavis. Joining them were several dozen New Hanover sheriff's deputies and local police. As Ben debarked from the plane, a detective read the warrant to him, there on the runway, and escorted him to a waiting police car. The cops did not allow his attorney to ride with Ben, who was hurried downtown for bail proceedings and made to post $10,000 bond. The next day's *Hanover Sun* ran a banner headline: "'Big Bad' Ben Surrenders."

After Christmas Ben returned to Portsmouth to continue the boycott. The older community leadership was cooperating with the young. Makeshift classrooms were set up in churches. The kids would picket the official schools in the morning and study at church in the afternoon. In mid-January 1972, the police turned the dogs loose on the students again. Until then the school boycott was about 75 percent effective, but after the police dogs bit the students, everybody walked out of school.

Ben would often commute the four hours from Portsmouth to Wilmington in those days. On the day when the police dogs went after the students the second time, Jim Grant and Marvin Patrick were with Ben in Portsmouth. That evening, as they pulled into a courtyard to drop off some students at home, they noticed an unmarked police car enter the courtyard behind them. Ben was on the passenger side in front and got out to approach the police. The police demanded Ben's driver's license. He told them that he wasn't driving the car, he didn't have to show his license, he had broken no laws, to charge him if they thought he had or leave him alone. Two other unmarked police cars came into the courtyard but by then the people who lived there had come outside to see what was going on. The police were far out-numbered, and got back in their cars and drove off.

Usually Ben stayed in the homes of various students or church members but, since his friends from North Carolina, Jim and Marvin, were with him, he joined them at the Holiday Inn. Tired from the day's events, they went right to bed. They were already asleep when the door suddenly flew off its hinges and a crew of police pushed into the room, their guns drawn. The young men were forced to line up against the wall for a body search. "Can you picture it?" asked Ben later. "There we were, naked or in our underwear, and the police are patting us down for weapons. They got so frustrated that we weren't armed, they tore the room apart looking for guns. They brought a camera crew up to the room to take mug shots. We hadn't even been busted yet."

Ben was placed under arrest—the others were released—for running a stop sign, failing to produce a driver's license when driving a vehicle, disorderly conduct and disrupting the public schools. Four misdemeanors. He was handcuffed and taken down to jail. At the jail were David Simmons, president of the United Black Students Association in Portsmouth, and his mother. Young Simmons was bleeding from the head where the police had beaten him. They had gone into his house and dragged him out. He was sick with flu and under doctor's care that day, and had not even been in the demonstration at the school. Mrs. Simmons was also under arrest for assaulting a police officer. When the police came to their home they pushed her aside as she answered the door and knocked her down when she blocked their path, hence the assault charge. The Commission put up Ben's $2,000 bond. His trial was put off to August.

In February Ben decided to catch the Muhammed Ali-Joe Frazier fight on a closed-circuit movie screen at North Carolina State University's Reynolds Coliseum in Raleigh. On his way out of the Coliseum with a friend, Ben was approached by a young white man whom he took to be a student. The stranger said something to the effect of how good the fight was, Frazier winning and all. Frazier had been built up in the press as the "good Black man" as opposed to the "militant," talkative Ali. Ben said he didn't think the fight was all that great but the white man kept on talking of what a good fight it was, and then, "Frazier sure shut that n-----'s mouth." Ben turned on him and told him to shut up. The man said, "I know who you are. You're that loudmouth Chavis and I'll shut your mouth like Frazier did Ali."

Ben started walking faster but the man followed him outside. On the sidewalk the man told Ben he was a police officer. Ben said he didn't believe him and told him to get lost. Moments later as Ben reached his car in the parking lot, turned on the motor and started to back out, a half dozen police cars, blue lights spinning and sirens blaring, pulled into the lot. An officer went to Ben's door, his gun in hand, pulled Ben out and told him to put his hands in the air. He was being arrested for assaulting a police officer. The white man from the Coliseum appeared and Ben was placed in handcuffs. Frank Ballance, a Black attorney whom Ben had known from Warrenton, witnessed the arrest and followed Ben down to the police station. Bond was set at $500.

When the trial was held three weeks later, Ballance represented Ben. The "assaulted" policeman admitted Ben had not touched him, but had assaulted him "by fear," because the cop thought Ben had a knife or gun. When he was forced under cross-examination to admit that Ben had actually carried no weapon, he argued that Ben had assaulted him with his mouth by calling him names. The case was dismissed, although the officer remained on the Raleigh police force. For Ben, his job as organizer was becoming as risky as a sack race in a minefield.

On Monday, February 21, 1971, Ben was in Charlotte to address a Queens College symposium. He told the students that "the system" in the United States was not working for Black people, that they had to begin looking elsewhere for models, that some day he hoped to go to Africa to study its liberation movements first-hand. When District Judge C. H. Burnett in Wilmington read the news report of Ben's remarks in Charlotte, he raised Ben's bond in the Wilmington Three case from $10,000 to $100,000 on the grounds that Ben might jump bail and flee to Africa. The raising of bond came in a preliminary hearing to find probable cause in the case. Ben was now being held for $100,000 charged as an "accessory after the fact of murder," while Donald J. Nixon who was accused of the murder itself was released on $3,000 bond. Ben sat in jail for 10 days while his attorneys fought for a reduction of bond. When a Superior Court judge finally brought it back down to $15,000, the Raleigh *News and Observer* said the reduction "seemingly indicate[s] the change in attitude in Wilmington, which early this year won a special state award for its effectiveness in dealing with racial problems."

Finally out of jail again, Ben flew to Gary, Indiana, for the First Black Political Assembly, hosted by Mayor Richard Hatcher. Ben was a spokesman for the North Carolina delegation and succeeded in getting the assembly to pass a resolution condemning the all-white Wilmington city government as illegal, due to its uncut umbilical cord stretching from the 1898 massacre. Since the Reconstruction government was forcibly overthrown, not a single Black had been elected to the city council or county commission. The day after the assembly adjourned, March 13, Ben returned to Raleigh and drove directly to Wilmington.

As soon as he crossed the bridge leading into town, police squad cars began to tail him. After picking up Marvin Patrick at home, he went directly to the Temple of the Black Messiah. Within minutes the Temple was surrounded by police. Patrol cars moved in, choreographed with June Taylor precision. Ben came outside to see what the fuss was about, and was arrested again, this time for five felonies: burning with incendiary devices, conspiracy to burn with incendiary devices, assault on emergency personnel, conspiracy to assault emergency personnel, conspiracy to commit murder. In Battle of Britain tones, the arresting officer told Ben that he was being held for the burning of Mike's Grocery during the siege of the Gregory Congregational Church 13 months before, for assaulting eight police officers, and for conspiring to murder Harvey Cumber, the white man who was killed as he fired into the church.

It was nearly midnight when they booked him and set bond at $75,000. In less than four months Rev. Chavis had been indicted for 12 separate crimes, busted five times, and had to post bond of nearly $200,000. (This brief record which begins with the "accessory after the fact of murder" arrest, does not include the false arrest in Raleigh after the Ali-Frazier fight, nor several dozen arrests for parading without a permit and other misdemeanors growing out of demonstrations.) While he made his one phone call to attorney Ferguson in Charlotte, the police brought in Marvin Patrick, Connie Tindall, James McCoy, Jerry Jacobs, Willie Earl Vereen and Ann Sheppard. All but Ann Sheppard were high-school students, activists in the Wilmington school boycott. The same charges brought against Ben were being brought against Marvin Patrick. The other four students were charged with arson and conspiracy to assault emergency personnel. Ms. Sheppard was charged with conspiracy to burn property and conspiracy to assault emergency personnel. Four other Black students were arrested soon after. Joe Wright, Wayne Moore, George Kirby and Reginald Epps were charged with conspiracy to assault emergency personnel and conspiracy to burn property. All were placed under $50,000 bond except Ann Sheppard whose bond was $20,000.

While awaiting a probable cause hearing, they were left in the Wilmington jail, notoriously filthy with rats and roaches ever present. Protests against the conditions by the young defendants brought macing and gassing of the inmates. Ben was gassed on three separate occasions. One morning fires broke out and the guards refused to extinguish them, leaving the prisoners to suffer from smoke inhalation until they could finally smother the flames.

On March 30 the preliminary hearing was held. Thousands of supporters stood in the streets in front of the courthouse. The courtroom was packed with friends from the Commission for Racial Justice, the Temple of the Black Messiah, and from East Arcadia, Elizabethtown, Burgaw and even from as far away as Portsmouth. Again Judge Burnett was presiding over Ben's fate. Their relationship was becoming as frequent and monotonous as *As the World Turns.* The hearing proceeded as expected, except for when the state's main witness Allen Hall, a former mental patient being held on unrelated criminal charges, jumped from the stand and lunged for Ben in an attempt to hit him. Eight deputies hustled Hall into a side room; others surrounded Ben.

Predictably, at the end of the hearing Burnett bound the 11 defendants over for trial. Though they had only had a preliminary hearing and not a trial and were presumed innocent in the eyes of the law, the men and woman were shackled in leg irons, waist chains and handcuffs and returned to the Wilmington jail. All were to remain there for months in a form of preventive detention, awaiting bail or trial.

VIRTUALLY every county prosecutor's office in North Carolina is all-white. In 1976 of 140 district court judges, only 4 were Black. Two of 60 superior court judges were Black. The 9 appellate court judges and 7 supreme court judges are all white.[12] Among the state's many legal peculiarities is the absence of a statewide public defender's office, although the law allows the hiring of private prosecutors; nor does North Carolina allow for sentence review. A Black community organizer accused of burning down a barn, say, will draw 25 years imprisonment, while a white man who kills another will get 3 to 5 years. That Black organizer might on appeal get a new trial or a pardon, but he cannot win a reduced sentence on the books.

Small wonder that prisoners see the judge who presides over the system of justice as "a political henchman of political bosses," as one pardoned former inmate testifies. "After all, a judge is a lawyer who may or may not have been a success in the practice of law. He is appointed or selected as a judge. If he knew anything about crime and punishment before assuming this powerful position, it was probably because he had been successful in 'getting convictions' as a prosecutor. In theory, every man is entitled to 'his day in court.' The theory is that he must be proved guilty of the crime with which he is charged. The theory is that the prosecutor, representing the 'people' has the duty to bring out all of the facts—to get the truth. However, anyone who has watched a prosecutor work will have to admit that his every word is designed to 'put the prisoner behind bars' and that truth and the individual rights of the prisoner are secondary considerations to what he considers his prime objective of 'getting a conviction.' "[13]

The theory of equal justice under law, supposedly a national credo, in reality cuts against the American grain, in the phrase of Dwight Mac-Donald. In North Carolina, with over one million Black people, only 100 Black lawyers were practicing in 1975. The Bar Board of Examiners had no Blacks, with the result that less than half the Black law school graduates ever passed the Bar exam. In 1971, 9 out of 29 Black graduates passed the Bar while all of the whites who took it passed. When Blacks do pass, they practice before predominantly white juries. Even in majority Black counties like Bertie County, Blacks have been permitted to serve on juries only since the 1960s; still today, only 20–25 percent appear on jury panels and even less serve on the final juries.[14]

The racial composition of the police departments is even more unbalanced. In 1972 in the city of Charlotte with a 30 percent Black population, only 22 of 522 police officers were Black, none of them in positions higher than patrolman, the lowest level in the police department.[15] The North Carolina Highway Patrol included in 1974 only 18 Black patrolmen of a total of 1,160 or 1.5 percent.[16] (Not one woman could be found in the Patrol.) By comparison, the Alabama state police was 4.5 percent Black.[17] Colonel Edward Jones, then chief of the state patrol, disclaimed racism in the agency: "Our Blacks do a good job. We had only one boy who caused us problems," he boasted in a tone reminiscent of antebellum days of yore.[18] That the daily random violence by police and state patrolmen is visited mainly on Black communities throughout the state is not incidental to the statistics cited. The Charlotte police force, like its brethren in other cities and villages, does not discipline officers for brutality, only for abuse of police standards, e.g. being on the take.

In 1976 Charlotte Police Chief J.C. Goodman led the fight against a civilian review board. In February of that year a Black 18-year-old Marine recruit, Kenneth M. Brown, died from blows landed by three policemen brandishing billy clubs in the Charlotte municipal airport. The NAACP and other community organizations called for suspension of the officers involved and the establishment of a civilian review board, but Chief Goodman would have none of it. "In police work," said the chief, "suspension connotes something wrong." The setting up of a civilian review board, he argued, would destroy department morale.[19]

A new form of official violence sweeping the country, complete with television hero-worship, was the SWAT squad, which no major city prone to paramilitarism could be without. Raleigh's SWAT is known as the Selective Enforcement Unit (SEU); its assignment is "strategic restraint." To selectively enforce the law and strategically restrain the lawbreaker, the SEU, with all its military hardware, goes wherever it cares to tread. In 1976 the SEU showed up at high-school games where violence off the field was anticipated, at Central Prison where more violence was anticipated, at courthouse demonstrations in support of Joan Little where still more violence was anticipated. No violence ever occurred. Unanticipated, violence-wise, was a two-hour standoff on Raleigh's Poole Road when a mental patient and 40 police officers exchanged hundreds of shots; or the fatal collision in April 1975 between a carload of teenagers and an unmarked SEU car rushing to the scene of trouble.[20]

The State Bureau of Investigation (SBI), North Carolina officialdom's pride and joy in law enforcement, had 8 Black agents of a total 260 in 1974. This was considered a great leap forward by then bureau director Charles Dunn who assumed the job in 1969 when there were no Black SBI agents out of a total of 57. Dunn conceded that the SBI composition created problems: "We have people in law enforcement who shouldn't be. We have a lot of sympathizers with the Klan and similar groups, but no real activists among our people."[21] Since all SBI agents carry shotguns and Magnum .357s, the distinction between a Klan sympathizer and an activist is not always easy to discern.

The SBI cultivates its image as crime buster as assiduously as its federal counterpart. One North Carolina crime victim was asked if she was afraid. "Why should I be?" she answered, "I have put my faith in God and in the SBI."[22] Under Dunn, a political protege of former Governors Luther Hodges and Dan Moore and U.S. Senator Robert Morgan, the SBI grew in five years from an annual budget of $750,000 to $4.3 million, an almost 600 percent increase in appropriations. "Today our crime laboratory is considered one of the best in the country. Our investigators are aggressive and as well trained as any officers," said Dunn, as he preached the gospel according to St. J. Edgar to local church assemblies.[23] When monies funded by the U.S. Justice Department's Law Enforcement Assistance Administration (LEAA)—which supplies SBI equipment and training—are included, the SBI budget was $6 million.[24]

The LEAA, which has been called "the Justice Department's Pentagon" because of its supplying of local police with military armaments, also has characteristics of a Justice Department Ford Foundation. Established in 1969 by a Nixon administration hell-bent on law and order, LEAA started with $63 million to help local cops learn the new war technology developed in Vietnam, for application now in the ghettos and barrios. By 1971 the LEAA budget had multiplied nearly 800 percent, to $480 million. The 1975 budget surpassed a billion dollars. Altogether, by 1976 the LEAA had spent $4.4 billion in taxes. Yet crime remained at record levels and LEAA officials conceded that they "simply do not know what works to reduce crime." One LEAA project was to reduce in two years the number of crimes in eight large cities by 5 percent. For this they spent $160 million; the target cities had an average 10 percent increase in violent crimes and a 43 percent increase overall at the end of the two years.[25]

In 1972 alone $400 million was spent by LEAA on developing still newer electronic spying techniques. Hidden surveillance systems monitored the streets around the clock in a number of cities. The now convicted John Ehrlichman prepared for the now pardoned Richard Nixon a document, "Communication for Social Needs," which unfolded a plan to require the installation of FM receivers in every radio and TV set, every automobile and boat, to enable the government to propagandize at will at any moment of the day or night.

Other LEAA contingency plans developed included the training of armies of informers, children in the Boy Scouts and youth corps, to spy on their own families; several hundred human experiments in behavior control; the walling off of so-called high-crime areas which are invariably those urban areas mainly populated by people of color and which do not include San Clemente, the La Costa del Sol country club in California run by the Teamsters pension fund, or the New York financial district; the development of SWAT squads in every burg from the Atlantic to the Pacific; the arming of city cops with hollow-nosed "dum-dum" bullets, outlawed by international law for use in warfare but legal in the United States if used by police against the poor. Law and order has become lucrative: Chicago's and New York's finest take in $100 million and $350 million respectively, enough to qualify for *Fortune*'s 500. More than half a million people earn their keep as coppers for 40,000 police departments throughout the country.

A former LEAA official, Martin Danziger, asked whether all the materiel being developed for control of dissidents and protesters was necessary, replied, "The business community has taken a substantial interest in them, and I have faith in their judgment."[26] North Carolina's business community was not atypical. From an initial LEAA outlay of $1,058,000 for North Carolina in 1959, funding grew to $15,982,000 only four years later.[27] A typical LEAA project was the $300,000 subterranean Emergency Communications Center run by the Durham police department, with an immense data bank wired into those of the FBI, the National Criminal Information Center, National Law Enforcement Teletype System and Computerized Criminal History, all federal police networks also funded by the LEAA.

Durham's police were led by Chief Jon Kindice, a graduate of the International Police Academy (IPA) and classmate there of Dan Mitrone, the fictionalized character of the movie *State of Siege* who, on behalf of the CIA, trained the Uruguayan police and army in the rudiments and subtleties of torture and counter-insurgency. Kindice was himself the "Public Safety Advisor" in South Vietnam's Quang Ngai Province after leaving the IPA in 1967. Quang Ngai encompasses My

Lai, where 350 civilians were massacred during Kindice's tenure. In 1968 he participated in the CIA's Phoenix program to destroy the South Vietnam National Liberation Front's infrastructure by assassinating more than 20,000 suspected local leaders. Later Kindice became advisor to the chief of the Saigon regime's National Police and Ministry of the Interior. From Vietnam Kindice brought his newly acquired knowledge home to California, where he worked out of the Sacramento sheriff's office through which he received riot control training and other courses. "I had a knack for interrogations," boasted Chief Kindice.[28]

The man who hired Kindice was Durham's Director of Public Safety, retired U.S. Army Lieutenant Colonel Esai Berenbaum, another former Vietnam officer, who taught the Green Berets at Ft. Bragg's JFK Center for Special Warfare. Still another Vietnam veteran in the leadership of the Durham police was Lieutenant Colonel William Robbins (U.S. Army, Ret.), chief of the department's auxiliary services. Lt. Col. Robbins served in Da Nang as senior advisor to the Saigon military's prisoner-of-war camp for the I Corps area, which includes Con Son Island, site of the infamous tiger-cage prisons. Robbins also commanded the military police battalion which manned the roadblocks in Santo Domingo during the 1965 U.S. invasion of that country.

These are the men whose jobs are made more pleasant and manageable because of ample funding and plans of operation supplied by LEAA. The LEAA is itself directed at the top and staffed on the bottom by dozens of "former" CIA agents and retired military officers. A survey conducted by the 200,000-member Retired Military Officers Association in 1972, showed that 30 percent of those responding were now working in federal, state and local governments. Like General John Tolson, who moved from commanding officer at Fort Bragg to North Carolina Secretary for Military and Veterans Affairs, the Kindices, Berenbaums and Robbins's who people the local police departments, SBI, highway patrol and prisons are bringing "pacification" home to the Tarheel state.

Late one evening, after two more weeks in the county jail and still more mace and gas attacks by the guards, Rev. Ben Chavis was moved amid absolute secrecy and intense security precautions, to Wake County Jail in Raleigh to face trial with Jim Grant on the federal charges. "Federal marshalls conducted the transfer with such speed," reported the Wilmington *Star-News* the next day, "that officials of the New Hanover Sheriff's Department were not aware of the move till it took place."

The hearings for pre-trial motions gave more than a hint of what was to come. Defense attorney James Ferguson charged racial discrimination in the jury selection, pointing out that only 6 of the 41 potential jurors called were Black. The clerk's office explained that the prospective jurors were chosen from the voter registration lists of those who had voted in the 1968 elections, that is, for Richard Nixon, George Wallace or Hubert Humphrey. Many of the counties from which the jury lists were picked were charged with voter discrimination under the 1965 Voting Rights Act. Ferguson also objected, without success, to the extraordinary security measures such as two-way radios in the courtroom and the seating of a marshall's deputy at the defense counsel table.

The trial was peculiar from the start, even by New Southern standards. Ben and Jim were on trial for aiding two "fugitives," and the fugitives, Al Hood and David Washington, were in the courtroom throughout the trial free of any charges. The "federal fugitive" charges against them were dropped, setting up a trial of two men for "aiding" fugitives who no longer were fugitives in the law's eyes. During pre-trial motions, charges against Hood and Washington for possession of firearms, unregistered destructive devices, and making destructive devices without paying taxes on them were dropped, when the government offered no resistance to motions offered by their defense attorney. The charges against Ben and Jim of illegal possession of destructive devices remained standing, even though neither had ever been found in possession of such devices and the case originated with the arrest of Hood and Washington in a car full of dynamite. An underwhelming case at best.

As the trial developed, Hood and Washington rather than Ben and Jim were to prove the key figures for the proceedings. The fix was apparent from jump street. Hood's attorney of record was a former U.S. attorney, W. Arnold Smith. Smith acknowledged early on that the federal government had been trying for "a long time" to prosecute Ben but had not until now "been able to get the goods up enough to prosecute him." A special prosecutor assigned to the case, David Long, was formerly assistant to U.S. attorney Warren H. Coolidge. Regarding the dropping of charges against Hood and Washington, Long argued that the timing was "the main thing" and that it was Coolidge's idea. Coolidge refused to discuss why the charges were dropped.

On the opening day of the trial, Hood refused from the stand to tell defense attorney Ferguson where he obtained the cars and money he used between September 1970, when he and Washington returned from Canada, and February 1971, when he was arrested in Charlotte. "I'm not going to tell you," he answered Ferguson. When Ferguson pressed him,

Hood said, "I don't remember." Ferguson: "You don't remember what anybody did but James Earl Grant and Ben Chavis?" Hood: "I remember what's necessary for this case." Stanley Noel, the Alcohol, Tobacco and Firearms agent who put together the prosecution's case and who had, in Ben's college days, monitored his anti-war activities and broken down the door to Ben's apartment, also had a selectively faulty memory. He told Ferguson he couldn't recall making the statement that he was going to get Ben Chavis if it was the last thing he did.

Later in the trial Washington admitted that he lied initially in a statement to the FBI when he told the bureau that the dynamite found in his car at the time of his arrest belonged to Joseph Goins, the third passenger. He lied, he said, because he "wasn't under oath" and "didn't think [he] had to tell the truth." When Ferguson questioned Washington as to why he had decided to tell his story to the authorities, the witness said he was "tired of running" from "that organization." When asked by Ferguson what "organization," Washington replied, "That organization that you and Grant are in right now." Ferguson pressed again for an answer and Washington said it was "the same organization that pays for everything Jim Grant does." The exchange was cut short by the judge and the prosecution rested its case.

That was it. The case against Ben and Jim rested entirely on the bizarre testimony of Hood and Washington. Asserting their testimony was "incredible and unbelievable," the defense decided not to call any witnesses. When the verdict was returned it was equally "incredible and unbelievable." Ben was found not guilty on all counts, but Jim was found guilty on both counts, despite the fact that the "evidence" and testimony against them were exactly the same.

After a plea for leniency based on Jim's record of work with VISTA and other community projects, and the fact that he had no criminal record, the judge sentenced Jim to the maximum 10 years in federal penitentiary, 5 years on each count to run consecutively. On the day Ben was found innocent of all the federal charges, the New Hanover County grand jury returned indictments against him and the Wilmington 11 on the charges for which he was arrested the month before. He was returned in shackles and chains to New Hanover County Jail.

Jim's appeal bond was set at $50,000 cash. The amount was appealed to the Fourth Circuit Court of Appeals which ordered the trial judge to accept 10 percent collateral. Through the efforts of family and friends, $5,000 was raised and Jim was released 10 weeks later on Friday afternoon, July 7. Three days after that he was to be tried in Charlotte in connection with the burning of the Lazy B stable.

Hood and Washington would also play the central role in the Lazy B trial, in which the defendants—Jim, T. J. Reddy and Charles Parker— would come to be known as the Charlotte Three. Charitably, one is reminded of Humphrey Bogart's answer in *Beat the Devil* to Robert Morley's query as to whether another character was a liar. "Let's just say," said Bogie, as we might say of Hood and Washington, "she uses her imagination rather than her memory."

Amid its many Rotarian boasts, Tarheel official propaganda holds that "North Carolina *is* Textiles," a claim not far off the mark. If you're bathing with a North Carolina washcloth in the morning, you've undoubtedly bedded down in North Carolina sheets and will be dressing in North Carolina corduroys or denim. The textile companies are fast becoming multinationals, but textile manufacturing is still centered in the U.S. South and the bulk of it in North Carolina. Of the million textile workers in the United States, nearly 300,000 work in North Carolina.[29]

Although the country's first cotton spinning mill was built in Rhode Island in 1770 and New England fast became the textile center for the new nation, Alexander Hamilton was predicting as early as 1775 that eventually it would be necessary to "take the cotton mill to the cotton field, to move mills south near the source of raw materials." By the early nineteenth century more textile goods were being manufactured in the South than being imported into the region. In 1810 the value of home textile production in North Carolina was $2,989,000 compared to Massachusetts' $2,219,000. In 1817 Colonel Joel Battle formed the Rocky Mount Manufacturing Company on the Tar River. The Rocky Mount Mills, still operated by the Battle family, is today the South's oldest operating textile plant.[30]

Alexander Hamilton's prophecy and Colonel Battle's faith were borne out: North Carolina did indeed bring the mill to the cotton, with the result that half of all U.S. textiles are manufactured in the state. Textiles have long dominated North Carolina industry, accounting for just under 45 percent of all manufacturing employment. [31] In the Piedmont—the central section of the Carolinas which has historically been the industrial belt of the state—manufacturing employment often exceeds 50 percent of the total employment, an industrial working-class concentration on the level of Detroit and Pittsburgh. The bulk of those blue-collar workers are in textiles.

As the Piedmont's R.J. Reynolds is the capitalist world's largest tobacco manufacturer, so is Burlington Industries the largest textile company in the capitalist world. Its 87 offices, terminals and plants, and its 44,000 workers in the state make Burlington the largest single industrial employer in North Carolina.[32] With its record $2.1 billion in sales in 1973, Burlington's volume was roughly twice that of each of the next three largest producers.[33] As Burlington says, "that's a lot of money." The textile industry has its official folklore. According to Burlington handouts, back in 1919, J. Spencer Love drifted down to Gastonia, just west of Charlotte, from Boston. A 22-year-old Harvard-educated war veteran, Love founded Burlington Mills four years later. A man whose apparent enthusiasm for cotton goods and textile profits was bounded only by the seven seas, Love lifted Burlington from a company with 40 plants in three states at the outbreak of World War II to a multinational firm during the war. The corporation increased its sales by 166 percent in the course of the war and began to acquire plants in Cuba and Australia. The marvels of war production are well appreciated in Burlington's board rooms. Today the company has plants in Canada, Colombia, Finland, France, Italy, Japan, Mexico, South Africa, Spain, Sweden, Switzerland, the United Kingdom, West Germany and Puerto Rico.

J.P. Stevens and Co., Inc., second only to Burlington as a textile monopoly, with operations on four continents, was started in Massachusetts in the early nineteenth century but following the second world war moved South "in a good way" because of "favorable economic conditions" and "good labor supply."[34] Of its 83 manufacturing plants in the United States today, 66 are in the South, 25 in North Carolina. Like Burlington, Stevens has a nose for the larceny of war profiteering. So acute is its smell that Robert T. Stevens, former president and chief executive officer of the company, was chosen by President Eisenhower to be his secretary of the army. One needn't stretch the imagination to figure out Stevens' amendment to his Pentagon chief Charles Wilson's dictum that "What's good for General Motors is good for the country."

Also sharing the action in the Piedmont are Cone Mills and Cannon Mills, both native Tarheel corporations. Cone, today the world's largest manufacturer of denim, corduroy and flannel, reached net sales of more than $372 million in 1972. Moses and Cesar Cone, two traveling salesmen of dry goods riding the Southern circuit after the Civil War, having tasted the beer, wanted to own the brewery. They built their first manufacturing plant in Greensboro in 1895 and that city remains the corporate headquarters for Cone.

While the Cones were traveling through the South, James Cannon was staying in one place—a general store in Concord, N. C., in which he held a partnership. Desperate poverty gripped the area in the wake of the Civil War. Cotton, known as "white gold" before the war, had been driven down in price. Cannon's idea, according to contemporary Cannon Mills propagandists, was to open mills near the source of raw material, to spin cotton into cloth, thereby providing jobs and prosperity for the area.[35] Such charity, of course, began at home. The result of this private war on poverty is a present-day corporation of 17 plants, 15 in North Carolina, some 25,000 employees, and net sales in 1973 of $355 million.

North Carolina's industrial revolution took place in the Piedmont for several reasons. Agriculture was far inferior here to that of the Coastal Plain. And the early mills required water-power sites more available in the hilly Piedmont than on the flat eastern shores. Water is as necessary to textile manufacturing as fibers. After yarn is spun it has to be bathed in water and starched to strengthen it for weaving. The needs of the textile industry to expand brought new techniques. In 1898 the first hydro-electric textile plant in North Carolina was built on the Yadkin River. Just two years later, one of every twenty-five mills in the state was using electric power. As W.J. Cash wrote in *The Mind of the South,* "Under the touch of Buck Duke's millions, hydroelectric power sprang into being, and by 1910 the energy of a million horses was pulsing in the wires of Dixie. And literally a hundred lesser industries made their appearance. By 1914, and apart from the cotton mills, there were at least 15,000 manufacturing establishments of one sort or another in the South."[36]

In 1905 Duke organized the Southern Power Company with offices in Charlotte, as a result of his partnership in the Catawba Power Company, formed six years earlier. Duke soon bought out his partners and owned Southern Power by himself. He had hoped to sell electric power whole-sale to the Charlotte Consolidated Construction Company for re-distribution while selling directly to the textile mills. The local company balked at the agreement. Duke, using his personal philosophy of "If you can't join 'em, beat 'em," acquired Charlotte Consolidated. Southern Power entered the retail market permanently. In 1910 Duke chartered the Piedmont and Northern Railroad, also powered by electricity, to provide transportation for all industries within the service area of Southern Power. The textile industry rapidly expanded and soon finished cotton goods were being shipped North.[37] Duke raised most of the two million dollars needed to get the Southern Power Company started. Its suc-cessor, Duke Power, now has over two *billion* dollars in financial assets and has become the sixth biggest utilities monopoly in the country.

If there is joy in the board rooms of Duke Power, for the paying customers there is nothing to cheer but cheer itself. In the six years between 1969 and 1975, Duke stiffed its customers with nine separate rate hikes. North Carolina is "the only state that has passed a law specifically driving its Utilities Commission toward basing rate-making decisions on economic predictions," which almost certainly means "unfair and higher electric, telephone and natural gas bills for Tar Heel customers." The law, passed by the state General Assembly in March 1974 was "heavily lobbied by the state's major utilities and was written at the suggestion of a Duke Power Co. vice president." The economic predictions on which rates will be based are supplied by the power companies themselves. On April 29, 1974, *The News and Observer* quoted Charles D. Penuel, assistant vice president for Southern Bell Telephone Company in Charlotte says, "Certainly North Carolina has the best and most specific law in this regard."

Duke power users who paid $14.72 monthly in 1970, paid $20.50. Four years later, a jump of nearly 40 percent. Two more rate increases that year brought the rate rise to 50 percent since 1970. Duke's profits for 1975 were in the neighborhood of 25 percent, a handsome neighborhood to dwell in.[38] Actually, profits are much higher but hidden through a device known as "allowance for funds used during construction (AFDC)." According to *Business Week,* utilities companies report phantom profits through AFDC, which gets interest costs on new construction off the income statement, where they cut into profits. Duke Power reports greater phantom profits than any other company in the United States, paying out a dividend to investors which is four times actual operating earnings. Duke dividends as a percent of actual earnings are *427.3 percent.*[39] This is nearly twice as high as the next placed utilities company in phantom profits—Carolina Power and Light (CP & L) in eastern North Carolina—with 219.6 percent. CP & L's phantom profits, in turn, were nearly twice that of New York's Consolidated Edison with its 117.3 percent.[40]

Both CP & L and Duke, of course, place the burden of rate increases on the individual consumer rather than industrial customers, a practice not limited to North Carolina, but one pursued to new frontiers in that state. In 1972, for example, residential customers, using only 23.3 percent of Duke's kilowatt supplies, contributed 36.3 percent of Duke's total revenues. Industry in the area, using 44.8 percent or almost twice as much electricity, paid less money, 31 percent of Duke's revenues. Duke has historically sold dearly to working people and cheaply to industry. Duke senior vice-president D.W. Booth has said, "It has been the policy of the Duke Power Company since its beginning to encourage the influx of industry in the Piedmont Carolina" through the use of low industrial rates. The practice was begun by Buck Duke himself. Using his tobacco profits to begin his power company, he parlayed his winnings by also investing in textile mills that would locate in the Piedmont and use his cheap electricity. (In 1974 Duke Power owned 59,000 shares of J.P. Stevens, worth some $1.7 million.)[41]

The growth of industrialization and electrification in this century have given North Carolina its New South image. To achieve this growth took and continues to take large outlays of capital, in amounts only the largest banks have available. The banks in turn demand increased profits, even though investment in monopolies such as utilities is hardly a gamble. In effect the banks own the power supply, and the homeowner or apartment-dweller who pays his 25 or 30 bucks a month to the power companies is actually paying back the banks. In North Carolina, which has been shown to lead the nation in such profiteering, this is particularly true. Not coincidentally, the state contains the two largest banks in the South, to go with its utilities and industrial giants.

Dominating the Charlotte skyline is the 40-story glass-sheathed tower of the NCNB Corporation, the biggest banking concern in the South.[42] The corporation, controlling about five billion in assets, is parent to the North Carolina National Bank which is chaired by Luther B. Hodges, Jr., son of the former governor. More than size, NCNB shares carry the highest price-earnings multiple of any big bank in the country, including New York's Citicorp.

Until the last decade, North Carolina banking was dominated by the Wachovia Bank and Trust Company, with headquarters in Winston-Salem. NCNB was formed in 1960 out of a merger of two other North Carolina banks with the stated purpose of giving Wachovia some competition. In 1973 NCNB moved past Wachovia in assets and deposits; and in the first quarter of 1974 surpassed Wachovia's net income, $7.29 million compared with the latter's $7.17 million.

For the most part, the ruling class of North Carolina provides a textbook example of the interlocking directorate. The Wachovia board included, for example, William S. Smith, chairman of R.J. Reynolds Tobacco Co.; while NCNB's board had the chairman of R.J. Reynolds Industries, Colin Stokes. Similarly, Burlington Industries put its chairman, Charles F. Meyers, Jr., on Wachovia's board; and its executive vice president, William A. Klopman, on NCNB's. Belk Stores, the largest retail store chain in the South, also based in Charlotte, placed its president, John M. Belk, on Wachovia's board, and its executive vice president, Thomas M. Belk on the board of NCNB.

Such corporate incest gets more complex: Duke Power Company's board included, among others, a R.J. Reynolds vice-president who was *also* on the board of Wachovia Bank. Also on Duke's board was Burlington's finance committee chairman, Howard Holderness, who in turn was on the board of Wachovia Realty Investments. Carolina Power and Light meanwhile enjoyed the directorship of Wachovia's president, John F. Watlington, Jr.

Running through these corporations and banks of course are representatives of the Wall Street stockholders—Citibank, Chase Manhattan, Manufacturers Hanover, Lehman Brothers, Morgan Guaranty, and so on. For example, Walter L. Lingle, Jr., former Proctor and Gamble executive vice-president, served on the boards of *both* Burlington Industries and R.J. Reynolds.[43]

In his classic work, *Southern Politics,* V.O. Key, Jr. described this ruling class as a "progressive plutocracy," a profit-minded business and banking elite that favored industrial development and higher education because they were good for business. The plutocracy was "progressive" because it brought a piece of the South out of the age of the mint-julep on the patio overlooking the savannah, and into the industrial revolution. Hence the "New South."

The history of North Carolina's industrial development is a classic example of baronic rule with mill villages and financial enterprises run as fiefdoms. The city of Durham was formed in the image of Buck Duke and the Duke forture is represented everywhere—Duke University, the American Tobacco Company, the Duke Endowment, Duke Power. In Winston-Salem the Reynolds family dominates in a like manner. Burlington Industries ran the city of Burlington until the company became too big and moved to Greensboro which it now helps run, while keeping control of Burlington city. Throughout the Piedmont, villages sprang up next to the mills, with company-owned shacks to house the workers and company stores to take back their paychecks and then some.

Of course North Carolina's industries and banks went the way of the nation's capitalism in the 1930s and 1940s. With the Great Depression and the inability of private enterprise to escape the crisis without the help of the government apparatus, there has been a merging of the state with the banks and industry. In North Carolina now, towns and villages are no longer owned and controlled by the companies. Rather the state and local governments—influenced by and acting in the interests of capital—manage the lives of the people.

There is at least one exception to prove the rule: Kannapolis, immediately north of Charlotte and the eighth largest population center in

North Carolina. Situated on an old cotton plantation in Cabarrus County, Kannapolis grew from the mill village built by Cannon Mills. Now home for 40,000 people, Kannapolis includes more than 19 square miles of residential sections, schools, churches and shopping centers surrounding Cannon's one-square-mile manufacturing-shopping-housing complex. The town has installed a $5.5 million sewerage system, built a high school and has a police department nearly 100 men strong. But Kannapolis is not a city; it is an unincorporated municipality owned by Cannon Mills. The Kannapolis police are on the payroll of the company. "Cannon virtually runs Cabarrus County," says company Vice President Ed Rankin. "We've got our own representative in the state General Assembly. And we also have a piece of Rowan County."[44] Rankin was himself Governor Dan Moore's director of administration, and private secretary and speechwriter for governors William Umstead and Luther Hodges.

If Kannapolis is run by Cannon, and Durham and Winston-Salem by Duke and Reynolds, the capital city of Raleigh is the province of all the corporations and banks. V.O. Key wrote in 1949, "An aggressive aristocracy of manufacturing and banking, centered around Greensboro, Winston-Salem, Charlotte and Durham, has had a tremendous stake in state policy and has not been remiss in protecting and advancing what it visualizes as its interests. Consequently a sympathetic respect for the problems of corporate capital and of large employers permeates the state's politics and government. For half a century an economic oligarchy has held sway." As if to verify the Marxist perception of "state-monopoly capitalism," Key continued, "The effectiveness of the oligarchy's control has been achieved through the elevation to office of persons fundamentally in harmony with its viewpoint. Its interests, which are often the interests of the state, are served without prompting."[45]

Apologists for this ruling class—Tom Wicker of *The New York Times* has called it "the Confederate Mafia"—speak of its paternalism in worshipful tones that evoke the expectation of background voices by the Mormon Tabernacle Choir. The Piedmont of the mill village was a place of shiny dreams, the industrial counterpart to plantation life. The transfer of rule over the lives of working folk from private hands to the state apparatus is an experience still within the memory of most North Carolinians. Much residue from the good old days remains: The oligarchy still talks—like Citizen Kane—of giving the people their rights as if it is payment for services rendered.

The peruser of North Carolina's corporate annual reports will discover early on that the fine line between "community relations" and "public relations" has been erased. Community relations programs *are* p.r. And there is no one so adept at public relations as those that rule North Carolina. Before the turn of the century, Buck Duke became one of the nation's biggest advertisers, alarming even his business partners with the amount of money spent on advertising. Duke designed the "sliding package" for carrying tobacco, the container that became the predecessor of the breakfast cereal box. Immigrants arriving at Ellis Island in New York were given free Duke sample brands.[46]

Public relations thus became one of our few native art forms like jazz, handpainted ties and frozen foods. In North Carolina, from the people who brought us "I'd walk a mile for a Camel," came also the "New South." A few years ago, according to textile industry press flacks, Robert D. Walters of Burlington Industries heard that the Boy Scouts of America were about to drop the textile merit badge for lack of interest. "Walters disliked that so much he almost single-handedly mobilized the textile industry 'to support their own badge.'" Soliciting industry leaders, the American Textile Manufacturers Institute and Phi Psi fraternity, Walters and his colleagues revised the "Textile Merit Badge Handbook" which, he says, "puts this dynamic industry in the Space Age where it belongs." Since that day when he got "the stay of execution," Walters says that Burlington alone awarded 1,500 merit badges in the Piedmont in 1973, more than in the rest of the United States all together.[47]

Such good deeds are often cited by corporate and state public relations officers to describe a ruling class whose purity of soul would try the patience of St. Francis. Cone Mills, for example, distributes a 12-page five-color brochure, "What We're Doing About It," meaning the company's efforts to preserve the environment, without once mentioning byssinosis, the "brown lung" disease that cripples textile workers in epidemic proportions. Duke Power had a campaign to convince Piedmont consumers that "radioactivity is not a dirty word." Radioactivity, it was explained, "exists in everything—trees, flowers, buildings, furniture, animals, even you. It always has. It's just natural." Without quite suggesting that Hiroshima might have qualified for a 1945 Model Cities program, Duke has a program to induce visitors to its Keowee-Toxaway nuclear plant near Clemson, S.C. There the company has carved out a landscape of lakes and forests for nature lovers to enjoy among the radiation emissions.

During the Cold War days of the 1950s, when ideological combat against socialism jerked U.S. school children about on "free enterprise" prayer mats, one point that was constantly driven home was that capitalism, like radiation today, is "just natural." You are a capitalist, the kids were told, if you owned your own house, car, books, even your own pencil. Like much of the pedagogical paraphernalia that went the way of the U-2, Bay of Pigs, Vietnam and Watergate, such teaching methods have long disappeared from much of the public education system in the United States. But in North Carolina they, like the atom bomb drill, have been retained. Public relations in this least challenged corner of state-monopoly capitalism sells not just its products but the system itself.

Backed by the banks and corporations, the North Carolina Legislature passed a law in 1974 requiring all high schools to give instruction in the virtues of capitalism. The bill amended a 1955 law mandating instruction in harmful and illegal drugs. The new law had bipartisan backing. The Rev. Dr. Billy Graham, North Carolina's most famous clergyman, has never been tentative in praising them that help themselves to others' labor: "I would not fault the wealthy, for at the death of Christ, it was a rich man who bought the burial spices and assisted in the final preparation of his body for the tomb. I recognize, of course, that most of his disciples were not men of material wealth, but Jesus had no implied criticism of the wealthy as such."

Duke Power continues to earn more than its share of profits, but its carefully created image of a company with a heart, the Bambi of utilities, has been tarnished. In a recent special edition of *Duke Power* magazine, the company describes the difficulties of winning the public: "For one thing, Duke Power is a monopoly. . . . The public's distrust of big business in general and monopolies in particular, evidenced by the growing strength of consumer activists, appeared to be an insurmountable obstacle. . . ." Asked to define the single most improtant objective of the company's advertising efforts, one officer replied: "Duke Power is not a monopolistic, impersonal corporate giant . . . but a dedicated group of friends and neighbors serving the public and the future of the Piedmont Carolinas."[48] Adopting the title, "Your Friendly Neighborhood Power Company," Duke distributed, "Hi, Neighbor" lapel buttons, "Welcome, Neighbor" doormats, and a 45 rpm record of "The Duke Power Suite."

New emphasis on selling "the system" itself came with the consolidation of the merger between the monopoly corporations and the state apparatus in the 1930s and 1940s. North Carolina was, like most of the South, particularly desperate during the Great Depression. The New Deal was looked to for relief by the citizenry. But the growth of the federal bureaucracy under the New Deal, combined with the transformation to a permanent war economy following the Roosevelt years, changed North Carolina forever, perhaps even more than the rest of the country. Because the major corporations in the state were all-powerful and unchecked by any counterveiling force, they would control the state government more completely and with fewer concessions to popular need than elsewhere.

C HARLOTTE, with 250,000 people, is the biggest city by far in North Carolina, nearly twice the size of Greensboro, the state's second city. The Queen City is to North Carolina roughly what New York City is to the United States—the commercial, banking and cultural capital, as well as the largest population center. Here can be found the home base of Duke Power Company, the North Carolina National Bank, the American Textile Manufacturers Institute. Lying on the South Carolina state line, at the foot of the hills that rise to become the Great Smokies, Charlotte is the main overland shipping center in the South, being an overnight drive to the Gulf ports and the docks of Philadelphia, New York and Boston. The city is important enough for John Belk, former chairman of the National Retail Merchants Association and chairman of the Belk stores, the largest privately owned chain of department stores in the country with 400 stores in 14 Southeastern states, to have served as mayor.

Back in 1965, a Black father named James E. Swann led a group of nine other Black parents into federal court in Charlotte and won an order for widespread crosstown busing to desegregate the Charlotte-Mecklenburg County school system. In 1971 the United States Supreme Court upheld that ruling by Judge James B. McMillan, making the school bus a legal tool for desegregating schools elsewhere in the country as well. Judge McMillan is modest about his landmark decision: "Heck, I was bused as a child in Robeson County. Everybody who attends school in North Carolina has been bused. Busing isn't the question, whatever folks say. It's desegregation." A young Black poet made the same point. "It ain't the bus, it's us."

Anti-busing rallies in 1970 in Charlotte drew as many as 10,000 participants. Within a year, more than 20 private "academies" were organized for 10,000 white students, one of every six white children in the county. The offices and home of Julius Chambers, NAACP attorney who brought the Swann suit (and partner of James Ferguson, lawyer for the Wilmington 10 and Charlotte Three) were destroyed by bombs. bused, and local officials supported the attacks. It is instructive to study the words of Superior Court Judge Frank Snepp spoken in 1974, three years after busing was already an accomplished fact, for a reflection of white ruling-class attitudes: "The Black lower classes," Judge Snepp told an interviewer, "have a violent and raucous life-style. They use violent language. A certain type of Black is wont to carry a knife as part of a life-style. They tend to feel that what happens to them is because they are Black, not because of what they've done. . . . The NAACP has organized chapters in the schools to act as espionage agents to report anything that might be made into a racial issue. Thankfully the school system has its own trained police department security force. . . . Busing brings unsavory elements into the decent community. Little hoodlums beat up white children. I've got a young 12-year-old boy, a very gentle boy. Now that he's in junior high school he says he hates Black people. . . . White students have now begun carrying chains and knives to school. You can understand why, with so many Blacks."

An epilogue to the brouhaha was provided on May 20, 1975, when President Ford came to Charlotte's Freedom Park for a Freedom Day celebration. Ford, who led the mob against busing for desegration, as his predecessor led the mob for "law and order," told the crowd of 50,000 of "America's capacity for unanimity and diversity, for courage in the face of challenge, for decency in the midst of dissention, for optimism in spite of reverses, and for creativity in adaption to the rapidly changing world in which we live today. North Carolina is a showcase of a state that reveres the values of the past while leading the way toward a progressive future." During the rally, Mrs. Billy Graham snatched from a young man a sign bearing the Revolutionary War slogan, "Don't Tread On Me."

After a year of trouble in the Charlotte-Mecklenburg schools, Jim Grant was indicted together with T.J. Reddy, Charles Parker and another man, Clarence Harrison, on charges of having burned down the Lazy B stable in Charlotte in September 1968, more than three years earlier. The Lazy B was the riding stable that Reddy, Parker, Ben Chavis and other students at Johnson C. Smith had integrated in 1967. When, a year after the civil rights incident, one of the barns burned, killing 15 horses, no mention of arson was reported and no link made between the two events. This was to become one of the oddest cases in a criminal justice system noted for the bizarre.

From the beginning, Jim, T.J. Reddy and Charles Parker were perplexed with the indictment linking them to Clarence Harrison. None of them had ever seen Harrison nor even heard his name before this. When the court read the charges at the time of pleading, the three men said "not guilty" as expected. But Harrison pleaded "guilty" to burning down the stable. The presiding judge, Frank Snepp (of the above enunciated view on Black schoolchildren and busing) asked Harrison if he was aware of what he was saying and if he knew that the charge carried a sentence of two to thirty years. When Harrison answered affirmatively to both questions, Judge Snepp allowed him to leave the courtroom, continuing his bond until the time of sentencing. No sooner had the admittedly guilty man walked away when Snepp ordered the other three men into the sheriff's custody for the rest of the trial. The judge refused to give a reason for his decision to revoke the bond of the Charlotte Three.

During the pre-trial motion period, defense attorney James Ferguson argued and presented evidence to prove that in Charlotte Black people were systematically excluded from grand juries and thus the grand jury that indicted the Three was unfair. Jury lists are drawn from voter registration lists and, while Blacks in Mecklenburg County were 21 percent of the population, they were only 14 percent of the registered voters. Snepp denied the motion, arguing that the "opportunity (for jury selection) is there if Blacks would register to vote."

Some 25 supporters of the Charlotte Three held a brief picket line outside the courthouse on opening day. This brought a court order from Snepp forbidding picketing or distributing handbills in the vicinity of the courthouse because such actions "tend to influence or intimidate" witnesses and members of the jury. Only after some stern counseling in constitutional law from federal judge James McMillan did Snepp rescind his order.

When the jury was chosen, it consisted of eleven whites and one very old Black woman who was hard of hearing and said she was employed "in my white lady's house." The prosecution used its challenges to eliminate every other prospective Black and Jewish juror.

The case against the Three was virtually nonexistent. Fire Department District Chief K. D. Helms, who originally investigated the Lazy B fire, told of a bottle, presumably an arsonist's weapon, found the day after the fire near another Lazy B barn that was unharmed by the fire. Helms testified that he emptied the contents of the bottle into a can which he sent to the FBI laboratory in Washington, D.C., for analysis. The empty bottle was given to the Charlotte Police laboratory for a fingerprint check. No fingerprints were found on the bottle, which Helms stored in a closet after its return from the lab. At the time of trial, Helms could not find the bottle and had no idea of its whereabouts. The FBI analysis of the bottle's contents found bits of solid matter similar to candle wax. Helms told the court that he found no evidence of arson around the burnt barn.

The state's case rested entirely on the testimony of Al Hood and David Washington, who had been the chief witnesses against Ben and Jim in the federal case ten weeks before. Hood and Washington testified that they had participated in burning the Lazy B and attempted to link the Three to their act. At one point Hood referred to the 1967 civil rights demonstration at the stable but said he thought it occurred in 1968 just before the fire. Washington said from the stand that there was a rehearsal for the arson in Biltmore Park and that T.J. had used a waterbomb to show what he was going to do to the stable. Hood, testifying to the same incident, said T.J. used a real bomb which exploded in the park. Hood also admitted that he had lied to law enforcement officers before and to everybody else "at one time or another." Washington was an equally reliable witness, admitting he had been tried and convicted of so many crimes he couldn't even remember all of them. Asked "Would you lie today if it would benefit you?" he replied, "I can't say what I would do."

In 1974 Judge Snepp, reflecting back over the trial two years before, told an interviewer that, "Hood and Washington are not exactly A-1 citizens but they realized they had to tell the truth." Whether or not he is a valid judge of law is a matter of dispute but Mr. Snepp is clearly no judge of character. Hood gave at least three different versions on three different occasions about who made the firebombs used in the Lazy B fire. And none of his three stories were in agreement with any of Washington's own set of conflicting stories as testified to in court, even though both men swore they were present when the bombs were made.

In court on July 12, 1972, Hood testified he couldn't see who threw the firebombs. Hood: "Well, the side that I was on was closed off. . . . I could not see the barn." Washington, who agreed with Hood that they were standing next to each other at the time, swore in court the same day that, "Both doors to the barn were open. . . . I had a pretty good view of the inside of the barn."

As to who made the firebombs, Hood told federal agents on July 21, 1971, it had been "T. J. Reddy and Jim Grant" and in a separate statement the same day, "T. J. Reddy and Clarence Harrison." To the court a year later, July 12, 1972, Hood said it had been "T. J. Reddy, Charles Parker, possibly Clarence Harrison." Washington was equally at variance with himself. In two separate statements on July 12, 1971, he said, "I saw T.J. (only)," and later "Grant and T.J. Reddy." In court a year later Washington fingered Jim Grant alone.

When the state finished presenting its case, the jury had to consider the sole evidence that a fire had occurred four years earlier and two criminals, who were not charged with the crime, had admitted committing the crime along with the defendants on trial. The jury never heard mention of the fact that Clarence Harrison had also been charged and had already pleaded guilty to the charge.

Among defense witnesses were Joe Hahn, a Pennsylvania philatelist at whose home in State College, Pa., Jim was staying at the time of the alleged arson; Andrew Brown, a Penn State student when Jim was in graduate school, whom Jim visited on the night the state of North Carolina claimed he was out tossing bombs at a barn in Charlotte; Brown's college roommate, Phil Coleman, who verified the testimony of the visit; and Professor Wells Keddie of Penn State, whom Jim met with in the afternoon of the day of the fire. Keddie brought his 1968 appointment calendar with him to court.

The prosecution's response was to attempt to discredit the witnesses. Hahn, for example, was accused of being "a card-carrying member of the American Civil Liberties Union." Brown, who is Black, was asked what "Black-oriented or other militant organizations" he belonged to. And as with the other witnesses, he was questioned as to whether he belonged to "The Marxist Study Club", "The Pennsylvania Socialist Society" and other nonexistent organizations.

Character witnesses for T.J. Reddy were all known and respected Charlotte citizens. The prosecution spared them no less than Jim's university associates. Dr. Robert Miller, for example, was asked if he hadn't attended a conference in Chicago which opposed the Vietnam War and supported Black power. "Yes," Dr. Miller responded, "that was a conference of the Lutheran Church."

Despite the weakness of the prosecution case, the verdict, given the time, place and circumstances, came down with the inevitability of nightfall. The Charlotte Three were pronounced "guilty as charged." Judge Snepp, pleased with the verdict, proceeded to deliver to the defendants a sermon stuffed with homilies as stale as leftover cornbread. In announcing the astonishingly severe sentences of 25 years for Jim Grant, 20 for T.J. Reddy and 10 years for Charles Parker, Snepp described the stable burning as "One of the most inhuman crimes I have ever heard of," referring to the horses killed in the stable fire. Less inhuman apparently, in the eyes of the North Carolina courts, were the burning in 1965 of a Mt. Airy store in which an employee was killed by a businessman who received only 5-8 years; the firebombing of a Charlotte grocery store one month after the Lazy B fire by a white man who was sentenced to 3-5 years with a recommendation of work release; the burning of a home in which his ex-wife was living by a Charlotte man who got 4-5 years; the burning of three Hendersonville schools by a white volunteer fireman who received 5-10 years in December 1971, a month before the Charlotte Three indictments were handed down; the burning of six barns in Mecklenburg and Cabarrus counties by four white youths who were given sentences ranging from 8 months to 2 years. In fact, in the ten-year period of 1965-74 only one burning case drew harsher sentences than that of the Charlotte Three, and that was for seven separate cases of arson by the same person. Wrote Washington *Post* columnist Coleman McCarthy, "When compared to the 20 years Lt. William Calley (who now walks free) got for murdering 22 Vietnamese civilians, the severity [of sentencing] is even more striking. Fifteen horses in Charlotte are apparently worth more than 22 human beings in My Lai."

As for the admitted Lazy B arsonists, Hood and Washington were of course never tried for the crime; Clarence Harrison was sentenced to 7 years, 5 of them suspended. Judge Snepp, in explaining the harshness of the sentences for the Three, said they were beyond rehabilitation because they "are educated men." Nevertheless he distinguished between Charles Parker whom Snepp viewed as an impressionable dupe, and Jim Grant whom he considered an "organizer and leader." Snepp called T.J. Reddy "a man of promise, of talent," but said the talent had been misdirected. It was as if T.J. had wandered into church, made a sacrilegious joke and now the priest was trying, ever so patiently, to set him straight. He accused Reddy of being able to mold people's minds and scolded him for doing so to bad ends. Later, writing from prison, T.J. wrote his "Judge Poem."

> . . . .Judge says he thinks I am intelligent, creative
> Said I *had* a future
> But since those voodoo dolls keep looming in his mind
> And his fears keep mounting
> Judge Snepp snips snaps at my heart
> Labels me tactician, conspirator, overeducated revolutionary
> Beyond rehabilitation
> Gives me a 20-year sentence
> And allows those who confess to the crime
> We are accused of
> To escape prosecution
>
> Judge deals with life
> In terms of lovelessness
> My only crime is my love of freedom
> the color of my skin

But in America's courtrooms
I am left at the mercy of laws
Designed to try me into submission
But I cannot live your lies, judge
I can't smile while you heap racist laws on me
And have you expect me to be grateful for them

Judge said I am something of a romantic
And, yes, I confess I am
I love life, I love love
And I am romantic minded
Knowing that in the midst
Of all the hatred and death
My love of life is all I have left

(From *Less Than a Score, But a Point:* Poems by T. J. Reddy, Random House, New York, 1974.)

Four

If the poor are too well off they will be disorderly—
Cardinal Richelieu

I N 1924 Buck Duke left the Duke Endowment as his legacy to attract industry to North Carolina. Thirty years later the state's first self-proclaimed "businessman in the statehouse," Governor Luther Hodges, made industry-hunting the first priority of the state government. An entire division of commerce and industry in the state's Department of Natural and Economic Resources is now devoted to industry-hunting, working with and complementing the efforts of the local entrepreneurs and Chambers of Commerce and the industry-hunters for Duke Power, CP & L and the banks. In 1973, for example, 104 new plants, representing an investment of $267 million, were brought into the state.[1] An additional $200 million was invested in existing plants. A quarter of the total new investment came in textiles and lumber, as did half the new plants and two-fifths of the new employees. But 45 percent of the new investments were in chemical, plastics and rubber plants.[2] Moreover 80 percent of the new industrial plants were outside the Piedmont, the bulk in the traditionally agrarian East.

This development is according to plan. North Carolina is the 12th state in the country in population. All the first 11 have large urban areas. North Carolina has only four cities with more than 100,000 people and only one, Charlotte, with a quarter-million. Official state statistics consider concentrations of 2,500 persons or more as "urban areas." The "Statewide Development Policy" prepared under Governor Robert Scott in 1972 saw "the growth of smaller centers of population" as its "primary objective." Growth in "places which were closest to where people needed jobs if they were to remain" in North Carolina became "the basis for all investment planning efforts." The trend, planned by the state in cooperation with the corporations, is for a decentralization of manufacturing employment, dispersed to increasingly smaller population centers.[3]

This policy—increasing industrialization by keeping people on the farms—seems illogical as a flight of fleas. But inherent in the plan is the great obsession of those who make policy for North Carolina—preventing the organization of its workers.

"Our main selling point is good labor," says the man whose job for Duke Power is to induce Northern industry to open plants in North Carolina. "Our workers aren't spoiled by organizations, although there are always a few bad apples. A big selling point is that we have no unions to speak of. So we can get a machine worker to turn out 1,600 items a day for $3.00 an hour where in Detroit he's limited to 400 items a day for $5.00 an hour."[4]

Wachovia Bank's former president, Archie Davis, is proud as a grandee with North Carolina's labor conditions. "Face it," he says, "the greatest advantage we enjoy is Taft-Hartley's 14b. 'Right to work' is the greatest attraction industry has to come here."[5]

In 1974 Carolina Power & Light, wanting nothing left to guesswork, surveyed 100 companies to find out why they had moved to North Carolina. The single greatest advantage listed by the most companies, 56 of them, was the "quality and quantity of labor supply" in the state. On a four-point scale, three of the five assets rating above a "three" were the "acceptance of the company by the employee," 3.3; "labor laws," 3.2; "labor attitude" (attitude to unions), 3.1. (The CP & L study results were kept confidential, shared only with the state government industry-hunters.[6]) Said CP & L's industrial developer, "A non-union labor force is an excellent reason for industry to come to North Carolina and that is why they do come."[7]

Union organizers and company spokesmen alike cite as the main objective reason for North Carolina's low rate of unionization the lack of large concentrations of people. It is hard to organize when workers are scattered, and when they live close to the soil. Mill hands go to work in the factories from their small farms. They maintain their farms so as not to be dependent on industrial wages. Shortly before he died in 1974, ex-Governor Luther Hodges, a former textile executive, recalled, "The mill villages were an outgrowth of plantation life and tenant farming. We were out to foster a good trusting relationship between the farmers coming into the mills and the companies."[8] Scott Hoyman, southern director of the Textile Workers Union of America, agrees with a qualification. "The absence of big cities means that there is no real working class or, rather, there is a rural working class, and rural workers are family-oriented. The workplace is not looked at in business terms but in family terms. This was true until recently. But now industry has run out of farmboys, and consciousness is beginning to change."[9]

The proletarianization of those "farmboys" through technical education has for 20 years been the first priority of the North Carolina school system. For a state that derives much of its progressive reputation from the image of Chapel Hill and Duke University, North Carolina's public schools are just about last in nearly every way. The CP & L survey of what attracts Northern industy to the state found that the schools were considered the biggest disadvantage.[10] "It is impossible to attract sophisticated industry to an unsophisticated labor force," reported CP & L's industry-hunter. "Of course the military bases in the east provide industry with semi-skilled workers, not readily available elsewhere. But our greatest inducement is our community college system which trains workers free of charge for new industries."[11]

During World War II the concept of the community college gained wide acceptance among U.S. educators. With the massive return of GI's, community college systems were rapidly developed across the country. North Carolina, which needed them most, was slowest to act.[12] The state's first junior college was set up in Asheville in 1927 but operated until 1949 without a campus of its own, moving from high school basements to children's homes or wherever space was available. During the war, junior colleges were also established in Charlotte and Wilmington. But that was the extent of North Carolina's community college system until the late 1950s.

In 1957, during Governor Hodges' drive to bring industry to the state, a system of "industrial education institutes" was agreed upon. The state might continue to suffer from intellectual malnutrition, but would no longer go without a working class schooled in technical education. A network of community colleges and technical institutes was built throughout the state. Its purpose was singular: "Equipping the individuals with the specific skills and knowledge required by a clearly defined job in a particular company. . . . [The program will] open the doors of industry to the entire educational services of a community college."[13] Some 56 institutions are now in operation; North Carolina's taxpayers paid more than $115 million between 1963 and 1970 to train workers free of charge for the monopolies.[14] Former Governor Terry Sanford said proudly, "We have mobility. An extension unit can be established for a class in one or more subjects in a nearby county, as needed. There is virtually no limit on the industrial and technical courses offered. We tell industrialists we can teach anything. Our courses range from bricklaying to poultry technology to welding to practical nursing."[15]

There are no entrance requirements to the community colleges. If you want to work at Burlington Industries as a fabric weaver, just enroll at Guilford Technical Institute. Your taxes will pay for your apprenticeship, saving Burlington the cost. The community college system's 1974 budget was $65 million, to accommodate an enrollment of 400,000 students. "And folks can stay on the farms," said community college administrator Joe Sturdivant. "About 95 percent of the people in the state are within a 25-mile commuter range of a community college."[16] Official promotional material claimed that "the strategic dispersal of these institutions throughout the state insures prompt and efficient service, wherever an industry may be located."[17]

The concept of state-monopoly capitalism is seen in bold relief in this public school system, paid for by taxes, completely at the disposal of the corporations. "A complete customized training package is tailored to the particular needs of each company. . . . For valid reasons, the participating company may prefer to use some of its own personnel as instructors. The State, however, will pay the salaries of all instructors. . . . the State will reimburse the company for 50 percent of the non-salvageable materials expended in the training effort, up to a maximum of $100 for each new job. . . . North Carolina's industrial training program makes a conscious effort not to infringe on the company's right of selection. However, at the company's request, the Employment Security Commission will test and screen job candidates. Only those applicants meeting the physical and mental criteria established for a particular job will be referred to the company for further evaluation."[18] With such a predisposition, the community college system not unnaturally now offers courses in "management development" for company foreman and administrators. The curriculum includes classes in the "Science of Human Relations," "Art of Motivating People," "Work Measurement" (wage rates, incentives, etc.), "Motion and Time Study," and "Labor Laws for Supervisors."

It is hardly surprising that Charlotte's First National Union Bank concludes that "throughout the past century" labor is the main factor in drawing industry to North Carolina. "Labor has traditionally been plentiful, trainable, willing to work for modest wages and non-union." Nowhere in the country is the labor force less unionized. Only 6.8 percent of North Carolina's working class is organized. Only South Carolina's 8.6 percent approximates that low figure. Each year the state ranks as the one with the fewest strikes. In 1967 North Carolina lost .04 percent of its total estimated working time due to strikes. The average time lost for all states was .25 percent. Hardly coincidental is the fact that the state is also the lowest in the nation in take-home wages for blue-collar workers. In 1969, for example, Tarheel workers in manufacturing averaged, *before taxes,* $105.88 per week. And in the major industries, wages were less than that worst average in the country. Textile mill workers averaged

$99.17 weekly before taxes (in the yarn mills, $94.51); apparel workers, $74.97; lumber and wood production, $85.27; furniture, $102.86. These industries account for nearly 75 percent of all manufacturing employment, and act to constrain wages in other sectors of the economy as well.[19] (All figures cited here and elsewhere in the book are from the period of the late 1960s and early 1970s, the years that Ben Chavis and his co-workers were being politicized and organizing others and the state was putting them on trial. The situation has not changed substantially since then. In January 1978, for example, the average manufacturing wage in North Carolina was $4.18 an hour, 44 cents below the Southern average, and $1.60 or nearly 30 percent below the national average.)

In 1975 a special study on the earnings of North Carolinians by the Department of City and Regional Planning at the University of North Carolina was quashed by the State's Office of Planning, which had originally commissioned the study. Small wonder: the state's own scholars showed that North Carolina, 8th in the country in industrialization, was 50th in industrial wages. And the earnings gap is growing: In 1971 the Tarheel industrial worker was paid $21.34 per week less than the average industrial worker, nationally; in 1975 he was paid $53.57 less. What's more, "North Carolina's anti-union stance is a major reason for the state's low earned income," and to move up the ladder "the state needs more unionization." But while the state's wages lag behind, "profits are higher than the national average" in 19 of 22 industrial sectors.[20]

What this means for the corporations is obvious: In 1973, with North Carolina workers taking home barely $5,000 a year on the average, value added per worker—i.e., corporate profits per worker—averaged more than $15,000. That is, North Carolina corporations and banks were making three dollars off a worker's labor for each dollar he was paid. Moreover, surplus value would increase at a rate of 5.4 percent a year in North Carolina, as compared to 4.8 percent for the United States as a whole.[21] Furthermore, Black family income in North Carolina is about half that of white, awesome evidence of the profitability of racism.[22] With such a rate of exploitation available, North Carolina's manufacturing employment increased 54.4 percent between 1960 and 1973, compared with 18.4 percent for the United States as a whole.[23] Obviously the monopolies know there is gold in them there mills.

Such are the ravages of a "free" economy that the first minimum wage law passed in the state—in 1959, 12 years after passage of the "right-to-work" law—required wages of at least 75 cents an hour. In 1960 North Carolina's per capita income was $666 below the national level. Ten years later, the difference had increased to $726. Bank projections for 1980 estimate that average wages in the state will reach $6,500, or below present national poverty levels.[24] Because textiles and apparel alone account for 1.5 million workers or 50 percent of North Carolina's working class, wages in this sector determine the economic status of all the state's labor. But the 1975 average annual family income of Southern textile workers, $6,380, lagged $3,186 or one third below the estimated $9,566 needed by an urban family of four to maintain a modest living standard, according to the U.S. Bureau of Labor Statistics. Their average hourly wage in 1975 trailed the national factory average by $1.40; in 1974 the gap was $1.17.[25] Again, only 15 percent of North Carolina's textile workers are in unions.

It is axiomatic by now that the absence of a strong trade union movement guarantees the presence of widespread poverty for working people and their families. North Carolina, with its lowest rate of union-ization in the country, again proves the axiom: Tarheel workers also have the lowest take-home wages in the United States. Although the state is highly agricultural, North Carolina has many more industrial workers per capita than the country as a whole: In 1973, 40 percent of the state's workers were in manufacturing, as compared to 26 percent of all U.S. workers.[26] But only 6.8 percent of the state's workers are in unions, while the national percentage is 28.[27] Consequently North Carolina workers on manufacturing payrolls take home the lowest average weekly earnings in the nation, $97.17 in 1970, compared to the statewide average of $120.36.[28]

Furthermore, in 1965 the most comprehensive study ever made of North Carolina's poverty showed that, "In no major N.C. industry did wages reach the average level . . . for the country as a whole."[29] In July Governor Terry Sanford initiated the North Carolina Fund to "experi-ment with and demonstrate new approaches to the problem of poverty." This proved to be the pilot project for the federal Economic Opportunity Act, Lyndon Johnson's "war on poverty." With some nine million dollars from the Ford Foundation and a couple of R.J. Reynolds family funds, the ruling class discovered—hold onto your hat—that working folks in the Tarheel state were poor. In fact, "about two families in every five meet one of the commonly used definitions of poverty—that of $3,000 family income or less."[30]

Moreover, in 1960, 50.6 percent of North Carolina's families had incomes under $4,000. The Conference on Economic Progress said that one-fifth of the nation lived in poverty in 1959, but in North Carolina *one-half* fell in the poverty bracket. Another 22.2 percent of the state's families earned between $4,000 and $6,000, the conference's definition of "economic deprivation." In all, then, 72.8 percent of all North Carolinians "lived under conditions of poverty or deprivation as defined by the Conference, compared with approximately 40 percent for the nation's population as a whole."[31] Significantly, *virtually all of these families were employed.* More than 9 out of 10 of these families had working male heads of households, with no distinctive difference between white and Black families, which supports the assertion that *low income, not unemployment* is responsible for poverty in North Carolina. Actually, 80 percent of those in the low-income categories were working *40 hours or more* per week. As an example of what James Baldwin once referred to as "democratic anguish"—the suffering of white alongside Black—"nearly half of the whites and one out of three non-whites worked more than 40 hours per week."[32] The latter figure was based on 1965 statistics after a decade of the most intensive industrialization in the state's history. After five years more of the same, North Carolina's average per capita income had risen to $3,218, still well below the poverty line.[33]

Aside from the obvious possibilities for growth in North Carolina, the labor movement would appear to have clear self-interest reasons for organizing that state and the entire South. Not only is there a direct correlation between the absence of strong trade unions and anti-labor and reactionary political representation in Washington, but the poverty and low wages in the state pose a continuing threat of runaway plants from the North, thus driving down Northern wages. That the trade unions have for the most part avoided or rejected the challenge speaks to the bureaucratic narrow-mindedness and "class-collaboration" of the top AFL-CIO national leadership under George Meany.

The effects of poverty in North Carolina also influence the education system in this state that points to Duke and Chapel Hill as its most treasured symbols of accomplishment. While North Carolina ranks among the highest states in the ratio of expenditures on public education to total personal income, that income level is so low that the state ranks below the national average in per pupil expenditures and teacher salaries. In 1970 the high school drop-out rate was 32.7, nearly one in three. Of North Carolinians 25 years or older, 10 percent had completed less than five years of school, twice the national average; 45 percent had never gotten as far as high school.[34]

Worse still, while only 48 percent of whites over 45 years old finished high school, the figure for Blacks was 38 percent. In 1967 the North Carolina Fund noted that of every five poor families in the state, "three are white and two are non-white."[35] James Baldwin has written, in another connection, that, "People are continually pointing out to me the wretchedness of white people in order to console me for the wretchedness of Blacks. But an itemized account of the American failure does not console me and it should not console anyone else."[36] Small consolation indeed are North Carolina poverty figures; the cited study also revealed that of every three white families, one lived in poverty, while three out of four Black families were so defined. In Robeson County, with the state's largest concentration of Indian peoples combined with a large Black population, almost 60 percent of all families earned less than $3,000 a year.

That Black workers are the "last hired, first fired" was borne out by the new labor force of North Carolina's industrialization campaign under Luther Hodges in the 1950s. Most of the jobs created by economic growth in that decade were taken by whites, mainly by white women. White women obtained over 126,000 jobs, nearly 88 percent of the new jobs created between 1950 and 1969. By contrast, non-white workers held 37,000 *fewer* jobs in 1960 than in 1950.[37] Even a state government study in 1973, which tended to minimize the extent of poverty in North Carolina, conceded that "approximately 44 percent of the state's non-white population was poor in 1970 compared to only approximately 13 percent of the white population."[38] Progress, in this state that considers progress its most saleable image, is slow in coming. A 1972 study of Black employment in the state's textile industry found less than 2,200 Black managers, foremen and skilled women workers in the mills. Black managers were only half of one percent of the total managerial force, although Black workers totaled nearly a quarter of the labor force in textiles.[39] Nor is change coming with even deliberate speed. Still another study—the human rights commissioner's alternative to fundamental social change—this one of the city of Charlotte, the most populous urban area in the Carolinas, finds that Blacks won't be living as well in the year 2000 as whites are now: "The chances of Blacks even reaching the 1970 levels for whites during the next 25 years are negligible," in this state where Black family income is half that of whites.[40]

Working people, Black and white, are driven into further impoverishment by the state's tax system, directed as are all state laws to favor the banks and corporations. A sales and use tax took some $335 million from the consumers in the years 1971–2.[41] During the same period, 74.8 percent of the net collections from state income taxes came from individuals, only 12.7 percent from domestic corporations, a bare 2.3 percent from the finance corporations.[42] If the banks were on welfare, the poor were virtually excluded from state aid. In 1974 in all of North Carolina, only 146,000 children and 64,000 social security recipients received welfare.

That was only 4 percent of the total population obtaining aid to dependent children, old-age assistance, and help for the needy blind or totally disabled. Neither unemployed workers nor the working poor (a majority of the working class) were eligible for welfare. Children were eligible only when one of the parents was missing, in which case the child received $41 per month in 1974. Thus a mother and four children—a family of five—would receive $164 a month, not including food stamps and medicaid.[43]

Those who decry the catechism of "welfare chiselers" and "rip-off artists" might note that old-age assistance recipients were fewer in February 1973—31,000—than in 1940 when there were 35,000. Average monthly payments per recipient amounted to $77.93. Medicaid and medical assistance payments are also in decline in North Carolina: In February 1971 these expenditures reached $9.36 million, in February 1973, $7.72 million.[44]

Some years ago former Secretary of Defense Charles Wilson, a General Motors executive who might have missed his calling as a fortune-cookie philosopher, said of the unemployed and those on welfare: "I have always liked bird dogs better than kennel dogs. You know, ones who will get out and hunt for food rather than sit and yelp." Mr. Wilson must smile down from his board room in the sky on North Carolina's welfare system which in 1972 served an average of 11,000 adults a month. That is less than half of one percent of all adult North Carolinians being helped in nursing homes, centers for the retarded, mental hospitals, etc.[45] Payments for public assistance expended per Tarheel resident amounted to $40.98 for the fiscal year ending June 30, 1971, barely half the national average. By contrast New York, which led the country, spent $167.56 per citizen on public assistance. But even the deep South led North Carolina: Louisiana, $67.71; Georgia, $65.81; Alabama, $65.76; Mississippi, $54.47.[46]

The state is no more generous in spending monies for public health departments. For the fiscal year 1972– 3 North Carolina allocated all of 55 cents per person; combined with federal and local funds, the health departments' per capita spending was $4.46.[47] By contrast, the legislature budgeted some $55.19 per capita for highway construction and upkeep in 1970. The results of such a priority of values are predictable: Not much has changed for the average Tarheel worker in 50 years when it comes to health care. In 1920 the state had 562 dentists, or 22 for every 100,000 persons; in 1970 there were 1,476 dentists or 30 for every 100,000. According to the Association of American Medical Colleges there should be at least one doctor for every 571 persons. In 1970 the national average was one per 711. North Carolina had one doctor per 1,063. And only 15 hospitals have outpatient clinics in this state of more than five million people.[48]

The consequences of a legislature in the service of the banks are more than only anti-strike bills aimed at labor. Working people as a whole, without the protection of a strong, aggressive trade union movement, are victimized in many ways. The division between white and Black workers—which assures the absence of such a labor movement—works to sustain that victimization, hitting Blacks hardest but also hurting whites. Infant mortality in North Carolina in 1972 was 22.6 per thousand live births; for whites it was 18.2 per thousand live births, for Blacks 32.4 per thousand. Between 1968 and 1972 the fetal mortality rate per 1,000 was 12.8 for whites, and nearly twice that, 23.4, for non-whites. Death rates that year were 9.1 per 1,000 North Carolinians. The death rate was 23 percent higher for non-whites than for whites—10.6 compared to 8.6 per 1,000. A non-white child up to four years of age was twice as likely to die as a white child of the same age. A non-white adult 23–44 years of age was three times as likely to die as the white adult of the same age group.

Figures for, say, tuberculosis and venereal diseases, both "poverty diseases," are telling:

1972	TOTAL	WHITE	NON-WHITE
Population	5,200,388	4,041,809	1,185,579
Reported TB cases	1,017	369	648
Reported VD cases	28,429	5,784	22,645

Thus, non-whites who are about 21.5 percent of the population had nearly two-thirds of the TB (or, proportionally, 10 times more TB than whites) and 80 percent of the VD (or proportionally 20 times more VD than whites).[49] Of North Carolina's legally blind persons, almost 42 persons are non-white, twice their proportion of the general population.[50]

Those who wax exuberant about the progressivism of North Carolina lose some of the gee-whiz quality in their voices when discussing the effects of poverty. In North Carolina in 1969, for example, more than 44,000 families earned a total annual income less than the cost of the economic diet alone, i.e., less than $1,200 for a family of four. A state Board of Health survey in 1971 found that only a quarter of the families eligible for food stamps were participating. The survey also found that 43 percent of the society's pre-school-age children and 27 percent of all households were consuming inadequate diets, deficient in Vitamins A and C, iron, calcium and protein. The greatest frequency of inadequate diets occurred among non-whites (47 percent compared with 29 percent for whites) but even among households reporting income of $9,000 or more, virtually all of whom were white, 21 percent had inadequate diets. Further, more than 40 percent of Black households in the industrial Piedmont and the rural east had substandard food preparation facilities, compared with only 3 percent of white households.[51] Nearly 14.3 percent of all housing units lacked some or all plumbing facilities. The national average was 6 percent. In North Carolina 38.6 percent of the Black population lacked some or all plumbing facilities.[52] Such were the social facts of New Southern life that Ben Chavis and his co-workers sought to change.

IT is perhaps sufficient commentary on New Southern justice to note that the brief formative years in which Ben and Jim Grant and T.J. Reddy came to positions of community leadership by organizing against war and for equal education witnessed a parallel development of criminal aptitude in Walter David Washington and Theodore Alfred Hood. The governments of North Carolina and the United States, in their zeal to persecute the community leadership, chose to embrace the criminals.

There is some evidence to suggest that Washington and Hood may have been operating as police agents as far back as 1967 when they set up a Black Cultural Association in a separate Charlotte neighborhood than that in which Ben's Black House stood. That the two informers formed a group called US, which in other parts of the country was clearly an arm of the police, at a time when the Black Panther Organization was organized in Charlotte, lends substance to this suggestion. As does their driving a carload of dynamite into a police roadblock at a time of racial tensions in Oxford. Nobody would ever accuse Washington and Hood of being brilliant master criminals, but such an act suggests an incompetence roughly on a level of being unable to catch water with a sponge. Leaving the country on the day of their trial, then returning immediately to Charlotte to surrender, and then escaping all prosecution in return for testifying against Ben and Jim and the Charlotte Three seemed to be some of the fanciest footwork since Gene Kelly was singing in the rain.

These two agents in the service of the government merit some examination. Washington's first conviction came in 1959 when he was twelve and was arrested for breaking and entering and larceny. Before his teenage years were over, he added new convictions for damage to property, assault and assault with a deadly weapon. In 1967 Washington received a medical discharge from the Marine Corps after half a year in Vietnam. Diagnosed as schizophrenic, he was declared 100 percent mentally disabled after trying to shoot his first sergeant. Since 1968 he has been receiving total disability payments from the U.S. government.

Washington pleaded guilty to armed robbery charges in August 1969, received a 20–25-year suspended sentence and was ordered to seek psychiatric help, keep a curfew between 8 PM and 5 AM for five years, and abstain from all intoxicants. When he was arrested in Oxford on the explosives charges in 1970, Washington was in violation of that probation. When he came to court for the probation violation hearing in May 1971, he brought along District Attorney Tom Moore, who was to prosecute the Lazy B case, and Assistant U.S. Attorney David Long, who prosecuted the Chavis-Grant federal case. Judge Robert Martin, who had presided over the trial of the Teels, the Oxford Klansmen who were acquitted for the murder of Henry Lee Marrow (and who would later act as judge in the Wilmington 10 trial), heard the appeal for Washington's continued probation. Martin agreed not only not to withdraw probation from Washington but also to drop all the conditions of that probation—reporting to probation officers, the payment of fines, curfews, etc. Martin acknowledged that Washington had violated all the terms of his probation but said they were not serious violations. A Charlotte Three appeals hearing in December 1974 disclosed that *at the time of Washington's testimony against Ben and Jim in the federal case and in the Lazy B trial, the informer was a suspect under investigation for five separate Mecklenburg County murders.* This fact was never disclosed to the defense attorneys. Washington was never charged with any of the murders.

Al Hood grew up and went to school with Washington and became his partner in crime. Before the Oxford dynamite arrest, Hood had been convicted of auto theft, assault with a deadly weapon with intent to kill, carrying a concealed weapon and assault on an officer. At the time of the Oxford bust, he was facing charges of armed robbery and of carrying a concealed weapon, as well as various probation violations. For his "work" on the Chavis-Grant and Charlotte Three trials, his $165,000 bond was reduced to $50,000 and then to a recognizance bond. All pending charges against Hood, including those unrelated to the Oxford incident, were dropped. Together, Hood and Washington had nearly 100 years in prison sentences facing them, all of which were wiped clean for their services to the prosecutors' offices. One could say of them, as William Powell's Nick Charles said in *The Thin Man,* "I don't like

crooks, and if I did like crooks I wouldn't like crooks who are also
stoolpigeons, and if I did like crooks who are also stoolpigeons, I
wouldn't like you."

The suspicion that Hood and Washington may have peen police agents
all along is given further credence by their seeming immunity to prosecution as their life of crime continued unabated even after the Charlotte
Three trial. On August 31, 1972, a month after that trial, Hood was
charged with narcotics possession and murder in the killing of a heroin
dealer while contesting control of the Charlotte area drug traffic. He has
never been brought to trial, remaining free on his own recognizance.
Four months later, on January 30, 1974, Washington entered a Charlotte
hospital with gunshot wounds in his heart and lungs. Two weeks after
that he was allowed to leave the hospital without ever having to explain
the details of the shooting, although the press speculated that it was in
retaliation for giving information regarding an armed robbery case to
police. Washington was in violation of his probation restrictions at the
time, as he had been for at least the previous five years. A few months
later he was back in Mercy hospital after shooting and being shot by a
store owner whom Washington was either robbing or enforcing a
syndicate policy upon. The police questioned him this time around, but
again he was released with the shooting going unexplained.

The old adage that holds that crime doesn't pay never took into
account the enterprising Hood and Washington. In the spring of 1974 the
Charlotte *Observer* reported that the two hoodlums received a minimum
of $4,000 each from the U.S. Justice and Treasury departments for their
testimony against Ben and Jim in the federal trial. The payments were
approved by the now convicted Watergate criminal Robert Mardian,
acting on behalf of the now convicted Watergate criminal John Mitchell.
The Justice Department alone paid out $3,000 each to Hood and
Washington as "relocation fees" to buy a ranch in Mexico after the Lazy
B trial. The $1,000 paid to each of the two informers by the Treasury
Department were described alternately as "reward" payments and "in-
formants' fees." Ironically, the last $1,000 payments were made by federal
agents at a time the state had an arrest warrant out on Washington for
probation violations. "Washington," reported the *Observer* on March
24, 1974, "had been cooperating with the FBI ever since the Oxford
arrest"—that is, even during the "flight" to Canada to avoid prosecution
which Ben and Jim were alleged to have conspired to aid—and had
"arranged through his attorney" to be arrested three months later on
December 27, 1970.

The amounts of U.S. tax dollars paid to Hood and Washington have not been fully verified. While the Justice and Treasury departments claim that they "were only able to find records showing payments of $4,000 for each man," an attorney who handled the negotiations insists they received about $15,000 each. The *Observer* reported, however, that "Three North Carolina law enforcement officers closely acquainted with Washington, say that in [1973] Washington has bragged to them that he received additional money. He gave each officer a different figure, ranging from $38,000 to $70,000. The officers all say they are inclined to believe him." It is known that in addition to the $8,000 paid the two as "rewards" and "informants' fees," $13,837.32 was given them for airline tickets and to house them and their families at an Atlantic Beach, N.C., resort for three months. Treasury Department requests for "expenditure of funds for purchase of evidence" were later made public. The Treasury requests were made by Stanley Noel, the agent who had monitored Ben's and Jim's anti-war activities in Charlotte for years, who had broken into Ben's house during his student years, and who had coordinated both the federal and the Lazy B cases for the government. The testimony of Hood and Washington was virtually the only evidence ever marshalled in court against the civil rights activists.

Twenty years ago Hollywood screenwriter Dalton Trumbo, writing of other political trials—those of the Communist Party leaders during the days of the Smith Act—described the role of police spies:

> No one will seriously question that they stood in relation to the FBI as employees stand in relation to a boss. A cook will prepare horsemeat or beef as the restaurateur requests; a carpenter will build a house as solid or flimsy as the contractor demands; a stenographer will type truth or fiction as his employer requires; and if any one of them fails to produce what is wanted, he will be discharged and his income will cease. The openly stated hostility of the FBI to the Communist Party justifies doubt that it would pay spies to secure information favorable to that organization. Indeed, it would not stretch credibility to suggest that the FBI requested damaging information about the Communist Party, and that any spy who failed to secure it would lose all value to his employer and quickly be separated from the payroll. The temptation to insure continued income by producing what is desired seems too obvious to belabor. . . .
>
> Many of the witnesses employed by the prosecution earn their living exclusively by testifying in political trials. If such trials stopped altogether, they would be out of work. They have no other occupation. Others who had not achieved a professional status nevertheless lived at government expense and were, in addition, paid substantial fees for their testimony. Their testimony was not, therefore, a disinterested act of citizenship; it was a commodity

for which money had to be paid. The government wanted to buy testimony and the witnesses had it to sell and a deal was consummated between them.

Over strenuous objections by the prosecution, which viewed the whole matter as a morbid intrusion into areas too sensitive for public scrutiny, the government was obliged to reveal the precise sum it had paid to its covin of witnesses. The sum . . . reveals how cheaply an American citizen can be deprived of his liberty. (*The Time of the Toad: A Study of Inquisition in America,* New York, Harper & Row, 1972, pp. 88, 90.)

If we substitute the words "North Carolina civil rights movement" for "Communist Party" and "Robert Mardian's Justice Department and Stanley Noel's Treasury Department" for "FBI," we have precisely the role of Hood and Washington in the Chavis-Grant federal trial and Charlotte Three case.

Assistant U.S. Attorney David Long, who prosecuted the federal trial, said that once Mardian and other Justice Department officials became aware of the case, they "were more interested in this case than in any others I prosecuted. . . . They had copies of all documents in their files in Washington and that was unusual." U.S. Attorney Warren Coolidge said that the monies paid to Hood and Washington were the only instance of assistance to federal witnesses in North Carolina granted during his four-year tenure. Throughout the Charlotte Three trial months later, the *Observer* reported, "Federal agents kept in close touch with the state case." One agent said within earshot of Judge Snepp on the last day of the trial, "There's an assistant attorney general in Washington waiting to hear what happened in this case." The only assistant attorney general in Washington that had kept on top of the prosecution from its inception was Robert Mardian. In keeping with the temper and thrust of Mardian's Intelligence Evaluation Committee and the FBI's Cointelpro operation, all federal secret memos regarding payoffs to Hood and Washington referred to Ben and Jim as "known Black militants" or "two of the top militant leaders in the State of North Carolina."

S HALL we pursue programs that would result in mixing the genes of the Negro race with those of the White race and so convert the population of the United States into a mixed-blooded people?" This was the burning question that so concerned Professor Wesley Critz George in 1962. The "programs" that were worrying this former head of the Department of Anatomy at the University of North Carolina Medical School, were court orders for school desegegation.[53]

This doctor of humane letters, department head at that New South showcase university, wrote like a hophead in sheets as he catalogued in the name of science virtually every crackpot myth of white racial superiority. Black people are "highly emotional" and "readily goaded by irresponsible leaders into violence." If mixed with whites, they "seem destined to bring about deterioration in the quality of our genetic pool." George examined "frontal lobes," "brain weight," "bone density" and a sorcerer's brew of other standards and measures for gauging white supremacy. The key test, however, the scale of scales, was the IQ test. "Some of us know Negroes who are intelligent, industrious, thrifty and dependable; but these are not qualities that characterize large numbers of the race. . . . Indolence, improvidence and consequent pauperism are qualities commonly ascribed to them."[54] Hence the classical argument for apartheid or even extermination: People of color are biologically different, those differences are far more than skin deep, "those people" are mentally inferior, racism is not ideological madness but rather an objective assessment of reality.

Worse, Black biological inferiority results in behavioral and moral inferiority. If "pauperism" is a natural quality of Blacks, so too is the "criminal instinct." A proportionally greater number of arrests of Blacks than of whites, wrote the good doctor, "seems to bear some relation to differences in personality and behaviorial characteristics of the two races. Among both ordinary citizens and psychiatrists one encounters the oft-expressed judgement that Negroes, both in this country and in Africa, exhibit a more unrestrained emotional life and lack of self-discipline than whites, and it is well known that the rate of arrest and conviction for crimes is much higher among Negroes."[55]

While only the occasional Shockley will utter such yesteryear ravings these days, the arguments of Dr. George remain the ideological under-pinnings of North Carolina's—and the nation's—criminal justice system. Black people, by their nature, are "the criminal element." Not victims of deprivation and discrimination, they are as Dr. George argued, "indo-lent" and "improvident." "The same qualities exist among some whites," concedes the professor, "but the incidence is much higher among Negroes."[56]

Racist pseudoscience has, in much of the country, given up the IQ ghost as an argument for white supremacy. North Carolina remains a throwback enclave. The U.S. Supreme Court ruled a few years ago in *Griggs et al.* vs. *Duke Power Co.,* that 13 Black workers had been wrongly eliminated from better jobs through the manipulation of intel-ligence testing. The court decided that any testing is unlawful unless it clearly gauges the necessary skills for a particular job.[57] With IQs on the defensive in the courts and in science, the same arguments are being forwarded in new forms; the old "mental defective" beans have been refried, to be served up as "learning disability."

The qualities that make for learning disabilities are essentially the same ones that North Carolina's eugenic laws have always used as the rationale for sterilization and castration, i.e., low IQ at an early age, the indication of life-long "mental defectiveness."

North Carolina's Eugenics Board was set up in 1938 during a period of great industrial expansion. In introducing the statutes for sterilization and experiments on the reproductive organs of working folk in the state, the Eugenics Board argued in an epigraph: "If recognized as an integral part of a broad system of protection and supervision of *those unable to meet unaided the responsibilities of citizenship in a highly competitive industrial system, it can be productive only of good.* "[58] (Author's emphasis.)

The board's secretary defined sterilization as "a means adopted by organized society to do for the human race in a humane manner what was done by Nature before modern civilization, human sympathy and charity intervened in Nature's plans." Referring to Sir Francis Galton, who developed the pseudoscience of eugenics in the late nineteenth century, North Carolina's sterilization pioneer said that several "methods of limiting or decreasing breeding among the undesirable human stocks have been advocated" by Galton's followers. "Among them are segregation of the unfit; restrictive marriage laws; birth control; eugenic education; and human sterilization."[59] For any who might miss the point, the state's leading advocate of eugenics quoted from the German Sterilization Statute of the time (the time, for those who lack historical perspective, is that of the Third Reich): "I. Whoever is afflicted with a hereditary disease can be sterilized by a surgical operation, if—according to the experience of medical science—there is a great probability that his descendants will suffer from serious bodily or mental defects. Hereditary diseases under this law are: 1) Hereditary feeble-mindedness; 2) Schizophrenia; 3) Manic depressive insanity; 4) Hereditary epilepsy; 5) Huntington's Chorea; 6) Hereditary blindness; 7) Hereditary deafness; 8) Serious hereditary bodily deformities. II. Furthermore those suffering from alcoholism can be sterilized."[60]

Lest there be doubts or curiosity about just what sorts of folks fall into these "hereditary" categories, the Eugenics Board conducted "A Study Relating to Mental Illness, Mental Deficiency, and Epilepsy in a Selected Rural County."[61] Listing the "*potential* mentally ill, mentally deficient and epileptic" (author's emphasis) by occupation, these potentially castrated or sterilized subjects were farm laborers, saw mill laborers, other laborers, textile workers, janitorial and other service workers, farm tenants, vehicle drivers, aircraft or munitions factory workers, furniture factory workers.[62] That's all. Only "other" and "none" were also listed. No banker's son or daughter could suffer from alcoholism or epilepsy only to face the surgeon's scalpel or the gynecologist's knot.

A look at the Eugenics Board statistics for the period 1954 to 1968, the years of the civil rights upsurge from the Supreme Court decision on school desegregation to the assassination of Martin Luther King, indicates that racism quickly supplanted the class bias inherent in the "science" of eugenics. A sharp increase in male supremacy, already deeply imbedded in eugenics, is apparent as sterilization of men virtually ended:[63]

Years	Number of Operations	Subjects under 20 Years*	Male	Female	Black	White
1954–5	556	214	131	425	198	357
1956–7	562	189	77	485	274	284
1958–9	535	151	43	492	315	209
1960–1	467	146	14	439	284	179
1962–3	507	157	14	493	323	170
1964–5	356	166	6	350	228	124
1966–8**	290	162	3***	287	188	96

*Under 20 means 10-19 years old.
**The 1967 state legislature removed epilepsy as one of the conditions for sterilization.
***Between 1969 and 1973 the Eugenics Board performed 358 more sterilizations, but no longer recorded the subjects' sex and color. In 1975 a new law took effect transferring authorization to order sterilization from the Eugenics Board to local district judges.

In recent years most of the "eugenics" sterilizations were conducted on adolescent Black women. Consent of the individual to be sterilized is not necessary but is considered helpful, according to the Eugenics Board's 1972 "General Decision Making Criteria." Most of those sterilized were declared "mentally defective," a category to fit those "with an I.Q. of 55," according to former Eugenics Board executive secretary June Stallings.

How then explain the apparent mental defectiveness in such great numbers among Blacks as compared to whites—a ratio of 10 to 1 in the past 20 years? Poverty, says Ms. Stallings: "Scientific research shows that infants with improper diets become retarded."[64]

But the Eugenics Board's own statistics show a clear class, racial and sexual bias. Indeed the notion of "eugenics" is scientifically akin to the ideas that Communists eat babies and Jews have horns. The poor are impoverished because that is their nature, the class structure of society is "natural," things are as they were meant to be, that's human nature.[65] Black people, particularly Black women, are disproportionately and increasingly "mentally defective," a condition that results from their impoverishment, which will not change. Attempts to change this natural state of being are the efforts only of outside forces, "agitators" in policemen's jargon. The political institutionalization of these ideas is fascism, writes Herbert Aptheker. "Its main propaganda device is racism. The ultimate logic of this are crematoria; people themselves constituting the pollution and inferior people in particular, then crematoria become really vast sewerage projects."[66] (When the United Nations convention on genocide was adopted in 1948, the fourth act of five constituting genocide was listed as "imposing measures intended to prevent births within the group.")

What is so unsettling about June Stalling's replies is that she sits, snug as a child in a mackinaw, reducing questions of life and death to banalities. Her response is on a par with the woman who helped oversee *lebensborn,* Hitler's attempt to create "a thousand year Reich" by breeding young German women with oval faces, blond hair and blue eyes, narrow noses and thin mouths, with SS officers of similar features, to arrive at a virtual pedigreed Aryan. Thirty years after the fall of the Third Reich, this woman recalled that *lebensborn* only provided homes for unwed mothers, that the emphasis on Aryan types was, you know, just a question of fashion. Some ages prefer blonds, others brunettes.[67] Dr. William B. Shockley, who has become something of a circuit rider in the cause of eugenics and a homegrown variety of *lebensborn,* is more candid. The future is threatened, Shockley argues, by dysgenics, defined as "retrogressive evolution through the disproportionate reproduction of the genetically disadvantaged. Or, down-breeding." The doctor suggests bonus payments be offered "to persons with low IQs who undergo voluntary sterilization."[68]

Even with its ring of scientific basis, "behavior modification" is still another way of linking "criminal behavior" to mental disorders.

Strange and mysterious indeed are the numerous ways it works its wonders to perform. Behavior modification has been defined by one psychologist as "the unethical utilization of any form of electrotherapy, chemotherapy, psychosurgery, psychotherapy, aversive therapy, rewards-and-punishment or other means or devices to alter the mood, behavior, personality or psychic state of an individual or a group." Tom Wicker writes that, "Nothing arouses the fears of prison inmates more than so-called 'behavior modification' programs, and no wonder. Behavior modification is a catch-all term that can mean anything from brain surgery to a kind of 'Clockwork Orange' mental conditioning; it usually includes drug experimentation, and in all too many cases it is aimed more nearly at producing docile prisoners than upright citizens."[69]

The Gideon for most behavior modifiers is B. F. Skinner's *Beyond Freedom and Dignity,* the thrust of which is based on the curious proposition that "housing is a matter not only of buildings and cities but of how people live. Overcrowding can be corrected only by inducing people not to crowd."[70] This suggestion is not too far distant from that which holds that the napalm victim is in part to blame for being in the wrong place at the wrong time. Further, we needn't ban napalm but must teach the victim to submit to the will of the bomber. As for Skinner's "overcrowding" example, three of his disciples, Dr. Frank Ervin, Vernon Mark and William Sweet, bring his thoughts to their logical conclusion in a letter to the *Journal of the American Medical Association.* The letter came in the wake of the Detroit ghetto rebellion in 1967, entitled "Role of Brain Disease in Riots and Urban Violence," and urged "diagnosing the many violent slum dwellers who have some brain pathology and treating them" [with brain surgery].[71]

Skinner himself sees in his "behaviorally engineered society" the control of the population in the hands of specialists, "police, priests, owners, teachers, therapists and so on."[72] Behaviorist James V. McConnell of the University of Michigan rubs his hands in gleeful anticipation: "I believe the day has come when we can combine sensory deprivation with drugs, hypnosis and astute manipulation of reward and punishment to gain almost absolute control over an individual's behavior." Preempting argument, the good doctor says, "There is no reason to believe you should have the right to refuse to acquire a new [personality] if the old one is anti-social."[73]

The key is, who is "anti-social" and again for the Skinnerist it is the napalm victim not the napalm bomber or manufacturer. UCLA's Center for the Study and Reduction of Violence conducted a study of "the family structure and unrest among the poor" in order to establish "models designed to control the activities of individuals and groups, including rioters." The Law Enforcement Assistance Administration admits to some 400 behavior modification projects in 1974 alone, including a $130,000 grant to the University of Puerto Rico for "neurological research into the correlations between criminal behavior and brain damage,"[74] although the Justice Department didn't suggest that Watergate resulted from mental retardation in the Oval Office.

Mr. Nixon's personal physician, Dr. Arnold Hutschnecker, proposed in 1970 the psychological testing of children under the age of nine to determine which were "criminally inclined," those with "violent tendencies" to be placed in special camps. This camp would be an alternative to slum reconstruction; in Dr. Hutschnecker's words, "a direct, immediate, effective way of attacking the problem at its very origin, by focusing on the criminal mind of the child."[75] Such testing now takes place in the hundreds of penitentiaries across the United States housing the largest prison population in the world, more so in North Carolina than in any other state. That testing, called behavior modification, has not yet been applied en masse to children but to their incarcerated elders, while the National Institute of Mental Health—part of the Department of Health, Education and Welfare—is funding several behavior modification programs for juveniles. Seven of the doctors tried at Nuremberg were hanged for experiments carried out on prisoners, but international law apparently does not pertain to those incarcerated in U.S. prisons and jails who are tested with a variety of toxins and diseases, subjected to electroshock and lobotomies, induced to take a host of chemicals and drugs, all for the greater good of research in controlling human behavior.

AFTER being found not guilty in the federal case with Jim Grant, Rev. Chavis was returned to prison to await the Wilmington 10 trial. During the trial with Jim, Ben occupied a cell in the Wake County Jail in Raleigh. Now, after a few days in the New Hanover County Jail in Wilmington, he was moved to Raleigh again, this time to the decrepit Central Prison. The absurdity of being in a maximum security prison while legally innocent and awaiting trial was matched by the cruelty of his surroundings.

About a quarter of the state's imprisoned felons are held at Central Prison, the state's only maximum security unit. Construction on the prison began in 1869 and still continues. As the rings of a redwood trunk reveal its history to the practiced eye, you can tell Central's history by the age of each additional building. A mental hospital is the latest structure. The foreboding red-brick prison, with all the attraction of a lanced boil, was built on the outskirts of Raleigh, but in the century since it was completed, the town has spread out, placing the complex right in the center of the modern capital city.

The main unit was designed to hold 500 men but has housed twice as many. In the "maxi-maxi" I and J wings and the west wing where the boredom is relieved only by the tedium, the 500 prisoners stay in their cells 24 hours a day except for meals and minimal recreation. In 1968 a prison rebellion ended in seven prisoner deaths and dozens of wounded, the worst violence visited upon prisoners in the country until Attica in 1971. In charge of restoring the authority of the prison administration was Sam Garrison, who is now warden at Central.

From the moment the slight 24-year-old Rev. Chavis walked through the gate, he was treated by the guards as "Big Bad Ben," a threat to their authority. Just before he arrived, a couple of inmates were brutally beaten and sent to the prison hospital for refusing to cut their "natural" hairdos. Ben's reputation preceded him with the other prisoners as well as with the guards. Some inmates approached Ben for help. Together they drafted and filed suits in federal court against the Department of Corrections, alleging discrimination against Blacks for banning "naturals." Though the suit was eventually withdrawn, prison policy changed and Ben himself was never asked to cut his hair.

Also being held in Ben's wing was Joe Waddell, a section leader of the Black Panther Party in Winston-Salem. Joe Waddell was only 20 years old and, like many young Panther members, enthusiastic about the Party. He would shout out the "10-point Program" of the Panthers, even during the evening "quiet hours." Such behavior was not calculated to win him a large following among the prison officials. It was known throughout the prison that some guards were laying for Joe Waddell. One day in early May, Ben, Joe and the other E-Block inmates returned to their cells from the recreation yard. It would be the last time that Ben and the other prisoners ever saw Joe Waddell. The authorities claim that he collapsed upon returning to his cell and was taken to the prison hospital where he was pronounced dead. The 20-year-old's death was attributed to a heart attack by the prison officials, but none of the inmates observed any signs of ill health during the recreation period. In any case, an autopsy to determine certain cause of death became impossible when the prison authorities removed all of Waddell's internal organs and bequeathed them to one of the nearby state hospitals for general experimental purposes.

May 26, 1972, was the first African Liberation Day celebrated in the United States and Ben was determined that Central Prison should not go without its commemoration. His leadership of the civil rights movement on the outside made him de facto a leader of the prisoners, who were becoming politically conscious throughout the country. Inmates from the other 71 prison units in the state, including the women's prison, wrote to him at Central. Using a post-office box in Raleigh and employing the services of a secretary at the Commission for Racial Justice, he began to organize the United Black Prisoners Freedom Movement. Because the only privileges allowed the prisoners at Central were eating and sleeping, the Black inmates agreed to forego the former as an act of solidarity, and held a one-day hunger strike on the first African Liberation Day the North Carolina Department of Corrections had ever seen.

Nine days later Rev. Chavis was transferred to the Pender County Jail in Burgaw. Local officials acknowledged that a fair trial in Wilmington for the Wilmington 10 was out of the question, so the trial was moved to adjoining rural, and predominantly Black, Pender County. Judge Joshua S. James was selected to preside. Attorney James Ferguson was again at the defense table. The prosecution was to be handled by James Stroud, a young assistant solicitor from Wilmington known for his sarcasm and prosecutorial zeal. The Klan-influenced *Hanover Sun* in a commentary under the banner headline "Here's to Jay Stroud" was to call the prosecutor, "One of the finest things that ever happened to the cause of law and order and justice in this area."

During pretrial motions the defendants moved for production of the evidence and disclosure of the witnesses against them; to quash the indictments based on the race and class bias of the grand jury; to sequester prospective jurors during the questioning period preceding jury selection; to disclose evidence favorable to the defense. Judge James denied each motion except the disclosure motions, which he granted in part. When jury selection proceeded as scheduled, a trial jury of ten Blacks and two whites was chosen. That was on Friday, June 9; opening arguments were to be heard on Monday. But Monday morning the prosecution moved for a mistrial because Jay Stroud was said to be suffering from a stomach ache or "intestinal flu," although the defendants agreed unanimously that the racial composition of the jury influenced Stroud's stomach more than any bug. Judge James acceded to the prosecution, announced a mistrial and dismissed the jury. A new trial was ordered for September.

With three more months to the new trial date, bond was reduced to $15,000 for Ben, $7,000 or $8,000 for the others. At the end of June they were released on bond. The movement was in disarray after months of incarceration of its leadership. Ben and the other defendants went back into the community to begin to rebuild. Ben returned to Raleigh briefly to organize a rally in solidarity with the inmates at Central Prison, protesting the macabre conditions from which he had recently emerged and in which more than a thousand remained. On July 22, the day of the demonstration, under orders of state Prisons Commissioner Lee Bounds, every prisoner at Central was placed in lockup. Machine guns were mounted on the walls of the prison and aimed at the streets outside. Orders were given to the guards to shoot any outsider who came within 150 yards of the prison. "We are aware," Bounds later told the press, "that this sort of thing (the rally) could adversely affect our operations here, so we were ready. We took such measures as I thought were necessary." Among Bounds' operations that might be adversely affected was the last remaining highway labor chain gang in the country.

In subsequent testimony before a hearing of the North Carolina Criminal Justice Task Force, Rev. Chavis reported that in Central Prison the prison guards regularly hosed down prisoners and their belongings with high-pressure fire hoses; and that the prison had erected an "animal cage," a two-by-six-foot wire mesh corridor from the cellblock to the cafeteria through which prisoners must walk "while young white guards are constantly picking at prisoners and harassing them." Governor Bob Scott's appointed secretary of the Department of Rehabilitation, George Randall, said he would not debate "with a man who doesn't know the facts about Central Prison."

But Bounds admitted that the fire hoses were used, although "only for control," not punishment. Bounds took credit for introducing the "animal cage," again as an advanced method of control. Of Bounds it can be said, as Saki wrote of Bernard Shaw, "He had discovered himself and gave ungrudgingly of his discovery to the world." Bounds did take issue with Rev. Chavis on one point: "The impact of the conditions of our prison system," argued the vexed Mr. Bounds, "rests evenly on whites and Blacks."

In August Ben had to return to Portsmouth to stand trial for the charges growing out of his January arrest—running a stop sign, failing to show a car registration card, disruption of public schools. When Ben showed that he had not been driving the car at the time of arrest, the traffic charges were dropped. But the court pursued the disruption of the schools charge. The magistrate, referring to Ben as a "trespassing pied piper," found him guilty and sentenced him to a year in prison and a $2,000 fine. Early the next year Ben would appeal the decision to a

Hustlings Court, where a jury would reverse the decision and find him not guilty. But for the next few months he would temporarily have his first conviction.

If the North Carolina civil rights movement had been set back by the arrests and prosecution of its leadership, the same could not be said of Leroy Gibson's Rights of White People, which continued to flower in the eastern part of the state. With Rev. Chavis back on the streets, ROWP had its number one enemy at large again. Ben began to get telephone threats at his home in Oxford and at the Commission office in Raleigh. State law enforcement intelligence agents approached him to say they had information that a group of Wilmington businessmen, upset over the loss of millions of dollars and new investments, had put out a $10,000 contract on his life. The agents were at a loss for an answer when Ben asked why they weren't arresting these businessmen for conspiracy to murder, but they warned Ben against returning to Wilmington.

On August 31 Ben had to be in Wilmington to consult with his co-defendants. That evening he returned to Raleigh to work on some papers at the Commission office in preparation for the upcoming Wilmington 10 trial. Arriving in the capital city at 10:30 P.M., Rev. Chavis went to his office in the downtown Odd Fellows building. Around 1 A.M. he came back downstairs, got into his car and headed for home. After driving for three blocks, he saw a blue flame, like an acetalyne torch coming from under the front seat. He braked the car, opened the door and jumped out. The whole interior of the car burst into flames, which enveloped the entire vehicle in a minute's time. An incendiary explosion knocked out the windows and threw Ben back. An ambulance came and rushed him to the hospital with first-, second- and third-degree burns on his right arm. Meanwhile, the remains of the car were taken to the Raleigh police garage. The city police announced they were turning the investigation over to the SBI. The SBI in turn passed the case on to the FBI, who turned it over to the Treasury Department's Bureau of Alcohol, Tobacco and Firearms. Stanley Noel, who organized the prosecution of Ben and Jim and the Charlotte Three, was put in charge of the investigation. Apparently the ATF hit a snag in this investigation, for no report was ever released, let alone a prosecution developed. The local police, SBI and FBI also remained silent.

Five

Law! What do I care about the law? Hain't I got the power?

Cornelius Vanderbilt

"Shut up," he explained.

Ring Lardner

NORTH Carolina's prison system is a hundred years ahead at being behind. With only five million people in the entire state, there are 77 state prisons, the most of any state in the country. Upwards of 14,000 inmates crowd the various units, the highest per capita prison population in the United States. New York, for example, a state with four times the number of people, has 15,000 prisoners or 7 percent more than North Carolina. The U.S. Justice Department listed the Tarheel state as having the highest number of inmates per 100,000 population—183—at the end of 1973. North Dakota with the lowest ratio had 28 inmates per 100,000 population. In the years since that report, North Carolina has consolidated its hold on its leading position in institutionalized repression, jailing more of its people than any other state, and jailing them for longer terms.[1]

If the country as a whole had North Carolina's ratio, there would be more than *five million* prisoners in the United States. Disturbing as is the overall figure, things are much worse for young people, and for Blacks and Indians. In 1974, almost 42 percent of the state's prisoners were under 25 years old. The ratio per 100,000 North Carolinians of, for example, 24 years of age, was 830, more than four times the statewide total that leads the nation. For Black men the ratio was 1,040 per 100,000, or five and a half times the general total. Thus, more than one percent of all Black men in North Carolina are imprisoned.[2] In addition, more than 16,000 North Carolinians (surpassing the total prison population) enter county and city jails each month.[3]

As the state shoe-horns several thousand additional new inmates into its prisons which contain only 10,000 beds, the Raleigh Archipelago has become a hell without fire. Four and a half thousand prisoners have no beds. In 1974, 650 prisoners under 18, some as young as 14, were mixed in the general prison population.[4] State corrections officials have proposed the construction of an additional four prisons to house another 3,000 inmates. Official state estimates are that by 1983, the shortage of beds for medium-custody inmates alone will be 6,000, as a "conservative" figure.

The estimates are based "upon past experience and the assumption that things will remain as they presently exist," a commentary at once on bureaucratic smugness and on a stagnant society.[5]

Women prisoners have special problems. North Carolina laws set a minimum prison sentence of 30 days for men, six months for women. A serious case of unequal protection exists, with decentralized programs of dispersal for men prisoners through the many prison units, whereas women are centralized at the lone state women's prison in Raleigh, making family visits more difficult as well as possibly being unconstitutional.

Another possible violation of women prisoners' constitutional rights is the use by prison authorities of pelvic examinations allegedly to search for contraband, which could be unreasonable search, cruel and unusual punishment and an invasion of privacy.

In June 1975, these and other grievances at the Women's Correctional Center resulted in more than four days of disturbances that left a total of 32 inmates injured at the hands of various prison and state police agents. Prisoner complaints included working conditions in the prison laundry, where they worked eight-hour days on aging equipment while temperatures often reached 120 degrees. State Prisons deputy director Walter Kautsky said, "The breakdown occurred because the inmates were allowed to have access to mop handles." After the protest was broken, 60 women were placed in "complete segregation," and 33 others were transferred to the previously all-male prison at Morgantown.

Unless things change soon, "it is likely that federal courts will intervene in the operation" of the state prisons, according to a report by the North Carolina Commission on Correctional Programs. The report found that the state prison system meets few of the standards set by the federal court which took control of the Alabama prison system out of that state's hands. Among the report's findings were that 71 of the North Carolina system's 77 prison units are overcrowded; that only six North Carolina units meet the court standard for Alabama; that only one inmate should be confined in a single cell with a minimum of 60 square feet; that if the Alabama standards were imposed, North Carolina's system could handle no more than 7,000 prisoners, less than half those incarcerated.

North Carolina's 77 prisons are part of the heritage of the highway chain-gang system. The state boasts one of the finest highway systems in the country and past chief executives and general assemblies are known to historians as "good roads governors" and "good roads legislatures." But rarely mentioned is the fact that for more than a century those roads were built and maintained by convict labor.

Before the Civil War, North Carolina had no state prison and held few prisoners. Some counties maintained jails which meted out punishment to offenders. No provisions existed for employing the labor of prisoners, except that free Blacks were hired out to pay fines and costs. Instead of imprisonment, law officials employed the pillory, the whipping post and the branding iron; the death penalty was also used promiscuously for dozens of offenses. Bigamy was punishable by branding with a hot iron the letter B upon the cheek. First offense manslaughter brought an M burned into the "brawn of the left thumb." Perjury in a capital case required that "the offender shall, instead of the public whipping, have his right ear cut off and severed entirely from his head, and nailed to the pillory by the sheriff, there to remain until sundown." Whipping was often the punishment for free Blacks for the same crimes for which whites were fined.[6]

In the aftermath of the war, the North Carolina constitution of 1868 established the state penitentiary and declared that the only forms of punishment in the state should be death, imprisonment with or without hard labor and fine. Actually the new constitution, considered reformist by official state historians, was a Confederate relic. A crime wave swept the state after the Civil War, they write, in which "there were added to the crimes by white people, which were the natural aftermath of war, the offenses of the newly liberated Negroes confused by the responsibilities of freedom." Widespread thievery of farm products "was partly due to the natural propensities of the Negroes, intensified by their necessities."[7] Such was the rationale by which state-sanctioned chattel-slavery before the war became, after the defeat of the Confederacy, state-sanctioned slave labor in the name of prison reform: "For a number of years the great majority of prisoners in both state and county prison systems were Negroes."[8]

In 1874, for example, 190 Blacks were sentenced to state prison, compared with 24 whites. The next year, 395 Blacks went to the state prison; only 45 whites were so sentenced. In 1898, of 952 state prisoners, 846 were Black, 105 were white and one was Indian.[9] The chain gang developed in this context. Before the Civil War, the only legal provision for sheriffs hiring out labor were those concerning free Blacks. Early in the nineteenth century, *free* Blacks were sold at auction until their labor paid back court-ordered fines and costs.[10] The first recorded road gang was organized by the military government at the end of the war. This story appeared in the Raleigh *Daily Standard,* September 27, 1865:

The military on yesterday picked up a large number of gentlemen of color, who were loitering about the street corners, apparently much depressed by ennui and general lassitude of the nervous system, and, having armed them with spades and shovels, set them to play at street cleaning for the benefit of their own health and the health of the town generally. This is certainly a "move in the right direction"; for the indolent, lazy Sambo, who lies about in the sunshine and neglects to seek employment by which to make a living, is undoubtedly "the right man in the right place" when enrolled in the spade and shovel brigade.

Immediately after the Civil War, the legislature of 1866–7 authorized justices of the peace to sentence offenders to work in chain gangs on public roads and railroads. As has been shown, the great majority of these prisoners were Black. The consolidated statutes of 1919 said that "Counties and towns may hire out certain prisoners." Statute 1356 read in part:

> The board of commissioners of the several counties, within their respective jurisdictions, or such other county authorities therein as may be established, and the mayor and intendant of the several cities and towns of the state, have power to provide under such rules and regulations as they may deem best for the employment on the public streets, public highways, public works, or other labor for individuals or corporations, of all persons imprisoned in the jails of their respective counties, cities and towns, upon conviction of any crime or misdemeanor, or who may be committed to jail for failure to enter into bond for keeping the peace or for good behavior. . . . [11]

The law served as the basis for the custom of allowing county commissioners to hire out prison labor to private individuals and corporations, a form of peonage as common to North Carolina and the South as rocking chairs on a screened front porch in summertime.

The Carolina chain gang contains the roots of the present prison misery. The vermin, the epidemics of tuberculosis and syphillis, hot and cold running dysentery, the random cruelty and torture by the "walking boss," the reported average life expectancy of five years for road-gang prisoners—these are the legacy of North Carolina's "corrections" system.

Boyd Payton, the textile workers' leader imprisoned in the 1960s for his leadership of the Harriet-Henderson Cotton Mill strike, described his days on a *modern* road gang in his book *Scapegoat*. As the prisoners rode to their assignment:

> As we bounced along on the boards fastened around the cage and intended for seats, the other members of the squad began my education as member of the "gun-squad." They listed the "don'ts" for me as follows: (1) Don't let the guard hear you cussin' or you'll get 30 days in the hole; (2) Don't cross the road from

where you're workin' or the guard can shoot you down for attempted escape; (3) Don't make any sudden moves like jumpin' or runnin' or stoopin' over like you was pickin' up a rock, or the guard can shoot you down; (4) Don't, never, approach within 10 feet of the guard or he can shoot you down; (5) Don't stoop over to tie your shoe without gettin' permission 'cause the guard might not feel as urgent about it as you do; (6) If you do get permission to go for a "crap" be prepared for the foreman to be standin' over you with a revolver and be careful not to make any sudden moves or he can shoot you down; (7) Don't, never, speak or wave to anyone who passes, or you'll go to the hole; (8) Don't ever get more than 10 feet ahead or 10 feet behind the rest of the squad; (9) Don't ever pick up an apple or a nut without permission of the guard and don't ever take anything from anyone passin' by.

The foreman was riding in the cab with the driver. I was told that they were both employed by the highway department but were under the jurisdiction of prison officials while supervising prisoners. "The guard is the 'top dog.' they told me, "but both the guard and the foreman like to be called Captain."

Then, as now, the prison labor had a singular purpose: "Without doubt," wrote two Chapel Hill professors half a century ago, "the motive underlying the establishment and the continuance of the county chain gang is primarily economic. . . . This system offers to the county an apparent source of profit in the form of cheap labor for use in the building and maintenance of roads. The average county official in charge of such prisoners thinks far more of exploiting their labor in the interest of good roads, than of any corrective or reformatory value in such methods of penal treatment. . . . The local criminal courts tend to be looked upon as feeders for the chain gang, and there is evidence in some instances that the mill of criminal justice grinds more industriously when the convict road force needs new recruits."[12]

Convict chain gangs were not ended in North Carolina until July 1973, and prison authorities have not dismissed the possibility of their return. State legislature discussions of the subject turn on the question of whether prisoners should be paid for their labor, even nominally. They never have yet in the state, and with economic hard times in the country, the likelihood is that they won't soon be paid. During the Great Depression of the 1930s, the state prison system became an appendage of the Highway Commission, both to cut down on the cost of government, and because the primary goal of the prison system was to maintain a 10,000-strong highway-construction army. In the 1950s, Governor Luther Hodges found that machines could build roads in less time and at lower costs than hand labor, that only 6,000 prisoners "could be economically employed in road work." He decided to set up a prison industries program to find new areas for this huge workforce that was forced to labor without pay. "Prison industries—as long as they did not compete with private industry—were recognized as being able to serve a useful and profitable part on the operation of our prison system," wrote Hodges later.[13] A soap plant was put into operation; a metal plant began making license plates; a sewing room was built at Women's Prison. Still the chain gangs continued and by 1970, North Carolina could brag of the finest highway system in the country, with more than 68 percent of all road mileage being paved. This compared favorably with the national average of 44.4 percent,[14] contributed heavily to the state's New South reputation, attracted still more industry and made Charlotte the overland trucking hub of the Southeast.

Most of the state's labor camps have, in their visitors room, inscribed and framed, the following exhortation, entitled "Loyalty": "If you work for a man, in heaven's name, work for him, speak well of him and stand by the institution he represents."

With the production of New South propaganda in itself becoming nearly a light industry under Hodges, still another "reform" was passed by the 1957 General Assembly with the prisoner work-release program. Under recommendation of the sentencing judge, misdemeanor prisoners could be allowed to work on regular jobs outside the prison, provided they returned each night and each weekend to their cells. North Carolina became the first state to introduce this "new star in the correctional firmament," in the words of critic Jessica Mitford. But the work-release program is also "a surprisingly useful and practical method of supplementing county jail and state prison budgets, providing sinecures for an inordinant number of guards and other 'correctional' employees, and supplying cheap labor to nonunion employers."[15] By 1974, there were some 2,000 North Carolina prisoners on work-release, the largest number and percentage of any state.

The first state to develop work-release on a statewide basis, North Carolina is also the first to allow sentencing a prisoner directly to work-release. Alongside the work-release program comes greater involvement of police and correctional systems in the community outside of prison. Several government agencies and private industries have planned programs for prison industrial work directed at returning prison industries to the private sector. One government report recommended "adoption of programs whereby private enterprise establishes factories manned entirely by committed offenders." North Carolina is a recipient of the federal Law Enforcement Assistance Administration's "Private Sector Correctional Program," coordinating private industry and prison work programs. At a time when the state could find no jobs for free labor, private concerns rushed to offer 3,200 jobs to convicts and parolees. A man who has to face prison with its arbitrary discipline at the end of each workday makes the "ideal" worker. A 1974 statewide survey of business attitudes found that industry liked work-release: "The work release prisoner . . . may be a more conscientious, dependable employee than the average free man."[16]

A system of forced labor has always been required by U.S. capitalism for the production of certain "unprofitable" products; to regulate the activities of a selected workforce which in turn could be used as a lever on the wages of the workforce at large; and to serve as a laboratory for development of new methods of coercion. Prison labor is the only domestic sector that produces a profit equal to or in excess of that enjoyed by multinational companies in the most exploited countries. Working without pay, under threat of severe discipline without restraint, prison labor earns private industry and government nearly 20 percent profit a year. North Carolina leads the country in prison industrial output per capita.[17] In 1973, with an average 1,000 prisoners working in the 11 prison industries, the Prison Enterprise System realized net profits in excess of $1.5 million.[18]

One explanation of North Carolina's having the largest per capita prison population in the country—12th in state population, Tarheel prisons house the 5th largest prison population—is that it is the only state in the country that houses misdemeanor offenders in the state prisons. One third of all state prisoners and two thirds of all new prisoners in a given year are misdemeanants, including public drunks.[19] The great majority of sentence-serving misdemeanants are mixed with the felon prisoners. Infractions of prison rules will bring maximum security to bear on misdemeanants as well as felons. And while guards can't shoot at a fleeing misdemeanant, they can shoot at fleeing felons, and fleeing prison is a felony—one of those Catch-22 provisions so vital to the *mishegoss* of corrections systems.[20]

But the imprisoned misdemeanant population does not entirely account for North Carolina's national lead in prison population, for the state also has the highest per capita felon population, according to state corrections commissioner Ralph Edwards, who comments, "Maybe we have better law enforcement."[21] Actually the lengths of sentences are getting longer and the felon population is increasing, including among young prisoners. In 1969, the state prisons admitted 300 under-18 felons; in 1973, the number had almost tripled to 850.[22] It is estimated that by 1979 the 1974 ratio of one misdemeanant to three felons will decline to the ratio of one misdemeanant to five felons, and by 1984 the ratio will be one misdemeanant to thirteen felons.[23] The projections suggest not leniency toward misdemeanants but quite the opposite—still harsher sentencing in years to come. Meanwhile, North Carolina has not yet instituted "time off for good behavior," a common practice in other states.

As barbaric as its treatment of adult offenders is, the state's approach to juveniles in trouble requires a Victor Hugo to adequately describe its horrors. Children diagnosed as having "learning disability" are "tracked" into juvenile prisons. Duke University psychiatrist J. S. Gallemore complains that the state's juvenile justice system is retrograde because it holds that criminality is synonymous with mental illness, and that punishment is rehabilitative.[24] Punishment of children in North Carolina, is endemic in the schools. State law provides that "Principals, teachers, substitute teachers, voluntary teachers, teachers' aids and assistant and student teachers in the public schools . . . may use reasonable force in the exercise of lawful authority to restrain or correct pupils and maintain order"; and further, that "No county or city board of education or district committee shall promulgate or continue in effect a rule, regulation or by-law which prohibits the use of such force."

In 1911, North Carolina established in state law the principle of *parens patriae* (the state's right to be a substitute parent) on the basis of providing for children or juveniles who, "by reason of infancy, *defective understanding,* or other misfortune or infirmity, are unable to take care of themselves."[25] (Author's emphasis.) Consequently, North Carolina imprisons more juveniles per capita than any other state, according to official figures.[26] By 1973 the state was spending more than $9,000 to house each imprisoned child, more than the cost of sending the same child to Duke University with summer vacation in Europe and weekly sessions with a private psychologist.[27]

Mason Thomas, a leading juvenile corrections expert at the University of North Carolina's Institute of Government, a sort of extension school for state and local officials, says that "the prison and juvenile training systems have been a method of separating powerless, poor Black people from the general population. The tendency to punishment is a way of continuing segregation."[28] In a brief history of the juvenile corrections system in North Carolina, Thomas wrote that a prime purpose of the juvenile prisons or training schools was for children to "receive moral training and develop middle class values."[29] The age of criminal responsibility was fixed at seven; children of this age could be prosecuted in the criminal courts.[30] The North Carolina Constitution of 1868 required the building of a state penitentiary which imprisoned children alongside adult offenders from the beginning. Only executive clemency—Thomas cites a governor excusing from prison a youth "sentenced to three years for stealing a goose valued at ten cents"—prevented children eight years old or more from incarceration at Raleigh's Central Prison.[31] Central Prison was built by prison labor and that same labor was sold or contracted to outsiders in order to make the prison self-sufficient. When the labor of women and children in prison proved not to be as saleable, the authorities moved to create a women's prison and the juvenile justice system.[32]

Juvenile courts and "training schools" have been part of North Carolina law since 1919, although juvenile offenders can and are still sent to Central and other state prisons by the courts. Undefined but included in North Carolina statutes as falling under the court's jurisdiction are children under 16 years old in the following categories: delinquent, truant, unruly, wayward, misdirected, disobedient to parents or beyond their control or in danger of becoming so, neglected, dependent upon public support, destitute, homeless, abandoned, or whose custody is subject to controversy.[33] A 1972 state law, which must count as a high point for a legislature almost wholly given over to lows, and in the estimate of penal reformers, is a considerable advance in North Carolina, requires that children less than 10 years old or those whose offenses would not be considered crimes if committed by adults, cannot be imprisoned until the court has exhausted all community-level alternative services. One of the more controversial questions before the state legislature is the continuing incarceration of juveniles for being "undisciplined," i.e., for committing acts which are not considered criminal for adults. Recent "reforms," for example regarding truancy from school, prevent imprisonment for first-time truants; these are placed on probation and are incarcerated "only" if they break probation.[34]

In a 1973 state legislative session dominated by "special interests" of the I'll-back-your-highway-You-support-my-bridge type, it was considered another small step for mankind when a statute passed limiting to five days the jailing of juveniles without a hearing.[35] Once imprisoned, however, no such limits exist. An earlier Bar Association report found that "juveniles who disrupt a class [in training school] are automatically locked up for five days" in segregation or solitary confinement.[36] Mason Thomas argues that "people—especially children—are locked up even though they pose no threat to anyone. Judges aren't tuned into people's needs—economic, personal, psychological. We deal with social problems by punishment. Part of this comes from our bible-belt morality. We separate children from their families in order to 'rehabilitate' them because the families don't have 'middle-class values and morality,' whatever that means."[37]

The 1975 General Assembly, in a holiday of generosity, passed a bill stating that youths under 16 must be held in a special "holdover" section of jail, isolated from older prisoners, and for not more than five days, before transfer to a juvenile prison. Until 1975, youth offenders of 14 and 15 years of age and sometimes younger could be held in county jails and placed in state prisons. Part of the reason was that there are only eight juvenile "homes" in the state but 190 holding jails.[38]

One of those "homes," the apple of the eyes of North Carolina's professional penologists, is the "high-rise" at Morgantown. The 11-story facility is designed as an institute for "behavior modification," the latest fad in the field of corrections, which refuses to acknowledge the failures of a society that needs fundamental change, opting instead to tamper with the individual subjects' heads. Camouflaged by garlands of psychological theories, behavior modification is underneath all the sweet rationales, still another way of forcing a prisoner to accept responsibility for his own poverty, deprivation, victimization. At Morgantown, behavior modification is literally built into the structure of the institution. Young inmates first brought here are immediately placed on the top floor in a bare room for a period of solitary confinement. Based on how he responds to his keepers, after a few weeks he is or isn't brought to the next floor down, where he is given a blanket. Similarly, depending on his behavior he works his way down to the other floors where he might acquire a cellmate, eventually access to a radio or television, until he finally works or "behaves" his way down to the ground floor and release from prison. The same program, where prisoners are put into solitary confinement upon entering the institute and are rewarded for docility with better conditions, was applied for a while at Springfield, Missouri, federal penitentiary, under the name Project START. If insufficient "progress" was shown by the prisoner after 18 months, he was then sent to a medical facility for treatment as a "chronic psychotic." That program was discontinued in 1974 after inmate protests, lawsuits, hunger strikes and congressional hearings. But local programs, such as those in North Carolina, continue.

U.S. Treasury agent Stanley Noel was present and accounted for at the Pender County courthouse in Burgaw that September 11, 1972, when the second Wilmington 10 trial was to begin. A man of cold steel-grey eyes which reinforce the appearance of one who might have viewed Buchenwald as merely an unpleasantness, Noel came to Burgaw for more than vicarious pleasures. He had pursued Ben Chavis from the time the young man became active in the student antiwar movement in UNCC, and had conducted no-knock raids of Ben's student apartment. Now, five years later, in a North Carolina state case, the federal G-man had prepared the prosecution's evidence just as he'd done in the state's case against the Charlotte Three. On behalf of his superiors he had finally managed to put away Jim Grant for 35 years in federal and state prisons; now after a half-dozen failures, he was going to get Ben Chavis for 34 years. Relishing his accomplishment, he would sit in court every day for seven weeks, now a participant, now a spectator, in the second longest trial in the history of North Carolina.

Also to be victimized as co-defendants of the Rev. Chavis were members of his church, high-school student leaders and community activists. Such are the requirements of "conspiracy" prosecutions and investigatory whimsy, that more than one person is necessary to "conspire," the more the better as it happens. Making up the Wilmington 10 in addition to Ben were Reginald Epps, the oldest of nine children, an usher and choir member at Wilmington's Price A.M.E. Zion Church, and member of the Student Human Relations Committee; Jerry Jacobs, who grew up in the Union Baptist Church and became an outstanding tennis player and instructor; James McKoy, a graduate of Hoggard High School, a musician and little league baseball coach; Wayne Moore, a graduate of the New Hanover County School and member of the Temple of the Black Messiah, whose mother is a community leader associated with Wilmington's NAACP, Ebenezer Baptist Church and Operation Headstart; Marvin Patrick, a member of the Temple of the Black Messiah and a Vietnam veteran at the age of 19; Ann Sheppard, the only white and only woman defendant, a friend of Rev. Eugene and Donna Templeton of the Gregory Congregational Church, a member of the Wilmington Good Neighbor Council, and mother of three; Connie Tindall, formerly part of the New Hanover County School Glee Club, an outstanding football player and member of the Ebenezer Baptist Church; Willie Earl Vereen, member of the Hoggard High School band and parishioner at the Temple of the Black Messiah; and William Wright, II, better known as "Joe" at the New Hanover County School he attended and the St. Thomas Catholic Church to which he belonged. All but Ann Sheppard and Connie Tindall were teenagers at the time of arrest; Ann was 34, Connie, 21.

Solicitor Jay Stroud's stomach ache was a thing of the past as the second trial opened. On hand to help out in addition to Treasury agent Noel, was Dale Johnson, a special prosecutor sent to Burgaw from Raleigh by his boss, Attorney General Robert Morgan. Morgan's record of prosecuting Rev. Chavis must have made him feel somewhat like the frustrated Hamilton Burger, who had to duel Perry Mason in the courtroom in each of Earl Stanley Gardner's creations. This time Morgan was determined to succeed. In addition to sending prosecutor Johnson from his own office, the attorney general dispatched Judge Robert Martin to Burgaw. Judge Martin, who had presided over the Teel trial in which the Klansmen who killed Henry Lee Marrow in Oxford went free, had also kept Walter David Washington on the streets after the latter's testimony against the Charlotte Three. It was Judge Martin who ruled over Washington's probation hearing when he was under investigation for murder and under indictment for armed robbery. Martin ruled that Washington's probation restrictions were no longer warranted, such had been the pace and thoroughness of his reformation. No such charity would be forthcoming from Judge Martin in the Wilmington 10 trial however.

Martin, who with Attorney General Morgan, had campaigned for the segregationist I. Beverly Lake for governor a decade earlier, did not figure to be disinterested and impartial in a case that centered around the struggle to desegregate the Wilmington school system. (Judge Martin told the author two years after the Wilmington 10 trial that he "harbored no prejudice" against Black people. "I was raised in a mainly Black county. I ate with them and played with them. We had an instinctive love for the Negro race. Why, my secretary is Black. That should show you how I feel about them.") For his part, Morgan played the prudent cruise captain, staying in the background except for at least one moment in the heat of the trial, when he came to Burgaw to lunch and confer with Judge Martin, an indiscretion both dismissed as a "social" meeting having nothing to do with the case at hand. Those who were not apt to take elected officials at their word, pointed out that tiny Burgaw is not so noted for its cuisine that the attorney general would drive 125 miles from Raleigh for a bite to eat.

The first week of the trial was consumed by jury selection. Over 100 prospective jurors were bused 80 miles every morning into Burgaw. Defense attorney James Ferguson asked the court to sequester the prospective jurors during the selection questioning so that they would not be influenced by one another's answers, especially in light of pre-trial publicity. The motion was denied by Judge Martin.

In that first week, the prosecution used 42 preemptory challenges to dismiss potential Black jurors without cause. The defense used up its preemptory challenges against jurors who were admitted Klan members or supporters, those who said they thought the defendants were guilty, and those who said they would not be on trial if they hadn't done at least some wrong. Eventually, though, the defense ran out of preemptory challenges and had to show cause. In this effort they were blocked by Judge Martin. The nature of the *voir dire* (jury selection) questioning and the trial to come can be determined by the following excerpts of testimony:

Q. (Prosecution) Let me ask you this. Have you heard or read anything with regard to any of these defendants in connection with these particular charges?

A. No, not these particular charges, no.

Q. And as a result of anything that you have read or heard have you formed any impression since you don't know anything that has gone on and you only have what you have read or heard to rely on, have you formed any impression about any particular or any of these defendants?

A. I have formed an opinion as to the character of one of the defendants.

Q. You have?

A. Yes, sir. That is, as a result of what I have read. It is not the result of any other source of information. Just what I have read.

Q. As a result of that impression you have of that particular defendant, do you think it would have any bearing at all in what your verdict might be in this case on the basis of the evidence that will be presented here?

A. If I had a difficult time in reaching a verdict it just might possibly help me in reaching a verdict, maybe, just might possibly. I am saying that the impression I have is an unfavorable one toward the defendant. I don't know the defendant personally. I have seen his picture.

Q. You have never seen him personally?

A. No.

MR. FERGUSON: Objection. We renew our motion to sequester the jurors on the *voir dire* examination.

THE COURT: Overruled. Denied.

Or, another example:

Q. Do you realize that anyone who will serve on the jury in this case will be required by law to render their verdict only on the basis of the evidence that is presented here under oath here in this courtroom. Do you understand that?

A. Yes.

Q. Would you be able to do that?

A. Well, I think maybe I could. I don't know. I have formed opinions and heard opinions formed about it. I don't know whether it would have any effect on me or not.

Q. Opinions about what, sir?

A. About this case.

Q. What about this case?

MR FERGUSON: Objection.

THE COURT: Overruled.

A. The case that is being tried here.

Q. You have an opinion as to the case that is being tried here?

A. Yes.

MR. FERGUSON: Objection; we renew our motion to sequester the remaining panel.

THE COURT: Overruled.

Scores of similar exceptions were made by the defense, which was holding to the American Bar Association fair trial standards that state, "Wherever there is believed to be a significant possibility that individual talesmens will be ineligible to serve because of exposure to potentially prejudicial material, the examination of each juror with respect to his exposure shall take place outside the presence of other chosen and prospective jurors."

Throughout the questioning Judge Martin catered to the prosecution's bent for constant references to the race of persons, e.g. "Do any of you know Mr. or Mrs. James Jackson, a Black couple who lived in that house owned by Mrs. Fennell?" or "Do any of you know Mrs. McKeithan, a Black woman of Wilmington who lived next door to Mike's grocery store?" But the judge was not so liberal in allowing defense questioning as to the jurors' possible racism. On at least 105 occasions, the judge sustained prosecution objections to such questioning by attorney Ferguson. The transcript provides the following examples among many:

Q. Now, ladies and gentlemen of the jury, it so happens in this case that nine of the defendants on trial are Black persons. The store that they are charged with burning is owned by Mike Poulos, a white person in Wilmington. Let me ask first if any of you presently have any feelings of racial prejudice against Black people. That is, would any of you more readily convict these persons because they are Black than you would if they were white? Do any of you feel more strongly about this case because the person whose store was allegedly burned was white? All of you feel that you could put that out of your minds and not let it influence your verdicts one way or the other in the trial of this case? One of the defendants in this action, Mrs. Sheppard, is white, a young white lady. Does the fact that nine Black men are charged along with one white woman give any of you any feelings about any of the defendants in this case which might be adverse to them or against them? Do any of you harbor any feelings of racial prejudice that you are aware of whatsoever? Have any of you ever belonged to any clubs or organizations which has as one of its tenets white supremacy?

SOLICITOR STROUD: Objection

THE COURT: Objection sustained.

Or, the following:

Q. Going back to Mr. Brown for a moment. I am sorry. What clubs or organizations in the community are you a member of, Mr. Brown?

A. I belong to the Burgaw Lions Club, Pender County Rescue Squad, American Legion, member of the Pender County Board of Education. I belong to several school groups. I belong to the Pender County Industrial Development Corporation. I have been a member of the Buckner Country Club, member of the Baptist Church. I am a Mason. That is all I can think of right now.

Q. Have you ever belonged to any club or organization that excluded Black people among its membership?

SOLICITOR STROUD: Objection.

THE COURT: Sustained.

Or, again:

Q. Have any of you ever been victims of a damage to property? Has anyone ever damaged your property that you know of? Any of your property burned by anyone? It happens in this case, ladies and gentlemen, and again I am just asking for your honest answers, that the nine defendants I represent are young Black men. The store that is alleged to have been burned was owned by a white man, Mike Poulos, in Wilmington. Does the race of the parties involved bother anyone? Does that give any of you any problems?

SOLICITOR STROUD: Objection.

COURT: Overruled.

Q. And is anyone bothered by that fact? I am really asking you if anyone feels more sympathetic to one side in the case or the other because of that fact? Do all of you believe in racial equality?

SOLICITOR STROUD: Objection.

COURT: Sustained.

Q. Is there anyone on the jury who doesn't believe in racial equality?

MR. JOHNSON: Objection.

COURT: Sustained.

Q. Would any of you more readily convict a person charged with a crime because he is Black than you would if he was some other color?

SOLICITOR STROUD: Objection.

COURT: Sustained.

183

The jury was finally seated after two weeks of selections, with ten whites and two Blacks, exactly the reverse of the ratio in the first trial.

The trial itself proved as frustrating for the defense attorneys as the *voir dire*. The state entered into evidence 88 photographs of the Gregory Congregational Church taken in 1972, a year after the siege of the church. That is, over defense objections, the prosecution presented "evidence" not of a 1971 "crime" but of a 1972 scene. Most of the state's case was about on the same level. During the armed siege of the church the previous year, emergency medical supplies were brought to Rev. Templeton's house next to the church for first-aid purposes. The medical supplies were later taken by the National Guard and were now presented in court as evidence that Ben and the students had been planning an armed rebellion all along and had set up a revolutionary hospital. The prosecutors passed the band-aids to the jury so that they could see them, then passed the scissors around, passed the gauze, the unguentine, the iodine. It took a whole morning of the trial for the jury to inspect these "revolutionary" medical supplies.

The only photos of Rev. Chavis the prosecution had were taken during a nonviolent march to the Wilmington City Hall asking for police protection for the Black community and for a city-wide curfew, and those taken during the funeral of Steve Mitchell a week after the siege of the church was lifted. The city had enjoined the mourners from having the funeral at Gregory, so they walked in formation across town to another church. Photos were taken of everybody in the funeral procession. These pictures were introduced in the trial and portrayed to the jury as a mob scene. Jay Stroud, aggressive in court but otherwise a rather dim bulb, told the jury, look, this is concrete proof, pictures don't lie, here's Chavis leading a mob. The photos showed the mourners, marching in twos, nonviolently. When the defense subpoenaed the photographer, it was discovered that he had been sent to Wilmington by the FBI, Defense Intelligence Agency and other federal snoop bureaus.

But the defendants suffered a serious blow early in the trial. The key witnesses were to be Rev. and Mrs. Templeton, who were flying back to North Carolina to testify. Their testimony would include vouching for the presence of Rev. Chavis and other defendants in their livingroom at the time of the fire at Mike's Grocery. Solicitor Stroud found out they were on their way and he sent some policemen to the Wilmington airport to arrest the Templetons on sight. The plane was to touch down in Fayetteville en route, and some friends of the defense took them off the plane and drove them to Raleigh to await discussions to decide how next to move. But the Templetons, fearful now of the consequences of testifying, left North Carolina again, taking with them the best hope of the Wilmington 10 for a court acquittal.

As in the Chavis-Grant federal trial and the Charlotte Three case, what the prosecution lacked in evidence it made up for with testimony from convicted criminals on the make for reduced sentences. Of 41 witnesses for the prosecution—most were police, firemen or other city employees who took the stand to say, yup, I was near the church that night, and I can tell you there were gunfire and destruction of property, but I can't identify the defendants and tell you if they did anything wrong—only one witness placed the defendants on the scene and implicated them in the damage that resulted. He was 18-year-old Allen Hall, who had been in and out of various mental institutions and was now in prison on a 12-year-sentence on charges of rioting during the siege of the Gregory Congregational Church. The other key prosecution witness was Jerome Mitchell, also 18, also in prison, for 40 years on unrelated robbery and murder charges.

When Hall was originally arrested, he signed a statement admitting that he had burned down Mike's Grocery, that he had shot at policemen, that he had shot Harvey Cumber, the man who died of gunshot wounds while he was firing into the church, and that he had committed these crimes alone. The police then sent him to a mental hospital until he agreed to testify against the Wilmington 10 in return for immunity from prosecution on the assault, arson and conspiracy to murder charges. It was Hall's agreement to the deal that brought the initial indictment.

By the time of trial, Hall had his tale down as pat as can be expected from a deranged teenager. The essence of his new story was that Ben Chavis came to Wilmington to organize a clandestine revolutionary rebellion, pitting Black people against white people; that Ben had virtually hypnotized Hall into doing the things he had admitted to; that in the church, Ben carried two machine guns, and that Hall and Marvin Patrick each had another; that they were under instructions to shoot at all white people, even the whites inside the church; that he burned down Mike's Grocery and killed Harvey Cumber on Ben's orders. Mitchell, who was not in the vicinity of the church during the entire week of the events in question, but who was allowed into the courtroom to listen to Hall's testimony, simply repeated Hall's story, as if verification from a convicted murderer and robber lent ample weight to secure a conviction. (Solicitor Jay Stroud was pleased enough with Mitchell as a snitch to use him in a trial of two other young Black men, Isaac Sherill Munk and Christopher Spicer, who were sentenced to death in Central Prison's gas chamber for the murder of a white man, on the basis of Mitchell's testimony on August 24, 1973.) Hall, a lifelong resident of Wilmington, and one who claimed to be in the church for the four crucial days in February, could identify only the 10 defendants as having been in the church with him, although he admitted there were some 200 other youngsters there as well. One of the defendants he named, Ann Sheppard, produced in court a letter Hall had sent her from prison, after he had agreed to testify for the prosecution. The letter was a threat to kill her if she didn't also testify for the state.

Under Ferguson's cross-examination, Hall's barking at the moon became apparent to onlookers. At times during Hall's three-day description of events that had taken place 19 months earlier, he told exactly how many bullets had been fired by various defendants during gunbattles with police, the number of firebombs thrown at buildings and the calibers of a dozen weapons. He couldn't say "right offhand" what detectives had said to him the day he admitted having committed the crimes, but he could "right offhand" quote precisely Ben Chavis' words of a year and a half before.

Ferguson showed Hall a transcript of a preliminary hearing in which the young convict testified he had never met Ben before February 5, 1971, and a later statement in which he said he attended several meetings with Ben earlier that year. Hall also testified on cross-examination that he had met with detectives and prosecuting attorneys several times before the trial and that he had visited the scene of the fires and shootings with them, but he could not recall the dates of these conversations and visits.

Ferguson showed Hall a statement he had signed months before the trial in which Hall claimed that on the night that Mike's Grocery burned down, he had bought a bottle of liquor and gone to an uncle's house where he drank and ate fried chicken. "You went out to the VFW and got drunk and don't know what you did on Friday night, isn't that right?" asked Ferguson. "No, sir," replied Hall.

The young mental patient became agitated as contradiction after contradiction in his testimony were brought out. He threatened to become unhinged, as he had during the preliminary hearings earlier that year when he jumped from the stand and swung at Rev. Chavis. Now, his anger was directed at attorney Ferguson. He bolted out of the witness chair and lunged at Ferguson. It took six deputies to subdue and remove the witness from the courtroom, and one juror was knocked down by Hall on his way out. When the court reconvened, one juror asked to be excused, citing heart problems, but Judge Martin chose to continue the trial, and warned Ferguson that he would be cited for contempt of court if he again "provoked" Hall.

The defense moved for a mental examination of Hall, and moved for a mistrial because of the witness's actions. At this point, the trial transcript reads:

> COURT: The court finds and concludes that the demeanor of the witness and the incident was precipitated in some degree by his long cross-examination, the rapidity of the questions, the tone of the examiner and that the motion for a mental examination of the witness is not required and the motion is denied.
>
> MR. FERGUSON: May we let the record show that we except to each and every finding of fact by the Court and to the conclusion of law.
>
> COURT: And also that the motion to strike the evidence of the witness is denied.
>
> MR. FERGUSON: I would like if I may, to state that we would like to call to the Court's attention that shortly after the cross-examination of the witness had begun and during recess of the Court we called to the Court's attention the fact that the witness was mouthing obscenities to me from the witness stand.
>
> COURT: And also I believe that I made the remark, I asked you was it audible and you said there was no audible sound.
>
> MR. FERGUSON: That is correct.
>
> COURT: The motion for mistrial is denied.

Among the more questionable of the prosecution's acts during the trial was its suppression of the right of discovery for the defense. Allen Hall had given a typewritten statement of his testimony to the prosecutors at the outset of the trial. As the prosecution is required to do, it showed this initial statement to the defense. However, in subsequent interviews between the prosecutors and Hall, the original statement was amended with notes by the prosecutor. The amended statement was denied to the defense. When Ferguson appealed to Judge Martin, the jurist read the notes himself but denied the defense the right to read them.

All of the contradictions in Hall's testimony were explained by Hall and the prosecution as having been "corrected" or "reconciled" in Hall's final statement, which the defense was not denied the right to read. Hall said that when he realized he had lied in earlier statements, he summoned Jay Stroud to the prison in which he was being held and dictated changes which Stroud noted in the margins of the original statement. Judge Martin ruled that the defense could not see Hall's corrected statements because they were, as the Raleigh *News and Observer* noted, "his own personal notes and were not meant for public examination." During Jerome Mitchell's turn in the witness chair the next day, to verify Hall's story, he also testified that signed statements he had given to police officers were false and "additions and corrections" had been made some time after the statements were signed.

In *Brady* v. *Maryland,* the key U.S. Supreme Court decision on suppression of evidence, the Court ruled: "We now hold that the suppression by the prosecution of evidence favorable to an accused upon request violates the due process where the evidence is material either to guilt or to punishment, irrespective of the good faith or bad faith of the prosecution." Now, in a case where the chief question was the credibility of the only witness the prosecution had who might tie the accused to the alleged violations, that witness's evidence was being suppressed by both the prosecution and the court. Since the supposed amended statement was the last recorded statement made by Hall, the jury was given the impression that regardless of any prior falsehoods or inconsistencies, Hall had made a final statement which was fully consistent with his testimony. And the defense was being told that it would not be allowed to show the jury that this "statement" in fact never did exist, or even that it was inconsistent with Hall's testimony. Judge Martin could not have more effectively rendered the defense powerless had he applied gags and shackles to the attorneys. The maneuver was so cute, as Dorothy Parker once wrote, it was enough to make one "fwow up."

Attorney Ferguson argued that the state was "emptying out the jails, the mental institutions and the training schools" to produce fabricated evidence to punish Rev. Chavis for his political leadership of the Black communities of the state He pointed out to the court that the state had based its case on a display of guns, some photographs taken months after the incidents in question, and the testimony of two convicted felons, Hall and Mitchell, who got their stories together when prosecutors arranged for them to meet at Cherry State Hospital in Goldsboro, where they were confined to undergo mental examinations. Ferguson's argument was to no avail. Toward the trial's end, the prosecution produced still another witness, a 13-year-old named Eric Junious, Jr., who had been imprisoned in a state training school after admitting to robbing a man selling newspapers. The teenage robber was called to support the contradictory testimony of Hall and Mitchell, an impossible task to start with and a miracle job for a 13-year-old. Eric Junious, Jr., proved not to be a miracle worker

Still, with a jury to the prosecution's liking, a favorable setting like rural Pender County in which the Klan and ROWP ran at will, a special prosecutor and special judge handpicked by the state's attorney general, Jay Stroud had easy pickings in presenting his closing arguments. Summing up the case against the young minister, eight local high-school students, and a white community worker and mother of three, the solicitor said that the defendants were "dangerous animals who should be put away for the rest of their lives." The state reserved special venom for Rev. Chavis, comparing him to Adolph Hitler. Both "filled their followers with hate . . . to make them do as they were told," Stroud told the jury.

After seven weeks of trial, the jury returned in less than an hour with its verdict. The Charlotte *Observer* reported on October 18 of that year, "The courtroom's tense calm was broken by the loud moan of a young Black woman who slumped forward in tears as the word 'guilty' was twice recited after the name of Willie Earl Vereen, a Wilmington 10th grader who has missed most of his classes and practice with the Hoggard High School marching band because he's been on trial since September 11." All 10 defendants were pronounced guilty as charged. Judge Martin announced that he would delay sentencing overnight and the Wilmington 10 were led from the courtroom.

The defendants were placed in chains and put on the prison bus that had been backed up to the courthouse door. Several dozen supporters of the accused gathered behind a line of patrolmen, to sing "We Shall Overcome" and to recite the 23rd Psalm. SBI agents on the scene reacted here were 10 defendants, 8 of them teenagers, who had never been The 10 were turned over to Department of Corrections officers, who then pulled out *their* pistols and told those praying and singing to get back. Ten highway patrol cars and half as many SBI and local police cars escorted the Wilmington 10 to the jail in Jacksonville, home of ROWP chief Leroy Gibson, thirty-five miles and a county away.

The next morning, they were awakened early, placed back in chains, put back on the bus, surrounded again by fifteen SBI and highway patrol cars and brought back to Burgaw for sentencing. Judge Martin asked for motions on sentencing and the defense requested lenience, arguing that here were 10 defendants, 8 of them teenagers, who had never been convicted of any crime. Mrs. Sheppard, they pointed out, suffered from hypertension and a jail experience could only be harmful. Ben requested that Ferguson not ask for lenience on his behalf because "I didn't want mercy from the state because I wasn't guilty." The prosecutors argued that the Wilmington 10 had to be put away for life, double the maximum, not to see the light of day again, to set an example, to teach society. One by one Judge Martin pronounced sentence: first, Mrs. Sheppard, 10 years; then the 8 teenagers 20–25 years; finally, Rev. Ben Chavis, 29–34 years, the longest sentence for arson in North Carolina history. All combined, the Wilmington 10 faced 282 years in prison.

Again they were placed in shackles and leg irons and led out of the courthouse to the bus. This time they were going to Raleigh, the men to

Central Prison where Ben Chavis and Connie Tindall would stay, while the others were sent to Odom Prison Farm; Ann Sheppard would again be incarcerated in Women's Prison in Raleigh. As they marched toward the bus, they could see sharpshooters on the roof of the courthouse. Later, leaving town, they saw through the bars of bus windows other police marksmen on the roofs of the armed encampment that was downtown Burgaw.

On the bus, the guards displayed their new weapons, M16s with infrared scopes, gifts of the Law Enforcement Assistance Administration in Washington. The guards told their young prisoners that they hadn't used the weapons yet and were just waiting for the opportunity to try them.

All 125 miles to Raleigh, Black people came out on the road to watch the prison bus and the cortege of a dozen police cars, and to wave good-bye to the Wilmington 10.

G OVERNMENT repression of the civil rights movement was patterned after years of persecution of labor organizers, stretching back decades, to much before the Henderson cotton mill strike in the 1950s.[39]

Not without reason. A reading of U.S. labor history shows North Carolina to have been the site of some of the longest and bloodiest strikes and pitched battles. Tens of thousands of Tarheel workers have been evicted from company towns, jailed, brutalized and murdered in this century for attempting to organize themselves.

In 1914, average hourly wages for Southern textile spinners ranged from 8 to 9 cents an hour. Hours had been charitably cut from 72 to 63 per week, including for women and children.[40] The world war provided a boom for the looms, particularly in the Carolina Piedmont. Gaston County adopted the slogan, "Organize a mill a week," and had built 105 mills by 1923. In 1929, it was the leading textile county in the South, and third in the nation, causing one union organizer to remark, "North Carolina is the key to the South, Gaston County is the key to North Carolina, and the Loray Mill is the key to Gaston County."[41]

The National Industrial Conference Board in 1920 computed that a minimum standard of living in Charlotte for a family of five would require $1,438 a year. But the average Tarheel textile worker's income was $730 in 1919, and dropped to $624 in 1921. Low wages became the magnet for Northern capital. One economist likened the Southern textile worker to the slave on the auction block. "Native whites!" he mimicked.

"Anglo-Saxons of the true blood! All English-speaking! Tractable, harmonious, satisfied with little! They know nothing of foreign-born radicalism! Come down and gobble them up!"[42] White mill workers' children were wage-slave counterparts to their Black chattel-slave fore-bears. A North Carolina mill doctor was asked, "How long do you believe it is safe . . . to employ a girl 12 years of age in a cotton mill?" He answered, not over 10 or 12 hours a day.[43]

Union organizing drives were sporadic and only intermittently successful. In 1919, the United Textile Workers shifted their main attention to North Carolina after several defeats elsewhere. In that year of postwar prosperity, the union had 43 locals in the state and claimed 40,000 members in North Carolina. But with the economic crisis of 1920–21, the mills started to shut down. Wages were cut by as much as 50 percent, the workers went out on strike, the strike waned without funding, and the workers returned to the mills under the gaze of the state militia, their wages still reduced by half, their union crushed.

If Gaston County was the largest textile county in the South, the Loray Mill—started by locals at the turn of the century but acquired in 1923 by the Manville-Jenckes Corporation of Pawtucket, R.I.—was the largest in the county. The Loray Mill was in constant turmoil as management sought a return to halcyon days of yore, while the workers became increasingly unruly. In 1927 the mill brought in a new superintendent, G.A. Johnstone, who immediately increased work loads, sometimes doubling them, discharged workers on a whim, reduced the workforce from 3,500 to 2,200 and cut wages by 20 percent. The Loray workers took to the streets the next year, convincing management to replace Johnstone.

The workers were hardly steeled in long years of class struggle. Gastonia lies at the approach to the Blue Ridge and, like most of the textile and furniture industry in North Carolina, the Loray Mill was established with an eye to lure mountain folk off their farms with promises of good cash wages. Come they did into these mill towns. Gastonia, dominated by Manville-Jenckes' Loray, was the prototype mill village. The company owned the general store, the churches, the recreational centers, the doctors, the teachers. The workers could not vote in local elections because they were not registered, or were registered in their home counties, or because they lived within the perimeter of unincorporated municipalities wholly owned by the mills. Manville-Jenckes could cut off credit at the company store, evict the worker and family from the company house, bar children from the company school, stop the worker from entering the company hospital, or even expel him from the company-owned church.

On New Years Day 1929, Fred Beal, an organizer for the newly formed National Textile Workers Union (NTWU) and a member of the Communist Party, came to neighboring Charlotte where he set up shop. With occasional forays into Gastonia, Beal was able to organize a NTWU nucleus at the Loray Mill. The company reacted predictably and swiftly, summoning up among the white city fathers the same hatred, as W.J. Cash pointed out, that gave rise to the Ku Klux Klan. Communist union organizers coming South brought a sense of déjà vu to a state that still collectively shuddered at the historical spectre of Northern troops securing Reconstruction.

A company informer exposed the union core-group in the mill and on March 25, 1929, Loray fired five union members. Five days later, a thousand workers voted to strike. The next day, a majority of both shifts refused to work. Union demands called for equal pay for women and children, union recognition and a $20 minimum weekly wage. The demands were called "beyond reason" by company superintendent J.A. Baugh. After four days of picketing, the state militia was dispatched to Gastonia on April 4, ostensibly to protect private property, a task for which they proved singularly ineffective. On the evening of April 18, a mob of masked men attacked the union's headquarters, smashed its windows, destroyed the commissary and virtually demolished the premises. While the mob raged, 250 militiamen slept less than 500 feet away. Eventually the militia was withdrawn but in its place the Loray Mill organized its own private army called the Committee of 100; plant foremen were deputized as sheriffs and policemen.[44] A reign of terror was launched against the striking workers.

The union appealed to Governor Max Gardner for protection, and warned, "If you don't have us protected, we know how to protect ourselves."[45] A tent colony was built to replace the destroyed union hall, protected by an armed security force of workers. Meanwhile the picket lines continued, suffering armed attacks by police and company thugs. A 72-year-old woman supporting the strike was thrown to the ground and beaten with gun butts. One striker was blackjacked and thrown unconscious onto a railroad track. Striking families were evicted from company houses and moved into the tent colony. The local press attacked the union, not only for its Communist leadership but for its advocacy of the equality of Black and white workers and its admission of both to membership. Although Blacks were 15 percent of the county population, few were allowed to work in the plant, except as sweepers. The Gastonia *Daily Gazette* published a front-page picture of an American flag with a snake coiled at its base, and the inscription: "Communism in the south.

Kill it." Flyers were distributed asking, "Would you belong to a union which opposes White Supremacy?"[46]

By June, Gastonia had become a garrison city. On the afternoon of June 7, some local police went out on a drunk, and ended up beating up and shooting a local restaurant owner. One of the marauders was an ex-officer who had been fired from the force for beating up a local woman but who had since been brought back into service to help crush the strike. That night, these officers were part of a party that included police chief A.D. Aderholt, which raided the workers' tent colony without a warrant. When they were blocked from entering, the police opened fire. Four policemen and one organizer were shot; Chief Aderholt was mortally wounded and died the next day. The Committee of 100 led by Major A.L. Bulwinkle, formerly and subsequently a U.S. congressman and attorney for the Loray Mill, raided the camp en masse. More than a hundred striking men and women were thrown into jail and beaten. Of these, 23 were held for murder or muderous assault. Beatings by the police and the Committee of 100 continued, but only one policeman was disciplined for excessive use of force, for beating a Charlotte *Observer* reporter whom he took to be a striker. The officer was immediately hired by Manville-Jencks as a security guard.

On the eve of the murder trial, the Charlotte *News* editorialized: "The leaders of the National Textile Workers' Union are communists, and are a menace to all that we hold most sacred. They believe in violence, arson, murder. They want to destroy our institutions, our traditions. They are undermining all morality, all religion. But nevertheless they must be given a fair trial, although everyone knows that they deserve to be shot at sunrise."[47] The prosecution staff numbered 10, including Major Bulwinkle; R.G. Cherry, state commander of the American Legion; and Clyde Hoey, a brother-in-law of Governor Gardner. Heywood Broun, covering the trial for *The Nation* magazine, observed that "the officials of Gastonia have been from the beginning no more than the hired musketeers of the mill owners."[48]

When one of the trial jurors went violently insane, the judge declared a mistrial and ordered a new trial for September 30. News of the mistrial unleashed a reign of terror in Gaston and surrounding counties. The strikers' headquarters at Gastonia and Bessamer City were destroyed by raids of 500 men. NTWU organizers were kidnapped, flogged or tarred and feathered, and seven were arrested for "insurrection to overthrow the State of North Carolina." A workers' rally was called for September 14 in South Gastonia, in response to which American Legion members were deputized to close all roads leading to the meeting. Three days before the rally, the Gastonia *Gazette* editorialized, "They have been warned to stay away. If they persist in coming, they do so at their own risk. This is the word from the good people of that community who have been law-abiding about as long as they can stand it."

On the night of the rally, a mob collected to prevent the meeting. A truck bearing 22 strikers from Bessamer City tried to enter South Gastonia and was turned back. Fifteen autos carrying strikebreakers set out in pursuit. After a five-mile chase the truck was stopped and a volley of shots was fired into the unarmed strikers. One of them, Mrs. Ella May Wiggins, a mother of five, was killed. A Gaston County grand jury refused to indict anybody in connection with the murder of Ella May Wiggins, but six weeks later after a national outcry, initiated by the International Labor Defense, Governor Gardner assigned a special prosecutor to reopen the case. Five employees of the Loray Mill were finally indicted. The Manville-Jenckes Company went their bail. When the case came to trial early the next year, all 5 were acquitted although the murder had been committed in the presence of at least 50 persons.[49]

The second trial of Fred Beal and the NTWU organizers in connection with the death of Chief Aderholt began in September 1929. By then the prosecution had withdrawn the first degree murder charge and had freed 9 of the original 16 defendants, including the 3 women. This left the prosecution with a conspiracy indictment, but that was shattered when the surviving police in the raid on the tent colony testified under cross-examination that when they arrived at the colony, everything was peaceful, and that they had brought with them a number of shotguns and rifles in addition to the regular police equipment. The state then made its case on the basis of the defendants' beliefs in communism, racial equality and atheism. One defendant was discredited by the sparmy-minded prosecutor with the words, "If teaching racial equality does not tend to impeach a witness, I do not know what would." Another defense witness was impeached for denying the existence of "a Supreme Being who punishes for wrong and rewards for virtues." In his summation to the jury, prosecutor E.T. Cansler argued, "The union organizers came, fiends incarnate, stripped of their hoofs and horns, bearing guns instead of pitchforks."[50] After 57 minutes of deliberation the jury returned a verdict of guilty. Judge Barnhill sentenced Beal and three other northern defendants to 17–20 years in the state prison; two Gastonia men received 12–15 years, the other, 5–7 years. One year later, on August 20, 1930, the Supreme Court of North Carolina upheld their sentences.

Southern justice had proven consistent. A North Carolina journalist wrote in summary of the Gastonia events: "In every case where strikers were put on trial, strikers were convicted; in not one case where anti-unionists or officers were accused has there been a conviction."[51] The state of labor relations that pertain today in North Carolina were established in those grim days of the Loray strike and its aftermath.

Actually, with the depression, things got worse. Calvin Coolidge in one of his moments that made folks wish he'd live up more to his nickname of "Silent Cal," once observed that "When more and more people are thrown out of work, unemployment results." The labor movement faced a crisis. The American Federation of Labor had refused to extend itself beyond narrow craft-union boundaries. The AFL's United Textile Workers had avoided Gastonia, in part because of the Communist leadership of the NTWU. "This aristocracy of labor," Haywood Broun wrote of the AFL, "is taking time out to consolidate its gains. If the communists did not organize the workers of Gastonia, nobody else would."[52] Southern textile owners, however, were not always discerning enough to make such distinctions, when it came to their workers. In his classic *The Mind of the South* (which might, more accurately, have been entitled, "The Mind of the White South"), W.J. Cash suggested,

> ... Almost the sole content of immediate actuality in these phantasmagoric [Red] terrors was, as is well known, just the peril of the labor movement, to the interests, real or imagined, of the ruling classes, and particularly the possibility of a labor movement that should stand to the left of the highly conservative American Federation of Labor as shaped by Samuel Gompers, William Green and Matthew Woll.
>
> And when that is clear, the case of the South becomes more explicable. If the Yankee manufacturer, long accustomed to labor unions, could be so wrought upon fears that he could without conscious hypocrisy, though of course not without the unconscious cunning of interest, see even the lumbering AFL as at least dangerously close to being Red, then it is readily comprehensible how the Southern cotton-mill baron, remembering unhappily its occasional forays into his territory, should get to see it as the flaming archangel of Moscow itself—why the organs of the Southern trade, such as the *Textile Bulletin* and the *Manufacturers' Record*, promptly set up the formula: labor organizer equals Communist organizer.[53]

Partially in response to the NTWU drive in Gaston and Mecklenburg counties, the AFL's United Textile Workers came to Marion in McDowell County, also in 1929 and met with a similar response. The Marion Manufacturing Co. and the Clinchfield Mills ran the mountain city as Manville-Jenckes ran Gastonia. None of the company houses in

Marion's mill villages had running water or toilets. The houses were built on stilts, with no wind-breaking foundations. Sinclair Lewis went to Marion to investigate and reported: "A four-room house, in which 12 people may be living, is just this: It is a box with an unscreened porch. It has three living rooms and a kitchen. In each of the living rooms there are, normally, two double beds. In these double beds there sleep anywhere from two to five people, depending on their ages."[54] Wages at the plants averaged less than $10 a week, and at least one case was discovered of a 14-year-old girl working more than 12 hours a day for $5 a week.

When an open meeting of the UTW was held in June, 22 union members were fired. Marion Manufacturing president R.W. Baldwin rejected demands to reinstate the fired workers, to reduce shifts to 10 hours, and to establish a grievance committee. With little help from either the AFL or the UTW, the plant's 650 workers struck. The Clinchfield workers, 900 of them, joined the strike. Clinchfield president B.M. Hart declared, "I cannot see that there is any difference between this so-called conservative union and the Communist union in Gastonia." As the strike continued, scuffles broke out on picket lines, and the company won an injunction against the demonstration. Governor Gardner, himself a textile mill owner from Shelby, again sent in the militia. Baldwin blacklisted more than a hundred workers in his plant. The pattern established in Gastonia was repeated. When, on August 31, Clinchfield strikers prevented a non-union worker from moving into a mill-village house, 74 strikers were arrested and charged with "a rebellion against the constituted authority of the State of North Carolina."

In the early morning hours of October 2, workers walked out of the Baldwin mill, because of harassment by the foreman. As they gathered at the plant gate to tell the day shift of the strike, Sheriff Oscar Adkins, a local merchant, fired tear gas into their ranks. His 11 deputies, taking the cue, shot at the backs of the retreating workers. When the shooting ended, 6 strikers lay dead, 25 seriously wounded. In an interview with the *Asheville Citizen* the next day, Baldwin said: "I understand 60 or 75 shots were fired in Wednesday's fight. If this is true, there are 30 or 35 of the bullets accounted for. I think the officers are damned good marksmen. If I ever organize an army they can have jobs with me. I read that the death of each soldier in the World War consumed more than five tons of lead. Here we have less than five pounds and these casualties. A good average, I call it."[55] Eight deputies were charged with second-degree murder. At the time, one of the defendants was put on $2,000 bond for shooting up the union headquarters. He and five other non-union workers in the Marion plant had been deputized by Sheriff Adkins. Pleading that they fired in order to suppress a riot, the deputies were found not guilty. One historian concluded, "Against the anti-union policy of the southern mill owners the United Textile Workers, affiliated with the conservative AFL, had fared no better than the National Textile Workers Union," under Communist leadership in Gastonia.[56] In the cemeteries where the murdered workers are buried, "there is no argument about the best method of running Southern textile mills," wrote Sinclair Lewis. The labor peace long sought by the textile owners turned out to be the peace of the graveyard.

Illusions of an impartial government, weighing equally the interests of labor and those of capital, were shattered. In Belmont, a militiaman ran an unmenacing striker through with a bayonet and killed him, but the authorities did nothing. Not one conviction was obtained in any major case of violence directed against strikers, not in the killing of Mrs. Wiggins, nor in the destruction of union headquarters in Gastonia, nor in the killings and maimings in Marion, nor in the kidnappings and beatings of union organizers in Elizabethtown, Kings Mountain, Charlotte or a dozen other towns and villages in North Carolina. But the Marion strikers who were arrested on the picket lines were given up to six months of hard labor; and the unionists accused in the Aderholt slaying, up to twenty years. The intertwining of the state and the corporation to determine not only labor conditions but the nature of the criminal justice system is a relationship that would hold, strengthen and become identical with time.

DURING Ben's first week back in Central Prison after the trial, a Black inmate leader named Charles Richardson was burned alive in his cell one night. Some white inmates, assisted by the guards, threw a five-gallon can of paint thinner into his cell, lit a broom handle, and set him on fire. The guards ignored his screams until he was thoroughly incinerated.

A few weeks later, another Black inmate, John Cuttino from Durham, was burned to death a few cells down the corridor from Ben. It was about 11:30 at night and all the inmates were locked in their cells, which left only the guards with an opportunity. Ben could hear Cuttino's cries for help and saw flames reaching out of the cell. Ben and the other men shouted for the guards but they didn't come for 15 minutes. By then, a partially burned Bible was one of Cuttino's few possessions left recognizable in the cell.

Because the smoke was about to suffocate other inmates on the upper tiers in the cellblock, the prisoners were taken outside to the yard. This was Ben's first opportunity to meet with the other inmates at one time. Since his arrival at Central the authorities had kept him from meeting with the general inmate population. When the guards saw the prisoners meeting in the yard, they ordered the men into the cafeteria. The guards knew they could shoot tear gas on the prisoners in the dining hall with much greater effect than in the yard. Some 400 men crowded into the cafeteria that was built to hold only a fourth that number. Ben got up and called the inmates together for some order.

After discussion, the men decided they were not returning to their cells. They wanted to meet with the warden and with Lee Bounds, the head of the state corrections department. The prisoners were aware of their peril. Bounds had ordered the massacre at Central in 1968 in which at least 6 inmates were killed and 50 were wounded. But the danger of returning to their cells—after the killings of the young Panther, Joe Waddell, and now Charles Richardson and John Cuttino—was also clear and present. Fletcher K. Sanders, the chief of security for Central's west wing, came into the cafeteria, walked into the middle of the inmates and ordered them to clear out of the cafeteria in 30 seconds. The hall fell silent. Then Ben stood up and told Sanders that they weren't leaving until they saw the warden and Lee Bounds, that they had violated no prison regulations, that they were ordered into the cafeteria by the guards and would stay until it was safe to return to the west wing.

Sanders appealed to the men not to listen to Rev. Chavis, and said that he was a troublemaker who would get them all hurt; that if they didn't leave in 30 seconds, he was going to deal harshly as only a prison security chief, left unchecked, can deal. Ben again said the men were not leaving. He accused Sanders of attempting to provoke them into doing something that would precipitate a repetition of the 1968 assault. Ben asked the inmates to sit and remain sitting. Only 2 of the 400 got up and left; one of them turned around on his way out and came back. A leader of the white inmates stood up and pleaded for his companions to stay, arguing that they had a stake in this resistance too because it wasn't safe for them in the west wing either.

Two hours later, an announcement came through on the loudspeaker to the effect that the warden wanted to see Ben Chavis in the yard. The inmates wouldn't let him leave, however. The assassination of George Jackson at San Quentin and the pogrom at Attica the year before were still fresh memories. One of the men in the cafeteria had a portable transistor radio, which was reporting a "rebellion" at Central Prison. The inmates had "captured" the cafeteria already, it was reported. The death of John Cuttino by fire that night was not mentioned on the news. But the men did learn that Lee Bounds was at the prison and had been there all night.

Bounds, who served the prison system for 21 years under Democratic administrations, started out in 1949 as a young law professor. After becoming involved in a case in which a chain-gang prisoner was hand-cuffed to his cell bars for 70 hours for telling another inmate that he was thirsting for a beer, Bounds soon joined the University of North Carolina's Institute of Government and found prominence as a penologist. Bounds recalls, "I just happened to hit it right. There had been a riot at Central, and the issue of reform was very much in the air." He counts among his great achievements the elimination of the stepchain. Knowing that an outright ban on leg-chains would be resisted by guards, he suggested that they be fastened on prisoners each day rather than permanently riveted on. The guards eventually found this inconvenient and eliminated the practice by disuse. By 1959, the balls-and-chains were banned altogether. Still Bounds, whom Will Rogers obviously never met, lamented the bad that comes with the good, "It was when we did away with the chains, the lash and other forms of discipline that we lost control of the population within the old dormitories. We had to herd them in and try to control them with the threat of shooting."

Now, the night of the death of John Cuttino, Bounds finally sent word he would meet with a delegation of the prisoners. Five were chosen: three Blacks including Ben, and two whites. Bounds explained right off that he was not at Central in response to their demands, but just kind of happened to be in the neighborhood. He would, however, hear them out. By then the prisoners had drawn up a list of ten grievances to present. They wanted an inmate grievance board, the right of inmates to have attorneys at disciplinary hearings, five fire extinguishers on each cell block, etc. Bounds replied that as a reputed penologist, professor at Chapel Hill and head of the corrections department, he was their superior, and worked and communicated on a different level. But what he had here apparently was not a failure by the inmates to communicate. Negotiations began which eventually resulted in the setting up of an inmate grievance commission, allowing prisoners to have their attorneys along for the hearing. And that day, five fire extinguishers were installed in the west wing at Central Prison, for the first time in its more than 100-year history.

Central is no worse than most of the 76 other units that make up the Raleigh Archipelago. Guards administer medicine instead of medics, and sick call is held only twice a week, with inspections conducted on desktops. Medical equipment and sterilization are unknown elements in these inspections. Inmates have a 10-month waiting period for false teeth. Until 1974, the entire prison system had no preventive medicine nor food dietician of any kind; one oral surgeon worked half a day a week. In recent years, unnatural deaths of prisoners have averaged one every four weeks, according to Charles Wilson, research director for the Department of Social and Rehabilitation and Control.

The Raleigh Archipelago has come into some notoriety in the 1970s, largely through the work of the North Carolina Advisory Committee to the United States Commission on Civil Rights, and through a number of lawsuits filed by the nascent North Carolina Prisoners' Union. In February 1976, the Advisory Committee, chaired by Rev. W.W. Finlator, issued a report of its findings after conducting public hearings, independent research and first-hand on-site inspections of several prisons. The Committee found that, while nearly 60 percent of the inmates are Black, the Division of Prisons had no Black superintendents at its 77 facilities; only 21.4 percent of the more than 5,000 employees were Black; among professionals, no women could be found. One full-time doctor and a quarter-time dentist were the only Blacks in the upper ranks. Sadism characterized the guards' behavior toward the inmates. Women were disciplined by denying them clothing until "her attitude changed." (Almost 20 percent of the staff at the Women's Correctional Center were men.) At Central Prison, fire hoses with nozzle pressure of about 70 pounds and pump pressure of about 120 pounds were used to knock down the inmates.

The Fourth U.S. Circuit Court of Appeals, ruling in January 1976 on a prisoners' suit, substantially upheld the findings of the Finlator Committee. Retired U.S. Supreme Court Justice Tom C. Clark, who sat as a member of the circuit court, said that Central's "Chinese cell" was "so bizarre that it is difficult to believe that such a situation could exist in our society." He said the cell is "reminiscent of the Black Hole of Calcutta." According to the court, the cell has "no bedding, no light and no toilet facilities, save a hole in the floor." Some prisoners have been placed in the cell for up to three months at a time.

Clark's opinion noted that federal courts are "most reluctant to interfere in the administration of state or federal prison systems," but argued that the abuses in North Carolina were so severe that the court was compelled to act.

WITH the violent suppression of the 1929 labor upsurge and the scarcity of jobs in the years to come, the textile barons "successfully combined the personal relationships of an agrarian society with modern personnel methods, re-established channels of communication with their 'people,' tutored overseers to shun arbitrary command, and cultivated in the factory an environment of living folkways."[57] Not that the re-established carrot eliminated the stick: A Senate subcommittee on civil liberties, headed by Robert M. LaFollette, Jr., found that twenty Southern textile firms laid out hundreds of thousands of dollars between 1933–37, the years studied by the subcommittee, for the spying and strikebreaking services of the Pinkerton agency and others. Of eighty corporations in the country that purchased more than a thousand dollars of tear gas and poison gas in those years, nine were Southern textile companies, two were textile subsidiaries of rubber firms, and one was an employers association in North Carolina's Alamance County.[58] The "cheap and contented labor" advertised by Southern textile and power company owners to attract Northern capital had proved to be a bit more quarrelsome than expected.

In 1935 the Congress of Industrial Organizations was formed and its drive for industrial unionization challenged the older, conservative and craft-oriented AFL. Moreover—and in no small part due to the Communist influence in the organizing drives—no CIO national union excluded Black members nor shunted them into "Jim Crow" locals. There was only one exception to this rule—the Textile Workers Union of America—an exception that helped to dictate the future course of labor and race relations for North Carolina.[59] By the end of the decade which saw labor organized as never before throughout the United States, virtually no mills in North Carolina were unionized.

Roosevelt's National Industrial Recovery Act, which lasted until 1937, demanded an industrial code recognizing labor's collective bargaining rights. The Tobacco Workers International Union of the AFL, which had until then been active only on the fringes of the industry, began to move into Winston-Salem and Durham. The momentum of the NRA period carried past 1937. Workers at American, Liggett & Myers, P.J. Lorillard all came into the union.

At R.J. Reynolds, the largest tobacco corporation in the capitalist world, the CIO's Food, Tobacco and Allied Workers (FTA), under Communist leadership, won a contract in 1944. FTA's Local 22 for years represented the largest single organized industrialized enterprise in the South. It was not a victory that came easily. The founder of the Reynolds monopoly, Richard Joseph Reynolds, came to Winston-Salem from the family plantation in Virginia. His father had been one of the largest slaveholders in the country, and his progeny were to carry over a similar set of labor relations into the twentieth century. Foremen were recruited from among the chain-gang guards on the country roads. Workers in the plants had no lunch facilities, no decent rest rooms, no sick leaves, no vacations, no seniority, no paid holidays, no job security. The big FTA organizing drive came in June 1943 when a sick Black worker dropped dead on the job after his foreman refused to let him go home. A sit-down strike began in the dead man's room and several other departments joined in spontaneously. Seven thousand Reynolds workers soon joined the union. When three years later they finally got a contract that granted more than union recognition, it provided a 40-hour week with time-and-a-half for overtime, paid vacations and holidays, grievance procedures, and the largest wage gains in the history of the industry.[60]

FTA militance, with Communist insistence, depended on the unity of Black and white workers operating as a single unit. Even the CIO top leadership in those days provided "colored hotel" accommodations for its Black convention delegates, and allowed for segregated toilets and drinking facilities in unionized Southern plants. After the world war, in announcing Operation Dixie, its Southern organizing drive, the CIO announced it would respect the "traditions of the South."

In a state where segregation was required by law, the FTA's Winston-Salem local with 10,000 members comprised an obvious threat to companies which as a matter of course play white against Black to keep wages down. Miranda Smith, a Black woman worker at Reynolds, earning 40 cents an hour in 1940, rose to the leadership of Local 22. A Communist Party militant, she eventually became director at the age of 32 of the FTA's south Atlantic region. She died shortly thereafter and was memorialized by the biggest funeral procession in Winston-Salem history, at which Paul Robeson sang to thousands of Black and white workers. It was largely Miranda Smith's leadership in the efforts at unity of the workers that brought the wrath of the companies, the state and the CIO bureaucracy down on the FTA.

Local 22 paid dearly for its efforts and its principles. In 1946 the union waged a bitter strike against the Piedmont Leaf Tobacco Company in Winston-Salem. The union was asking 65 cents an hour. Company-influenced police were especially brutal against Black strikers. Mrs. Margaret DeGraffenried, mother of four, was beaten by police during the strike and sentenced to three months on a road gang. Cal Roberson Jones, a worker at another tobacco plant, who happened to pass by the Piedmont plant, was beaten by police and sentenced to eight months on the chain gang. A white Local 22 organizer, Philip Koritz, came to Jones' defense during the beating, and was himself beaten and sentenced to six months on a road gang. Betty Keel Williams, a young woman striker, was given 30 days.[61]

The House Committee on Un-American Activities, which included among its members freshman Richard Nixon, came to Winston-Salem and set up shop at the Robert E. Lee Hotel. The Cold War was now in full force, the "first shot fired" directed at the Left within the trade union movement. Ten international unions were expelled from the CIO for their Left leadership, among them the FTA. Local 22 was targeted for destruction through raiding by other CIO unions. Scores of CIO personnel came to Winston-Salem to undermine the FTA. The first anti-Communist law of the Cold War period, the Taft-Hartley Law, made Communist membership and leadership in unions illegal and curtailed the right to strike. Taft-Hartley was passed in 1947, and immediately afterward North Carolina passed one of the first "right to work" laws in the country, outlawing the closed union shop. Armed with Taft-Hartley, the "right to work" law and the collaboration of the CIO national leadership, Reynolds Tobacco was able to "destabilize" Local 22, 25 years before that word became synonymous in government jargon with the forcible overthrow of legally elected bodies. In a 1950 National Labor Relations Board election at the R.J. Reynolds plants in Winston-Salem, Local 22 emerged on top with 3,223 votes. However, the AFL's tobacco union received 1,514; a CIO splinter union, 521; and "no union," 3,426. Reynolds refused to enter into collective bargaining with the FTA, and has now remained unorganized for a quarter of a century.[62] One result of the Reynolds open shop is a productivity rate about three times that of union shops.[63] According to former Reynolds vice-president Charles Wade, the FTA's union drive "was primarily a Negro issue," but "now we've licked that problem and there is no need for a union."[64]

It is no credit to the TWIU that today Reynolds, the open-shop employer, has the biggest Black employment—25 percent—in the tobacco industry, although even that is half of what it used to be. The TWIU originally signed "sweetheart contracts" over the heads of the workers at Liggett & Myers, Reynolds, American and Lorillard in the union's salad days during the first world war. But in the post-war period Reynolds reduced wages in its plants without resistance from the union; consequently, TWIU membership declined from 15,000 in 1916 to 1,500 in 1925.

The TWIU's segregationist policies have plagued its efforts to organize Black workers at Reynolds ever since. Hence, the FTA, under the initiative of the Southern Negro Youth Congress, was able to organize Reynolds and win the National Labor Relations Board election in 1944, where the TWIU could not. That defeat moved the TWIU to resolve in 1946 not to organize any local plants on a segregated basis. But the gap between resolutions and performances became an abyss in this case. In the 1950s new white workers were employed while Black TWIU members were laid off with little union opposition. The influence of the Klan and White Citizens Council in local union leadership led to the disturbing situation of at least token integration at non-union Reynolds and not even a token at unionized plants.

With new federal civil rights laws, some gains were made in the years 1964–68. A few Black workers were upgraded to more skilled positions, and the union merged its Black and white locals. Even so, Blacks remained the only janitors and the only shippers, except for their white foremen. With the introduction of mechanization, these jobs were gradually but substantially reduced, thus affecting mainly the Black workers. Whereas in 1940 Blacks constituted 54.9 percent of the tobacco workforce in North Carolina, by 1950 they were reduced to 42.3 percent, and by 1960, 31.6 percent. Today Blacks are merely 22 percent of the tobacco workforce in the state, which contains 46 percent of all cigarette workers and 35 percent of all tobacco workers in the country.[65]

THAT was November 30, 1972, when Ben led the prisoner delegation to meet Corrections Secretary Lee Bounds to secure some protection from fire. On December 16, the United Church of Christ paid a $50,000 appeal bond and Rev. Chavis walked out of Central Prison to begin the long appeals process for the Wilmington 10. The next day he flew to New York to participate in a conference that was preparatory to establishing a national organization to defend political activists and victims of repression. The meeting was initiated by remnants of what had been the National United Committee to Free Angela Davis and all Political Prisoners, which had built perhaps the greatest mass movement in history around a single prisoner. Angela Davis was herself on hand for the conference that day and Ben also met Charlene Mitchell, who had organized the Angela Davis defense movement. Other organizations that were helping put together this new movement included the National Conference of Black Lawyers, the Attica Brothers Defense Fund, Puerto Rican Socialist Party, Communist Party, the anti-war People's Coalition for Peace and Justice, Women's International League for Peace and Freedom, the Commission for Racial Justice and others. Ben had the opportunity to meet his counterparts from other movements and to acquaint them for the first time with the situation in North Carolina, which even the more knowledgeable among them still considered a New South showcase. The day-long meeting was an important experience for Rev. Chavis and his new companions, and together they agreed to begin work on a founding conference for their new national organization.

Meantime, in Wilmington things were still out of hand. The Rights of White People continued to build up their arms caches, hold park rallies with arms drills, and ride in caravans through Black neighborhoods to intimidate the people. With the release of the Rev. Chavis from prison, new assaults were launched against Wilmington Blacks. This, despite the fact that Ben had been assigned to direct the Washington, D.C.-Maryland office of the Commission for Racial Justice.

Ben still faced charges in the Wilmington Three case with Molly and Leatrice Hicks, and trial was scheduled for late Spring 1973, only a few months away. This was to be one of the strangest cases in the history of North Carolina jurisprudence, a history hardly void of anomalies. Molly Hicks had been one of the most active adults in support of the Wilmington student movement and Leatrice came out of that movement to join the Temple of the Black Messiah. In the wake of the violence at the Gregory Memorial Church in February 1971, Molly Hicks had asked for police protection for her house in which she and Leatrice lived alone. On the evening of March 13, Molly Hicks was at her Seventh Day Adventist church. Leatrice was asleep in the upstairs of the house. Three young Black teenagers, Clifton Eugene Wright, Jerome McClain and Donald Nixon, were downstairs in the parlor. As reported on the next day's news, someone knocked on the door, Clifton Wright went to the door and an unidentified white person blew his head off. Ben was at home in Oxford at the time, but three months later the FBI asked to interview him, Molly and Leatrice Hicks. The three agreed to the interview if it could be held in James Ferguson's law office in Charlotte. It was peculiar enough that Ben and Molly Hicks should have been questioned at all, since even the government agreed they were nowhere near the house at the time of the murder. When the FBI asked Ben who might have killed young Wright, he answered that he had no knowledge but guessed, given Molly and Leatrice Hicks' activities, it might have been an ROWP night rider.

When, months later, in December 1971, a week after the federal indictments came down against Ben and Jim Grant, Ben was arrested again, this time with the two Hicks women, they found that Donald Nixon and Jerome McClain were also in jail. In the months since Wright was killed, Nixon and McClain had become narcotics addicts and had pulled off a number of burglaries and robberies around Wilmington.

Now, in jail, they signed a statement saying that they had accidentally killed Wright, although the gun was never discovered and they had no idea where the murder weapon could be. Further, the Nixon-McClain story went, they called Ben in Oxford and he made up the story about the white man for them to tell the police; and Molly and Leatrice went along with the story. Hence the arrests of Rev. Chavis, Molly and Leatrice Hicks on charges of accessory after the fact of murder, with bond set at $10,000 each (and Ben's bail raised to $100,000 when he told a Charlotte meeting that he someday wanted to visit Africa). Meanwhile, McClain, one of the admitted "murderers" was released outright, and Nixon, who had also confessed, was let off with $3,000 bond on charges of involuntary manslaughter. What was so peculiar about the state's case was that by allowing Nixon to plead guilty to involuntary manslaughter, the prosecution and the courts thereby ruled that Wright's death was accidental. Yet they charged Rev. Chavis and the Hickses with knowledge of a murder which the state had already ruled did not really happen.

While Ben prepared his defense, he continued to work for the founding of the new national defense organization. In the call to the founding conference, the coalition argued that "North Carolina has particularly become a laboratory for new methods of racist repression." Here was a group that filled a great need as far as Ben was concerned—a group made up of diverse forces with long years of experience in organized mass defense of other victims like himself—Angela Davis, the Puerto Rican Nationalist Party leaders, the Wounded Knee defendants, the San Quentin Six, the Attica Brothers, the Soledad Brothers. Moreover this was to be a national organization, and heretofore national attention had not been paid to the repression gripping North Carolina. Had there been a national movement in defense of the Wilmington 10, they might have won their case, Ben thought. There were other reasons for the lack of national attention on the Wilmington 10 trial, not the least of which were popular illusions about North Carolina as a bastion of the New Southern liberalism, and the abandonment of the civil rights movement by Northern liberals when that movement came North. Further, there were the particulars of the case itself: These were, after all, political activists, not merely "victims" and one needed to support that activism rather than simply "take pity." That there were ten defendants rather than only one, around whose single personality support could be garnered, also presented problems. But more than anything else, what was missing was a national organization, whose purpose was to build a mass movement in defense of the Wilmington 10. Especially had this been needed at the trial level, the most favorable time to mount such an effort. Now it would be difficult for the Wilmington 10 in the appeals process, but the Wilmington Three case was still at the pre-trial stage.

Meeting in Chicago on May 11-13, 1973, what was to become the National Alliance Against Racist and Political Repression was founded by 800 delegates representing churches, trade unions, community organizations and campus groups, veterans' movements and political parties. The fledgling organization adopted a vast and varied program of activities to combat the many forms of repression, from police brutality to repressive legislation, from behavior control and human experimentation to the repression of labor rights. The conference agreed that in North Carolina could be found the most intensive and comprehensive wave of repression in the United States, and agreed to make North Carolina a national focus of its activities. Immediate attention would be paid to building national support for the Wilmington Three in their upcoming trial the next month. And Rev. Ben Chavis was elected a vice-chairperson of the new National Alliance.

On the eve of the Wilmington Three trial, a new wave of terror hit Wilmington. ROWP dynamite blasts leveled the offices of the Wilmington *Journal,* which had served the town's Black community since 1911. The rubble that was the *Journal* building stood only 50 feet away from an empty lot which had been the site of the *Record,* Wilmington's Black newspaper during Reconstruction, which was burned to the ground by the Redshirts during the violent overthrow of the Fusion government in 1898. An ad-hoc group, the Wilmington Committee to Defend Victims of Racist and Political Repression, began to rally Wilmingtonians to defend against further terror. It called upon national civil rights and Black leaders to come to Wilmington to show their support of the Wilmington Three and other victims. Among those who responded were Congressman John Conyers who sent a staff assistant; the Commission for Racial Justice under the leadership of Dr. Charles Cobb of New York; the Southern Conference Education Fund, which sent a full-time organizer, Judi Simmons, to work in Wilmington. Judi Simmons had also been elected a vice-chairperson of the newly-formed National Alliance Against Racist and Political Repression. The National Alliance sent one of its chairpersons, Angela Davis, and its executive secretary, Charlene Mitchell.

At the outset of the trial, defense attorneys asked that the charges be removed from the state of North Carolina and placed under federal jurisdiction. The defendants' petition argued that "the judicial system under which the defendants are required to be tried in New Hanover County, including the judges, the prosecutors and the prospective jurors and the police officers, is antagonistic toward the defendants and persons of their race"; and further, that a fair trial was unlikely for the defendants because of their designation "by the state to be civil rights activists who stir up trouble in the Black community by encouraging the Black community to actively assert its civil and constitutional rights", and that the Wilmington city government which was pressing the charges, was illegally constituted and had been since the 1898 coup d'etat. District Court Judge John M. Walker, who had earlier called for Lieutenant William Cally, the My Lai murderer, to "clean up" Wilmington, was sitting on the bench when the Wilmington Three petition was presented. After reading it, Judge Walker told the press that the government allows "these kind of people to operate, and if you declare the government unconstitutional, that means open season on everyone, doesn't it?"

The request for transfer to federal jurisdiction was dismissed but as the trial began, Solicitor Jay Stroud did move to reduce the charge against Rev. Chavis and Molly and Leatrice Hicks to "accessory after the fact of involuntary manslaughter." Public pressure was beginning to make itself felt. Angela Davis, who attended the trial for its duration, addressed a rally of 4,000 Wilmingtonians, the largest civil rights demonstration in the town's history. Even while she spoke to the throng, several blocks away ROWP bombs blasted a gaping hole in the front of the B'nai Israel Temple synagogue. The threats began to tell on the defense attorneys and some of their supporters. Some from the defense team and even some of his co-workers urged Rev. Chavis and the Hicks women to plea-bargain, to agree to say they were guilty in return for reduced sentences. But the defendants insisted they were innocent and that it would be a betrayal of themselves and the movement they represented to enter a false plea, however expedient it might seem to some of their friends.

The prosecution and the courts were under even greater pressure as national attention was brought on Wilmington for the first time, and as Wilmington Three supporters responded in the streets. Chief prosecution witness Donald Nixon told the court, under cross-examination, that even though he had pleaded guilty six months earlier to involuntary manslaughter in the killing of Clifton Wright, he had never been sentenced. Judge Robert D. Rouse, Jr., sitting while protests in the streets mounted with the appearance of Angela Davis, dismissed all charges against Rev. Chavis, citing the lack of any incriminating evidence for the prosecution. This left Molly and Leatrice Hicks to face a jury decision. Defense attorney John Harmon asked the jurors to use their common sense in their verdict. "You know who the state was looking for in this case," he said. "It wasn't these two women." The jury hopelessly deadlocked in deciding the fate of Leatrice Hicks and the case against her ended in a mistrial. Molly Hicks was found guilty but given a suspended three-year sentence. Donald Nixon, the admitted killer, never did serve time.

Ben went directly from Wilmington to St. Louis to attend the Eighth General Synod of the United Church of Christ. The Commission for Racial Justice had initiated a resolution to have the church put up the $350,000 bond to get the other nine Wilmington 10 defendants out of prison. The assembly passed the resolution and two weeks later all the Wilmington defendants were released on bond.

T HE textile monopolies have always led North Carolina against unionization, and North Carolina has led the country. In 1955, the National Right to Work Committee was formed by Charlotte's E.S. Dillard. Scott Hoyman, southern director of the Amalgamated Clothing and Textile Workers Union (ACTWU), says that companies, as a "style of life," won't enter into union contracts, much as "violent racism was once a style of life." A bit inhibited from directly using racism themselves, "the textile firms instead turn their mailing lists over to anti-Semitic, anti-Black trash sheets like the *Militant Truth*. J.P. Stevens is one company that supports this rag."[66] The *Militant Truth* is a frequently, though irregularly, published fundamentalist newsletter, which exhibits the thought process of a Klan-like White Queen, believing as many as six impossible things about Jews, Blacks and unions before breakfast.

Virtually all corporate spokesmen in North Carolina are by now reconciled, at least in public statements, to the demise of Jim Crow as a way of life. But they will bark at the skies and spit in the wind at the mention of unions. Charlotte corporation attorney Whiteford S. Blakeney, according to Hoyman, will drop a client if the client agrees to bargain with a union, thus proving he can wield an axe by chopping off his foot. Blakeney is a trustee of the National Right to Work Legal Defense Foundation, Inc., established in 1968, which works through the courts to complement the legislative lobbying of the earlier formed National Right to Work Committee.

The state legislature being as it is a wholly-owned subsidiary of the corporations and banks, Blakeney and his colleagues have found little trouble in maintaining "right to work" laws in North Carolina. State laws prohibit public employees from bargaining collectively with their employer, the state, and in turn prevent the state, cities and towns from

Nothing Could Be Finer

bargaining with public employees' unions. Laws to reverse these prohibitions have never even gotten out of committees of the General Assembly. Similarly, all efforts at allowing the "agency shop" have met with defeat in legislative committees, never reaching the floor for debate. Unlike the union shiop in which all workers must join the union in a plant under contract, and which is barred in North Carolina by its "right to work" bill, the agency shop does not demand compulsory membership in the union. Those who do not join the union still receive all the benefits of the contract—wages, vacations, pension, health plans, grievance protection, etc. Still the agency shop is too strong a threat to those who genuflect before the totem of "free enterprise."

North Carolina labor laws are a throwback to the years before industrial unionism, a stage not yet reached in this state. Workmen's compensation remains elective, not compulsory. Minors 14 and 15 years old can work up to a 40-hour week; employers who violate the law can be "penalized" with a fine of only 5–50 dollars. The state minimum wage of $1.80 per hour in 1975 does not cover establishments with fewer than four employees, state and local government employees, employees under 16 or over 65 years old, workers in the seafood or fishing industries, domestic workers, workers in charitable, religious, educational and non-profit organizations, inmates, news vendors, golf caddies, theater doormen, part-time employees, and a fistful of other categories. Violators of minimum wage laws can be fined 10–50 dollars.

North Carolina's complete suppression of a labor movement is generally explained away by corporate apologists as the result of "human relations" programs and of "paternalism." Back in the 1920s, under the sponsorship of Western Electric, sociologist Elton Mayo supervised a number of studies to develop "human relations" techniques in industrial settings. Mayo's results still serve as the basic tenets of corporate manipulation of workers' attitudes.[67] Mayo discovered that industrial society "is characterized by a social split, growing hostility and hatred between various social groups, and an absence of mutual understanding between employers and workers."[68] But, denying the Marxist premise of class struggle inherent in a class society, Mayo, according to William Whyte in his *Organization Man,* "sees conflict primarily as a breakdown in communication. If a man is unhappy or dissatisfied in his work, it is not that there is a conflict to be resolved so much as a misunderstanding to be cleared up."[69] The industrial map of North Carolina is dotted with employers associations, chambers of commerce and industrial developers who pride themselves on "human relations" expertise.

"Paternalism" they like to call it, the "identification" of boss with worker and vice versa. The ruling class goes to the country store to keep in touch, chew tobacco, talk to folks. Since the state is made up of small isolated towns, provincial to the core, to be a radical or pro-union is to face ostracism. The pat on the back, the turkey at Thanksgiving, the local gossip, the Boy Scout donation, the current dirty joke—these are the weapons which face the challenger to the prevailing system of doing things.

"Human relations" professionals urge the skillfull manipulation of "symbolic rewards" to acquire and secure the loyalty of workers. Sociologist Robert Dubin argues that "status pay is the 'cheapest' form of payoff for the organization. It involves only some kind of public recognition by a member of management of a person's particular merits."[70] Celebrations in honor of veteran employees, public commendations, special badges and bonuses, letters to the workforce from the employer at Christmas—all are "symbolic rewards" handed out with a wink as a matter of course by North Carolina's paternalistic corporations. Companies hand out 5-year pins and 10-year pins for lengthy service. After 30 years a worker will receive a $30 watch, a "symbolic reward" of a dollar for each year at the loom or the assembly line. Paternalism works in just this way: A textile worker making $1.80 an hour is weakened by "brown lung" disease, endemic to the industry, but continues to work for years because his wife is crippled with arthritis and the kids have to eat. He calls himself "middle class" and roots for the American Legion baseball team attached to the mill and looks to the day his boy can go the local community college to train for a more highly skilled job at the mill. By fostering a sense of identification with the company, management seeks to render trade unions superfluous: "There would be no point in a worker joining a trade union and fighting to defend his rights and interests if he were to believe that his employer himself was showing 'constant concern' for his welfare."[71]

A host of schemes are devised in this continual corporate campaign. Textiles Incorporated of Gastonia held an "energy saving idea" contest, and presented a $25 savings bond to the best entry in the plant. The American Textile Manufacturers Institute, Inc., with headquarters in Charlotte, publishes a monthly *Public Relations Pointers* newsletter to pass on new ideas to the textile barons for developing "employee rapport." Cone Mills sponsors a Junior Fishing Club for children of its employees. R. J. Reynolds publishes workers' favorite bake recipes in its bi-monthly magazine. All the companies welcome "workers' participation" in the form of suggestions for plant efficiency, but decision-making of course rests firmly in the hands of management. One supporter of "workers' participation" contends that "the self-government of the plant community can only be justified if it strengthens management. Its functions are not only limited; they are also strictly subordinate."[72]

While encouraging an I-got-plenty-of-nothing-and-nothing-is-plenty-for-me philosophy among employees, the textile industry leads all other industries in giving to churches, hospitals, and private schools. In 1973, about $8 million of donations were given by the textile industry to philanthropy, in a more traditional form of paternalism.[73] Such generosity of course is rewarded by the Internal Revenue Service each April 15.

Among the favorite objects of corporate charity in North Carolina is the church. Liberal donations to the local house of worship has for years brought sermons from the pulpit against trade unionism. Several companies in the western mountain bible belt offer chapel services in the plants before work. After the Civil War, says the textile union's Scott Hoyman, "The attitude toward industry in every part of North Carolina was that the companies were our saviors. In Salisbury, the local minister was picked to run the mill."[74]

The historic roots of religion in industry are as long as the history of the state itself. The North Carolina "Statute of Oaths" of 1777, stipulating that to qualify as a witness at a trial one must believe in divine punishment after death, was used to disqualify Communists and other non-believers as witnesses during the textile violence in the 1920s and 1930s.[75] During the Gastonia strike a mob singing "Praise God from Whom All Blessings Flow," rushed a boardinghouse where it seized three union organizers and took them to an adjoining county where they were beaten and abandoned.[76]

Liston Pope in his study, *Millhands and Preachers,* quotes a mill official, "Belonging to a church, and attending it, makes a man a better worker. It makes him more complacent—no, that's not the word. It makes him more resigned—that's not the word either, but you get the general idea."[77] H.L. Mencken used to figure that organized religion would always prove more effective than police force in neutralizing workers' strikes. "The gospel scheme is far more humane. More, it is far cheaper," wrote Mencken, who estimated that to put down a strike of 400 workers by force might cost $10,000–$15,000, whereas a good hell-raising revival would cost only $400–$500.[78]

Many workers live in isolated communities in North Carolina and belong to primitive pentacostal sects. For some, church services two or three times a week are the "only entertainment" available to them.[79] A good share of the Duke Endowment goes each year to maintaining the rural Methodist Church. Half of North Carolina's half-million Methodists today live in communities of less than 1,500 persons, and are eligible for Duke funds.[80] R.J. Reynolds has a chapel inside its huge Winston-Salem plant and maintains a number of preachers on its payroll. The tobacco monopoly acknowledges that it has "what we like to call a pastor-counselor, who has a personal ministry exactly like a psychiatrist, dealing with alcoholism, family problems and the like."[81] Such "pastor-counselors" are likened by union organizers to the traditional Christian missionaries, teaching colonial subjects to accept their lot on earth in return for *post-mortem* rewards in the sky.

The aggregate results of a half-century of company chaplains, "paternalism," and police and vigilante violence on behalf of the ruling class in North Carolina are fewer than 160,000 union members or about 6.8 percent of the state's production workers. Textiles remain the key to unionization in this state with one third of the country's textile workers, and in which textile workers make up fully half of all manufacturing workers. U.S. Senator Jesse Helms may try to resuscitate unrevivably exhausted anti-labor cliches ("Unless enough Americans somehow unite, I must candidly say . . . that freedom's days are numbered . . . I am gravely disturbed . . . about the very real possibility of a relative handful of union bosses grabbing hold of America's government . . .")[82] but the fact is that in his home state unions are without political power of any kind.

Some labor organizers hold that a "brown lung" movement can build the textile union in North Carolina the way the "black lung" movement turned around the United Mine Workers in the late 1960s. Brown lung, or byssinosis, is caused by inhaling cotton fiber dust, which builds up in the lungs to cause difficulty in breathing, uncontrollable coughing and gradual destruction of the lungs. Many public health officials rank brown lung as the leading occupational health hazard in the state. While textile companies argued that there has never been a diagnosed case of byssinosis in North Carolina, Dr. James A. Merchant of the state Board of Health reported that of three textile plants he studied in 1972, from 6 to 25 percent of the workers suffered from the disease.[83]

Another study found that brown lung has victimized 12–29 percent of all textile workers in the last decade, and up to 41 percent of the workers in the dustier areas of the mills. This study, at the same time, suggested collusion between the textile companies and the state health inspection teams: Seventy-six percent of the hazards found by federal inspectors had not been found by the North Carolina inspectors who visited the same plants and, further, "Administrators at the highest levels of the North Carolina Department of Labor have obstructed proper enforcement of the state's laws governing cotton-dust exposure."[84] Exact statistics on how many cotton mill workers have died from byssinosis are unavailable. But none have been compensated. No state or company plan exists for reimbursement of medical costs incurred from the disease.

In England, under pressure from the textile unions there, byssinosis has been compensable since the beginning of World War II. In the United States, though, textile owners argued that there was no such disease, that the workers only had severe bronchitis or asthma or smoker's cough. "We are particularly intrigued by the term 'byssinosis,'" editorialized the trade magazine, *America's Textile Reporter,* in 1969, "a thing thought up by venal doctors who attended last year's ILO [International Labor Organization] meetings in Africa, where inferior races are bound to be afflicted by new diseases more superior people defeated years ago."[85] Exposures by the textile unions and Ralph Nader raised the issue in the discussion preceding passage of the 1970 federal Occupational Safety and Health Act.

Tests on Atlanta Federal Penitentiary inmates working in a textile plant proved the existence of the disease to the resistant textile owners, who now claim to test their employees for byssinosis. Burlington, Cannon and Cone mills all work with Duke University Medical Center to treat the more obvious victims. But estimates for the number of afflicted North Carolina workers run as high as 70,000 and only 38 individuals applied for compensation between July 1971 and 1973.[86] The North Carolina Workmen's Compensation Act places on the victim the burden of proving one's byssinosis. Most doctors, ignorant of the disease which was not recognized until recently, diagnose it as emphysema. But not one industry spokesman has yet been heard to suggest that money be spent on steaming and washing the cotton before it goes through the carding process to keep the air in the mills free of dust particles. And the textile union is neither strong enough nor bold enough to mount a campaign to compel the industry to eliminate the causes of brown lung.

Until recently the textile union had pursued a strategy of organizing on a plant by plant basis, relying in large part on the National Labor Relations Board to rule in its favor on unfair labor practice charges. But the NLRB, made up of political appointees, is generally used by the textile industry to its own advantage. Difficult as it is to get the NLRB to call an election on union recognition, it is harder still to win such an election, not to mention winning a contract later. If the union collects enough workers' signature cards to hold an election, the company in question will fire key workers. If the union protests the dismissals to the NLRB, the company can usually count on a friendly hearing. When it cannot, it will appeal the NLRB ruling through the courts, tying up the case for years and destroying the union campaign by attrition.

However, in this state where one can be imprisoned for overworking a mule but not for overworking a textile worker, a change is on the agenda. Its first signs were seen in 1974, with the victorious 12-year campaign to unionize the 3,400 workers at the 7 J.P. Stevens mills in Roanoke Rapids. None of the Stevens' 46,000 workers in 89 plants have ever been covered by a union-negotiated wage agreement. Stevens, second only to Burlington as the biggest textile company in the capitalist world, is a skilled practitioner of intimidation, blacklisting, paternalism and violence against union efforts. Company agents in other plants have been charged with illegally wiretapping union organizers. The NLRB has ordered Stevens to pay back wages and damages amounting to about $1.3 million to 289 workers who had been illegally fired in the course of the organizing drive in the past dozen years.

The town of Roanoke Rapids was founded as a mill village at the turn of the century by a former Confederate Army officer, Major Leyburn Emry, who served as its first mayor. Emry owned the local power company, the mill of course, all the land in the town and the houses on that land, and all the forest around the town. He built Roanoke Rapids' first streets and first buildings, opened its only saloon and gave the land for its first church. Nearly 800 tenant houses were built on Emry's property, in which the mill workers lived. Emry later hired Sam Patterson to serve as his foreman and manager. Patterson eventually set up another mill as a joint venture with Emry, and as the major reached his seniority, Patterson became the town's landlord, merchant, mayor, school principal, police chief and political boss and patron. Folks who lived in Roanoke Rapids worked in the Emry-Patterson mills, lived in the Emry-Patterson houses, shopped at the Emry-Patterson stores, bought the Emry-Patterson produce, studied at the Emry-Patterson schools.

Eventually Patterson sold the town to his own lieutenant, Frank Williams, who eventually sold the by-then 6 mills to the Simmons Mattress Company, which in turn sold the mills to J.P. Stevens in 1956. But there remained the continuum of Roanoke Rapids as a company town, with all of its oligarchical structure. The parents of today's J.P. Stevens millhands worked for Frank Williams, and their parents worked for Sam Patterson.[87]

The union victory at Roanoke Rapids has by no means guaranteed a contract. Since 1974, the union has been bargaining for the contract to no avail, which has prompted the AFL-CIO to support a national boycott of Stevens products. (At another textile giant, Deering-Milliken, the union is still engaged in more than a 20-year-long legal struggle after winning an election in 1956.) Despite record-breaking profits—for the fiscal half-year ending May 1, 1976, net sales were $679.2 million, up 40.5 percent from the previous year[88]—Stevens refused to make a single economic improvement for its workers. The 33 officers and directors of the corporation receive an average of $100,000 each in direct payments from the company, plus profits, depending on the amount of stock they own. Board chairman James Finley made $462,000 in 1975, president Whitney Stevens, $325,000. Pensions for the Stevens chieftans come to as much as $75,000 a year. But the millhands face a different fate. Under Stevens' "profit-sharing" plan, a worker of 36 years' experience may receive a lump sum of $1,200 and a deadly case of byssinosis upon retirement. For the years 1970, 1971 and 1972, not one penny of "profit-sharing" payments was given to the workers.

Clearly Stevens prefers to defy the law rather than enter seriously into contract negotiations with the union. The $1.3 million the company has paid out in fines for its violations of the law since 1968 is nothing compared to the $104 million in government contracts it has received in the same years. Daniel Pollitt, who served as counsel for the Special House Subcommittee on Labor in Washington, said that Stevens and other southern textile companies laughingly refer to back-pay awards as the "hunting license" they need to continue their union-busting activities.[89] Thus, Stevens has become the number one labor law violator in the United States. As of March 15, 1976, 94 cases of labor law violations by Stevens were pending before the National Labor Relations Board. The NLRB has found Stevens guilty of flagrant and massive violations 15 times since 1964. Appeals by Stevens of these NLRB rulings have been rejected 8 times by the U.S. Cicruit Court and 3 times by the U.S. Supreme Court, which are not known for a pro-labor bias.

An August 1977 ruling by the Second Circuit U.S. Court of Appeals found the company in contempt of court "not once but twice, involving over 30 individual violations," which "have been described as massive, cynical and flagrantly contemptuous." The court said it would consider a proposed fine of $120,000 for any future violation and an additional $5,000 fine for each day that a violation continued.[90] Four months later an NLRB judge again found that the company failed to bargain in good faith in the Roanoke Rapids negotiations. Judge Bernars Ried said that Stevens' record "as a whole indicates that it approached these negotiations with all the tractability and open-mindedness of Sherman at the outskirts of Atlanta."[91]

The 1974 vote for the union by the Roanoke Rapids workers brought out the power of the company in North Carolina. Banks and finance companies reminded the millhands of their debts. New loans were refused until after the election. Stevens foremen, acting as deacons and ministers, preached against the unions in the local churches. Even Boyd Leedom, NLRB chairman under President Eisenhower, described Stevens as "so out of tune with a humane civilized approach to industrial relations that it should shock even those least sensitive to honor, justice and decent treatment."[92]

The fabric of social relations, specifically Black-white relations, in the area may be changed as the Stevens dispute is resolved, particularly as the 17-year-long effort to organize becomes still more protracted. Ever since the 1929 defeat of the NTWU at Gastonia, in part through the use of racism to combat the union's principled defense of racial equality, the textile unions tried to avoid the racial issue. With the influx of Black workers into the industry since the 1960s—due to pressures by the civil rights movement, and to the labor shortage as whites moved to more skilled jobs in the new industries coming South—textile union organizers have had to meet the issue of racism.

In 1950, Blacks did not comprise more than 10 percent of any textile mill's workforce in North Carolina. Black women were totally excluded, except occasionally as scrubwomen. No Black occupied jobs in the more preferable weaving and spinning departments, let alone white-collar jobs or supervisory positions. But by 1968 Black men constituted 15.9 percent of North Carolina's textile workforce, Black women, 9.7 percent. Still only 66 Blacks occupied white-collar jobs in the entire industry, the state's largest. Of these, 3 were managers, 3 were professionals, 7 were technicians and 53 were office or clerical workers.[93] In June 1976, J.P. Stevens was found guilty of gross discriminatory acts in its Roanoke Rapids plants by a federal district court. Among the court's findings were the exclusion of Black workers from clerical supervisory and skilled jobs. Black male workers with 12th-grade educations made less than white males with 3rd-grade educations; Blacks with 10 years' seniority made less than whites with two years.[94] At its plants in Roanoke Rapids during the union election campaign, the company posted on its walls pictures of huge Black men crouching over frail white women, and passed out photos of white murder victims in San Francisco's so-called Zebra terror campaign.[95]

State AFL-CIO president Wilbur Hobby, who personally interceded in the Stevens organizing drive, says that "whites leave the textile industry because the pay is so low and they can get more in the new industries coming here." This helps the unions because "Black people are more prone to organization, they're not so fooled by the myths of 'individualism.'" But there is a problem because "when a union moves in, and calls a first meeting, mainly Black workers show up, and then the company goes to the white workers and says, 'You all don't want to join a union dominated by *them*.'"[96] The Stevens campaign proved successful, because the organizing committee was made up of Black and white workers, operating on the basis of equality. At first whites stayed away from union meetings, victimized by a company campaign showing that the union supported school desegregation. The union's Scott Hoyman says that young whites as well as Blacks now "feel no obligation to the company. The companies race-bait and tell the whites that they will be run by Black union bosses, while at the same time the company is beginning to upgrade some Blacks to foreman. With the entrance of new industries—rubber, paper, etc.—the textile companies feel the pressure for more wages, benefits and rights. If a tire company pays $1.50 an hour more than a mill, the textile company will be pressured by whites as well as Blacks."[97]

The class interests of white workers mitigate in favor of unity with Black workers when they are clearly seen. Thus the civil rights and Black liberation movements serve white workers as well. The corporations, by their nature undemocratic institutions with all decisions made by a few owners, are restricted in their total control by any extension of democratic rights, including those that take place outside the plant gate. The companies understand this sometimes better than the unions. Thus the corporations, and the state apparatus under their control, have moved to neutralize and eliminate any suggestion of a civil rights movement as a threat to their economic dictatorship.

Afterword

I N A Christmas season statement in late 1973, the North Carolina Advisory Committee to the United States Commission on Civil Rights, under the chairmanship of Rev. W. W. Finlator, said in customary understatement:

> At the very time when the federal government is meeting with reversal after reversal in its efforts, across the nation, to harass student protesters and war resisters, and is frustrated by juries that refuse to convict on what seems to them trumped up charges, here in North Carolina our courts are meting out harsh penalties and giving unconscionably long sentences to political activists. While prosecution has failed elsewhere to gain verdicts of guilty, the success of North Carolina prosecutors in jailing socially engaged leaders has been both remarkable and alarming.
>
> It is difficult to avoid the suspicion that the administration of criminal justice in North Carolina could become politicized in its pursuit to ferret out, suppress and punish political belief and action. Brilliant, sensitive and talented young men such as Ben Chavis, an ordained minister and pastor from a home of culture and leadership, James Grant, a Ph.D. in chemistry who has been offered a faculty position in a state university, and T. J. Reddy, a poet and painter whose works are soon to be published by Random House, have been arrested, tried, convicted and given long jail sentences under circumstances that tend to revive the spectre of what was once called "southern justice." The harsh and seemingly punitive sentences, the excessive bail, the selection of juries, and, most shocking of all, the use by the State of discredited witnesses who have themselves been charged and convicted of heinous crimes and have then been given immunity and protection by the State, have the cumulative effect of convincing many people that a pattern and trend of legal repression may exist in North Carolina.

That same "cumulative effect" was evident on July 4, 1974, when the National Alliance brought nearly 10,000 people to Raleigh to protest against that "laboratory of racism and repression" in North Carolina.

More than half the protestors in the demonstration, the largest the South had ever seen since the murder of Dr. King, came from North Carolina— from the cities, the small towns, the countryside, from Charlotte and Wilmington and Tarboro and Oxford and Fayetteville. The Rev. Ralph David Abernathy, Dr. King's successor as president of the Southern Christian Leadership Conference, told the marchers: "I've come to march because the same foot of iron that seeks to keep me down as a Black man is seeking to keep us all down, whether we be Christians or Communists. And they want to divide us and they want to tell us something is wrong with some people because they are Communists. Well, I want to tell you right now that it's a pride and it's an honor for me to march with Angela Davis."

Speaking to the crowd, Angela Davis agreed with Rev. Abernathy: "They said people would not take to the streets any more, to raise their voices against racism and repression. Sisters and Brothers, how wrong they were! Look around you, and who do you see? You see Black people by the thousands; you see Puerto Ricans, Chicanos, Indians, Asians, white people. You see workers and students, marching together. You see ministers and Communists, nationalists and church people. We've learn-ed some very important lessons from our history. We've learned that if we want to be strong, we have to use the only weapon which the people who are politically powerless, and economically powerless, hold in their hand. Our weapon is unity; our battle is to organize."

Under pressure from many quarters, Governor James Holshouser announced right after the July 4 march that he could not consider executive clemency for the Charlotte Three until the defendants had exhausted all legal avenues of redress. The governor urged the defense to appeal through the state courts. Immediately an appeal was filed and arguments heard by Superior Court Judge Sam Ervin III. For nine months Judge Ervin held onto the case before ruling, in December 1975, that the secret federal payoffs to the informers Hood and Washington, one of the key questions in the appeal, were merely "harmless error." Immediately the defense filed a writ of habeas corpus in federal district court of appeals, and the appeals process dragged on. By now Jim Grant had been paroled by the federal authorities, after serving two and a half years at Atlanta Federal Penitentiary on the charge of aiding fugitives, and turned over to the state of North Carolina, where he was assigned first to the Avery County prison unit, then to Stanly County to serve his sentence in the Lazy B case. Finally in June 1976, after four years imprisonment, Jim Grant and T. J. Reddy were released on $50,000 and $10,000 appeal bond. Charles Parker was by now already on parole.

In December 1974, the state Court of Appeals turned down the appeal of the Wilmington 10. In the appeal, the defense listed *2,635* exceptions to Judge Martin's "admitting into evidence . . . testimony . . . which was irrelevant, immaterial, incompetent, remote, prejudicial and inflammatory." In rejecting the appeal, the appellate court was obliged to state that, "In our opinion some of the rulings constituted error," but nevertheless, "In our opinion the errors in the admission of State's evidence were non-prejudicial beyond a reasonable doubt." The court concluded its decision denying the appeal with these words, "In our view defendants had a fair trial before an impartial, patient and courteous judge and by a competent, unbiased jury. They have been accorded every reasonable request. The State's evidence was clear, and overwhelmingly tended to show the guilt of each defendant of the offenses with which he was charged. In the trial we find no prejudicial error. No error." What the court failed to note in its opinion was that the "impartial, patient and courteous" trial judge, Robert Martin, had been appointed to and was now sitting as a member of the Court of Appeals.

Six months later the North Carolina Supreme Court refused to even review the case. Among those sitting on that court were I. Beverly Lake, Dan K. Moore, and Joseph Branch, for years political cronies of Judge Robert Martin and Attorney General Robert Morgan, who had prosecuted the Wilmington 10. This left the U.S. Supreme Court as the last resort. In October 1975 the Wilmington 10 petitioned the highest court in the land. At a press conference called by the Commission for Racial Justice to announce the petition, National Alliance executive secretary Charlene Mitchell argued, "In fact the case of the Wilmington 10 should not have reached the U.S. Supreme Court at all. It should never have even been brought to trial. The wrong people, the victims rather than the perpetrators, were brought to trial. Just as they were wrongly tried, they were wrongly convicted; their appeal to the state appellate court was wrongly denied, and the state supreme court wrongly refused to even hear the case."

Then in January 1976 the U.S. Supreme Court "wrongly refused" to hear the case as well. Nixon appointee and Barry Goldwater confidant Judge William Rehnquist read the case for the high court and recommended rejection of the case without comment. The National Conference of Black Churchmen, under the presidency of Dr. Charles Cobb, stated the outrage felt by the legions of Wilmington 10 supporters. "It is hard to perceive," said the Conference, "of a greater inhumanity than this denial of the writ of certiorari imposes; it is hard to perceive of a greater abrogation of moral and judicial responsibility."

The Wilmington 10 now had to prepare to return to prison. During their period of liberty, they had remained active members of their communities. Rev. Chavis continued as director for the Washington, D.C., office of the Commission for Racial Justice and was a candidate for a master's degree in divinity at the Howard University School of Religion. Reginald Epps and Wayne Moore were now juniors at Shaw University in Raleigh, majoring in business administration and political science, respectively. Joe Wright was a political science student at Talladega College in Alabama. Jerry Jacobs married a school teacher and was a city employee in Wilmington. Ann Sheppard had remarried and was now working in Raleigh. James McCoy was an electronics major at Cape Fear Technical Institute in Wilmington. Marvin Patrick was now working in Oxford, Willie Earl Vereen in San Francisco, and Connie Tindall in Wilmington.

Washington *Post* columnist Coleman McCarthy asked, "What purpose is served by locking away the nine young men and one woman for a combined span of 282 years?" and answered himself: "A spirit of vicious retribution appears to be at work. None of the Wilmington 10 had a record of crime before his arrest, and none has had serious involvement with the law after. None jumped bail. Nothing in their behavior since their arrests in 1972 suggests that these are social menaces needing to be incarcerated to protect the community." At an 11th hour bond hearing before Magistrate Logan D. Howell, 236 affidavits were filed making that same point. The affidavits testifying to the good character and responsibility of the Wilmington 10 and asking for bond to be set while the federal appeals process continued, came from professors, attorneys, trade union leaders, clergy, city council members, mayors, judges and members of Congress. Support for the Wilmington 10 had come already from the Washington, D.C., City Council which had proclaimed a "Wilmington 10 Day" on May 31, 1975, from the Congressional Black Caucus and from the Archdiocese of Hartford, Connecticut, from the Baltimore Central Labor Council and the World Peace Council based in Helsinki, Finland. Among the scores of prominent community leaders who appeared in person to offer character testimony at the bond hearing were the Rev. William Oliver, chairman of the Commission for Racial Justice; the Rev. Ernest Gibson, executive director of the Council of Churches of Greater Washington; Dr. Lawrence Jones, dean of Howard University's School of Religion; and the Rev. A. Knighton Stanley, director of Bicentennial programs for the Mayor of Washington, D.C.

Magistrate Howell, however, refused to hear the testimony or read the affidavits. Receiving a fair hearing from the arcane judicial system of

North Carolina where justice for Ben Chavis and the Wilmington 10 are concerned, was as easily accomplished as freezing smoke rings. Appeal bond was denied and the ten young defendants were sent to prison for most of the remaining years of their lives.

T HIRTEEN months after the Wilmington 10 were again placed behind prison walls and barbed wire, the newly inaugurated President Jimmy Carter wrote to Andrei D. Sakharov in Moscow, "You may rest assured that the American people and our government will continue our firm commitment to promote respect for human rights. We shall use our good offices to seek the release of prisoners of conscience." The White House, the new president was saying to the world, would no longer be burdened by the corruption of Watergate and the barbarism of Vietnam. Human rights were to be the hallmark of this administration.

Two weeks after the Carter letter to Sakharov, another letter on the subject of human rights was written, this time to President Carter from the Rev. Chavis. Sent from his prison cell in McCain, North Carolina, Ben wrote, "As only one of the many American citizens who has been unjustly imprisoned not because of criminal conduct but as a direct result of participation in the human and civil rights movement in the United States, I appeal to you. . . to first set a national priority of freeing all U.S. political prisoners. . . . We are 10 victims of a racist and political prosecution. . . In fact, we are equally as well 'prisoners of conscience.' I pray that you will with speed respond positively to my request." The young minister's prayers and his letter went unanswered by a White House whose public relations credo holds that image, not substance, is the stuff of which presidents are made.

Spoken in tones as soft as the slyest innuendo, President Carter's human-rights sermons were meant to give the impression that his government had cleansed its hands of the blood of foreign aggression and the grime of corruption in high places. His Attorney General, Griffin B. Bell, who had 20 years earlier been the architect of Georgia's "massive resistance" to court-ordered school desegregation, was not prepared to be quite so firm with high government officials caught in criminal acts. Early on in the young administration, Bell accepted the recommendation of his department's office for professional responsibility to drop consideration of prosecuting FBI agents on criminal charges.

Nor was the FBI unique in exemption from "professional responsibility." Take, for example, Richard Helms, please. As Director of

Central Intelligence, Helms' career included, among other highlights, his personal involvement in assassination attempts against Fidel Castro; drug-testing and mind-control programs and ordering the files of these programs destroyed; tens of thousands of illegal mail openings; Operation CHAOS to disrupt democratic movements in the United States in violation of the CIA charter; withholding information on the Watergate coverup from the FBI and destroying evidence in the Watergate case; subverting and eventually overthrowing the democratically elected government of Salvador Allende in Chile. After establishing a record of lying under oath to congressional committees regarding the latter three crimes, Helms was charged with perjury.

Enter Messrs. Carter's and Bell's Justice Department, to seemingly act more as defense counsel than prosecutor. After months of negotiations, felony charges of perjury against Helms were reduced to the misdemeanor of refusing to testify fully and accurately. Even the misdemeanor charged carried a possible two-year sentence and $2,000 fine, however, so Assistant Attorney General Benjamin Civiletti urged upon the judge in the case, "with all the strength and conviction which I can muster on behalf of the Attorney General and the Department of Justice," that there be no jail sentence. Helms, entering his *nolo contendre* plea, stated his understanding that, "There is to be no sentence and I will be able to continue to get my pension from the U.S. government." Let off with a one-year suspended sentence and $2,000 fine, his attorney told the press, "He's going to wear this conviction like a badge of honor." Said Helms, "I don't feel disgraced at all." From the courtroom he went to a luncheon in his honor by former colleagues at the CIA, who gave him a standing ovation and passed around a wastebasket to collect the $2,000 he had been fined. So much for the deterrent effect of the plea bargain. Attorney General Bell, defending the arrangement a few days later, said that when his department urged that Helms not be sent to prison he had received no special consideration. "You can rob a bank and get probated," he said, adding that it was common for "first offenders" not to go to jail.[1]

This was hardly a persuasive argument to supporters of the Wilmington 10 who were apparently exempt from the Bell pronouncement. The young defendants, scattered throughout the Raleigh Archipelago, some to prisons hundreds of miles from their families, fought for their innocence and their freedom behind the walls while their families and supporters took to the streets outside. Several of the Wilmington 10 became active in the North Carolina Prisoners' Union, exposing abuses of inmates' rights by the authorities. For their efforts, they were placed in isolation or moved back and forth from this prison to that, like so many leaves in a wind. After a brief spell at Central Prison again, Rev. Chavis was moved to Caledonia prison farm in the rural east. Then after a few weeks and as punishment for reading the Bible to fellow prisoners and explaining their legal rights, he was put in leg irons and chains, placed on the back of a prison truck and transferred 200 miles to the McCain prison unit.

For "security" reasons, Ben was confined to a hospital section for prisoners with tuberculosis and mental disorders. At McCain as at Caledonia, he was allowed only to wear the gray "gun" uniform, signifying that were he to attempt to escape, he would be shot to death by prison marksmen using double barrel 12-gauge shotguns with number 4 buckshot. When various appeals and grievance hearings brought no relief, Ben embarked on a "spiritual fast and political hunger strike" which lasted 131 days.

Meantime the National Alliance was distributing a half million pieces of literature, mobilizing several thousand telegrams and letters to the governor, organizing delegations to the attorney general, soliciting articles in national magazines and arranging network television documentaries. In preparation for its National March for Human Rights and Labor Rights in Raleigh on Labor Day 1976, more than 100,000 supporters attended Alliance rallies across the country, while personal appearances on radio and television by Alliance leaders reached many millions more. As the demonstrators paraded in the streets of Raleigh that day, support actions were held in Jamaica, the USSR, Iraq, Greece, Denmark and the German Democratic Republic, the result of a call for an International Day of Solidarity with the Wilmington 10 and Charlotte Three by the World Peace Council based in Helsinki, the International Association of Democratic Lawyers in Brussels and the Womens International Democratic Federation in Berlin. In the next year and a half, the White House in Washington and the statehouse in Raleigh would receive over 500,000 signatures from its citizens demanding freedom for the Wilmington 10.

By the time Mr. Carter gave his inaugural address, he had already received an "Open Letter" from James Baldwin, printed first in *The New York Times* and then carried in newspapers from Rome to Raleigh:

> I have a thing to tell you, but with a heavy heart, for it is not a new thing. . . .
> If I know, you must certainly know of the silent pact made between the North and the South after Reconstruction, the purpose of which was —and is—to keep the n[----]r in his place.
> If I know, then you must certainly know, that keeping the n[----]r in his place was the most extraordinarily effective way of keeping the poor white in his place, and also of keeping him poor.

The situation of the Wilmington 10 and the Charlotte 3 is a matter of Federal collusion, and would not be possible without that collusion.

When those Black children and white children and Black men and white men and Black women and white women were marching behind Martin, up and down those dusty roads, trespassing, trespassing wherever they were, in the wrong waiting room, at the wrong coffee counter, in the wrong department store, in the wrong toilet, and were carried off to jail, they found themselves before *federally* appointed judges, who gave them the maximum sentence.

Some people died beneath that sentence, some went mad, some girls will never become pregnant again. . . .

Too many of us are in jail, my friend, too many of us can find no door open. And I was in Charlotte 20 years ago, three years after the Supreme Court made segregation in education illegal, when it was decided that *separate* could not, by definition be *equal*. Charlotte then begged for time, and time, indeed, has passed. . . .

I dared to write you this letter out of the concrete necessity of bringing to your attention the situations of the Wilmington 10 and the Charlotte 3 . . . Their situation is but a very small indication of the situation of the wretched in the country: the nonwhite, the Indian, the Puerto Rican, the Mexican, the Oriental. Consider that we may all have learned, by now, all that we can learn from you and may not want to become like you. At this hour of the world's history it may be that you, now, have something to learn from us.

The Baldwin letter was followed by a "60 Minutes" CBS-TV documentary on the case, a letter to Attorney General Bell from sixty members of Congress, support declarations from the NAACP, Congressional Black Caucus, National Urban League, National Council of Churches, Amnesty International, the International Federation of Human Rights, the World Council of Churches, resolutions by the city councils of Los Angeles, Denver, Honolulu, Milwaukee, Detroit, Hartford and Madison, editorials in a dozen of the biggest newspapers in the country, and demonstrations in front of federal buildings and Democratic Party headquarters and at U.S. embassies abroad. It was becoming difficult to take at face value the president's refusal to act on the basis of not knowing "all the facts" in the case. Before his first year in office would end, he would be told by Rep. Parren Mitchell, chairman of the Congressional Black Caucus, from the dais of the Fourth National Alliance Conference: "The injustice of the Wilmington 10 can no longer be tolerated by a nation that prattles about human rights . . . You hypocrite, you. You talk about human rights in the Union of Soviet Socialist Republics. Why don't you start with the human rights of the Wilmington 10. I don't fool myself. I, Parren Mitchell, could be in prison.

No one who's Black, Brown or poor is safe. No one who speaks out against the Neutron Bomb is safe. It is not just brother Ben Chavis, it is us, it is us."

I⊤ is an axiom in defense work that the earlier one enters a case, the better the chances for victory. Best of all is to prevent arrests, but if arrests have already occurred the movement can work to block indictments. Next best is to get the charges dropped and avoid a trial, and after that, to win at the trial level. If a trial results in conviction, the best the defense can hope for at that stage is reduced or suspended sentences. But it is generally conceded that once tried, convicted, sentenced (especially to long terms), and serving time, a defendant's prospects are slim at best. Especially is this so if your name is Ben Chavis (or Ann Sheppard or Willie Earl Vereen or Jerry Jacobs or Reginald Epps or Connie Tindall or Marvin Patrick or Joe Wright or Wayne Moore or James McKoy) and the entire police and criminal justice apparatus of the federal and state governments is aligned against you, and your case is unknown outside of your home town, and the general assumption of those who know of the case (including some who are supposed to be your friends) is that you may well be guilty and the best you can hope for is mercy from some future governor or court some years down the road.

Such was the situation when the National Alliance was founded and first began to mount a movement. Now four years later, this case of poor, young, unknown civil rights workers, already convicted, imprisoned and given up as lost in the most repressive state in the country, had broken wide open. Massive pressure from throughout North Carolina and the United States and around the world had created a new atmosphere where false witnesses, once intimidated, now felt confident enough to recant; and true witnesses, once too frightened to testify, now came forward with the truth; where those who in earlier times opposed or averted the campaign now initiated actions of their own.

The first big break came while the Alliance was mounting the Labor Day march in 1976, when Allen Hall, the chief prosecution witness, in a sworn affidavit, recanted his trial testimony. Hall now said that he had himself set the fire at Mike's Grocery in 1971. Facing a forty-year sentence, Hall had agreed to prosecutor Jay Stroud's terms to falsely implicate Ben Chavis and the other defendants in exchange for a reduced sentence. He had been coached in his testimony by Stroud, U.S. Treasury agent William Walden, and District Attorney Allen W. Cobb. The flavor of the case can be tasted by selections from Hall's recantation:

HALL: And so then like they told me what to say in Court because I had gotten mad and I had said that for them to just give me a gun, that I would kill Chavis, you know. And so Stroud said, no, uh, you couldn't kill him because if you kill him they would investigate because he is in a civil rights movement and so then they said that the best way to get him is through by law. He said, because law has so many quirks and turns in it and so like, I went along with that. So like, then after they had told me how to make Molotov cocktails and they had showed me what dynamite was, you know, and blasting caps.

ATTORNEY JAMES FERGUSON: Did you know anything about Molotov cocktails and dynamite before they told you about them?

HALL: No, because I had never been involved in nothing like that before.

FERGUSON: You hadn't seen Chavis or any of the other people who were on trial making any Molotov cocktails or bring dynamite into the church or anything like that?

HALL: No.

FERGUSON: O.k., go ahead and tell us what else happened.

HALL: And, ah, then, like ah, Mr. Walden, Bill Walden, he said that here goes some dynamite and some blasting caps and he said it was electro-dynamite. He said that he had found this in the basement of the church. And ah, he asked me had I seen it and I said, no I hadn't seen no dynamite in the basement of no church. And so, like, he said, no, you don't say that there because you lookin at the dynamite now, right. I said, yeah. He said, well then, that's the dynamite that came out from under the church. You supposed to say that you saw the dynamite in the basement of the church. And so, I said, well o.k. then. . . .

FERGUSON: Where was Ben when Mike's Grocery was burned?

HALL: In Reverend Templeton's house because, like ah, to the best of my knowledge, Ben didn't know nothing about it because half of the time, like ah, whenever the gas was there, half of the time, you know, Ben didn't even know it because they kept it hid.

FERGUSON: O.k. So are you saying then that Ben didn't tell anybody to burn down Mike's Grocery Store?

HALL: No.

FERGUSON: And he wasn't out there when Mike's Grocery was being burned?

HALL: No, he wasn't out there when it was being burned. . . .

FERGUSON: Were you promised anything by any of the officers such as the Solicitor or police officers for testifying against the defendants at the trial?

HALL: I was promised by all of them that I wouldn't get much time, and that I would be out in six months if I didn't get into anything.

A court hearing some months later revealed that during the trial Hall was housed at a beach resort with his girlfriend, whom Solicitor Stroud had brought from Asheville, 300 miles away.

Also housed with Hall was Jerome Mitchell, the second main witness against the Wilmington 10. As far back as June 10, 1974, while the case was still on appeal in the state courts, Mitchell had written the parole board: ". . . Back in September 1972, I testified for the state in the Chavis case. Which I can no longer go on with myself about. Because of the fact that I committed perjure [sic] against every person in that case. . . . I don't care what anyone else do. But I feel I was wrong. I want to do all I can to get this right. I am praying they can be free or get a new trial. . . . Please as soon as possible let me hear from you. I have done wrong enough. Please let me have my chance to help free those I lied on. Thank you." For three years, Mitchell's letter was suppressed by the state. Then in March 1977, after Hall's recantation was made public, Mitchell also made a public statement. Facing unrelated first-degree murder charges and a possible death sentence at the time of the Wilmington 10 trial, Mitchell had agreed to offer false testimony against the defendants in exchange for a promise of a six-month sentence. (Mitchell was eventually convicted of second-degree murder but served less than four years of his 30-year sentence before being paroled to a $3-an-hour laborer's job. After his recantation, he was arrested again, charged with trying to pass off a $10 bill as a $100 bill.) Like Hall, he would be coached in his testimony by Solicitor Stroud, Treasury agent Walden, and Wilmington police officers:

After staying at Wrightsville Beach for approximately a week or two, Allen and I were moved to a beach house on Carolina Beach. I believe it was an eight-room house. A man named "Tex" came one night and talked to us for a long time. He said he was in the Ku Klux Klan and he knew a lot of people and if we needed protection or financial aid he would assist. Most of this had already been brought out by Stroud. We stayed at the cottage until the trial was over. [Tex Gross, Grand Cyclops of the Knights of the Ku Klux Klan in eastern North Carolina, owned the beach cottage in which the prosecution housed Mitchell and Hall. Author.]

After I testified Stroud said I did a good job and if he got a conviction he was going to throw a party. After the trial we had a party at the cottage. We grilled steaks and drank whisky. . . .

To learn the testimony I studied the material Jay Stroud give me daily for approximately a month. That's all we had to do during the week. As time went on I kept reminding Stroud about his promise and he kept assuring me he would have me out in six or seven months if I testified. . . .

During the trial of the Wilmington Ten almost all my testimony was false. I told the truth about my name and some of my past, but all the details I gave about Chavis and the other defendants was false. I was not there at the church those nights and I did not participate in the burning of Mike's Grocery nor do I personally know who did. I testified to these matters only because Jay

Stroud promised me that I would get out of prison in six or seven months if I did. Jay Stroud prepared the statements for me because I didn't know anything about the burning of Mike's Grocery. That was the only way I could learn the details. That is, I had to study what was given to me because I didn't know anything about it. I never saw any fire-bombs or anyone making them nor did I ever see any of the Wilmington Ten with guns.

I am giving this statement to be of all truths to the best of my knowledge and beliefs. It is the truth so help me God.

Hall's and Mitchell's recantations brought forth yet another from Eric Junious, the third and lone remaining state's witness against the Wilmington 10. At the time of trial, Junious was a thirteen-year-old juvenile who was confined to a training school for having committed armed robbery at the age of eleven. In a sworn, notarized statement in January 1977, Junious said that he too was coached by Stroud, given a set of photographs of the Wilmington 10 and a list of their names, and trained to match up the two. In exchange for his testimony, the youth was promised and given a minibike and a job in a gas station owned by Stroud's cousin.

By now Robert Morgan, who as attorney general had overseen the prosecution, had replaced Sam Ervin in the United States Senate, where he joined the Intelligence Oversight Committee, a move not calculated to make human-rights advocates feel too comfy when the doorbell rings. If politics makes strange bedfellows, think of the possibilities of swapping: replacing Morgan as attorney general was Rufus Edmisten, Ervin's chief aide during the Watergate hearings. Apparently the buck stopped there, on the Potomac, for Edmisten, who now became chief defender of the Wilmington 10 prosecution and conviction, even after the recantations.

Nor were the recantations all the authorities had to squirm about. Now it was revealed that North Carolina's Good Neighbor Council, which had been responsible for inviting Ben to Wilmington and worked hand in glove with him there, had acted in collusion with the prosecution during the trial. In late 1976 Good Neighbor Council members and staff revealed that the council had resisted efforts by the defense, including subpoenas, to produce at the trial documents and records that indicated the innocence of Ben and his co-defendants. One council field worker said: "We were concerned about maintaining a low profile. We were very aware that our appropriations came from the General Assembly." So they dodged the subpoenas, pretty much sealing the fate of the Wilmington 10. The Rev. Aaron Johnson, a council member, now told the press in November 1976 that those records, so "highly favorable" to the defendants, had been stolen from the council office in Raleigh.

By 1977 Rev. Eugene Templeton and his wife, Donna, who had fled the Gregory Congregational Church and North Carolina in fear for their lives, felt strong enough to return to North Carolina to give the testimony they were afraid to give at the trial five years earlier. Now they told a Superior Court hearing that Ben, Marvin Patrick, Connie Tindall and James McKoy were with them inside their home in Wilmington at the time of the fire at Mike's Grocery. Others came forward to say that Wayne Moore was babysitting at the time of the fire, that Joe Wright was visiting relatives.

Moreover Reverend Templeton would now defend Ben's presence and activities in Wilmington to the press. Ben united the community, parents and students, said Rev. Templeton. "Chavis was a catalyst. It was the first time I saw that kind of interest on the part of the Black parents. He was able to generate genuine interest, genuine concern in their situation within the Wilmington community. For the very first time I saw enthusiasm and hope in those people. They believed they could really get things improved. I thought this was a very positive thing, and I told the deacons that. Never did I hear any talk of violence from Ben Chavis or anyone else."

With the only three witnesses against the Wilmingtoin 10 recanting, and defense witnesses coming forward to say that the defendants were in their homes at the time of the alleged crime, even one of the original jurors of the 1972 trial, Gretchen Simmons, could tell the press in 1977, "It's obvious, isn't it, that the case is completely blown." Still the state was unrelenting. At a post-conviction hearing in May 1977, forced upon the authorities by a determined outcry of public opinion, Superior Court Judge George Fountain listened to two weeks of testimony, including the recantations of Hall, Mitchell and Junious, and then took all of five minutes to rule against a new trial in a decision *The New York Times* called "breath-taking." Subsequent evidence showed that Judge Fountain's later 37-page written opinion was actually produced word for word by the state attorney general's office in violation of federal statutes.

That violation, together with the recantations and other new evidence produced since the 1972 conviction, plus the original defense papers alleging more than 2,500 trial errors, formed the basis of several appeals which sat in Federal District Court for more than two years while the Wilmington 10 sat in some of the worst prisons in the country. As the courts, acting in tandem with the executive offices in Raleigh and Washington refused to budge, the defense's best guess was that they were fearful to acknowledge that there had been a frame-up, and later a cover-up, in which some of the most trusted and highly placed state and federal officials participated. Careers were on the line for these conspirators from on high.

The stubbornness of the North Carolina authorities in refusing to confess error and wrongdoing again became apparent in January 1978 after the state appellate court refused to reverse Judge Fountain's decision in the post-conviction hearing. Governor James B. Hunt, under tremendous pressure as a result of the recantations and the mobilization of public opinion, had refused to deal with defense appeals for pardons of innocence for the defendants while the case was still in state court. Now with the appellate court decision, the legal appeals were entirely in the hands of the Federal District Court. Governor Hunt announced that he would make a statewide television address to announce his decision on the question of pardons, a decision which "would end this matter for all time" and "put this case behind us." Skeptics believed that he would not grant pardons—pressures from the Right and from powerful forces like Senator Robert Morgan would not allow that—but that he would commute the sentences to "time served," thereby releasing the defendants from prison and defusing the mass movement. Instead, using harsh prosecutorial language, Hunt told the state and the country that he believed the defendants were guilty and the prosecutors and the courts were honorable; that the sentences on one count were not consistent with his concept of the law, so he would reduce the sentences of the Wilmington 10 from a maximum of 282 years to 221 years. Predictably, what had been a storm of protest before Hunt spoke became a monsoon. Nearly three dozen daily newspapers complained in bitter editorials about the governor's "Monday Night Massacre." Most, like the Kansas City *Star* and the Cleveland *Plain Dealer,* were heard from for the first time. With North Carolina's abdication, all pressure now would be on the White House.

While President Carter offered his State of the Union Address in January 1978, the Wilmington 10 remained in prison. Jim Grant, T.J. Reddy and Charles Parker—the Charlotte Three—had just lost their appeal to the Fourth U.S. Circuit Court of Appeals. Al Hood and David Washington, whose testimony sent Jim and the Three to prison, remained on the streets to pursue their lives of crimes. Allen Hall, Jerome Mitchell and Eric Junious were back in prison, charged with various offenses. Treasury agents Stanley Noel and William Walden continued to work their wares in North Carolina. Their former boss, John Connolly, had been acquitted on corruption charges a couple years earlier. Richard Nixon, under whom the prosecution of the defendants began, had been pardoned of all his crimes. John Mitchell was free on a medical furlough from a sentence of 3–8 years for his Watergate crimes. His assistant, Robert Mardian, had his conviction reversed in the same Watergate conspiracy. Solicitor Jay Stroud, prosecutor of the Wilmington 10 and Wilmington Three, was named U.S. attorney for eastern North Carolina, in one of Richard Nixon's final acts in office, and later became prosecutor in Gastonia. Robert Martin, the trial judge, now sits on the North Carolina Court of Appeals. Robert Morgan remains a U.S. senator.

"Meanwhile," said Congressman Ronald V. Dellums in a speech to the House of Representatives while the U.S. Supreme Court was still considering the petition of the Wilmington 10, "the Reverend Chavis is a courageous man, as he has shown through scores of arrests and attempts on his life . . . The authorities will try to break him and he will not break. The consequences of prison resistance are well known to anyone with eyes to read the daily newspapers. . . . I think it is important for Congress and for the people of our country to understand that, in these days of investigation into the misdeeds of the intelligence community, real lives are at stake. The provocations against and persecution of the Reverend Benjamin Chavis and the Wilmington 10 by federal and local agencies were not 'simulated' attacks; they were not assassination plots that went awry or were called off at the last minute. Rather, they were calculated attempts against the civil rights movement of North Carolina, with consequences for the whole United States. To our shame they were attempts that have so far succeeded. They can only be blunted by an alert bar of public opinion and a Supreme Court intent on upholding justice in our land."

The struggle continues.

Notes

Introduction
1. Barbara Howar. *Laughing All the Way*, Fawcett World, Greenwich, Conn., 1974, p. 29.
2. See Joy Lamm, "So You Want a Land Use Bill?"; and James Branscome and Peggy Matthews, "Selling the Mountains," *Southern Exposure*, Fall 1974.
3. Author's interviews with John Coit, April 29, 1974, and David Flaherty, April 17, 1974.
4. North Carolina Department of Natural and Economic Resources, *North Carolina Historyland*, Raleigh, 1974, p. 19.
5. *The New York Times*, May 25, 1974.
6. North Carolina H.B. 1395, Chapter 1207, 1963. The bill was amended into extinction in 1965.
7. Author's interview, June 10, 1974.
8. Bergen County, N.J. *Record*, January 22, 1975.
9. Raleigh *News and Observer*, February 20, 27, 1974.
10. *The New York Times*, November 17, 1974.

One
1. V.O. Key, *Southern Politics*, Peter Smith, New York, 1949, p. 5.
2. Herbert Aptheker, *The American Revolution, 1763-1783*, International Publishers, New York, 1960, p. 220.
3. Herbert Aptheker, *American Negro Slave Revolts*, International Publishers, New York, 1943, pp. 231-32.
4. Ibid., pp. 243-44.
5. Herbert Aptheker, *To Be Free*, International Publishers, New York, 1948, pp. 18-19.
6. See Herbert Aptheker's *One Continual Cry*, American Institute for Marxist Studies, New York, 1965, particularly pp. 47-49.
7. Quoted in ibid., p. 12.
8. *To Be Free*, op. cit., pp. 144-45.
9. See James S. Allen, *Reconstruction: The Battle for Democracy, 1865-1876*, International Publishers, New York, 1963, pp. 74-75.
10. Quoted in Herbert Aptheker, *Afro-American History: The Modern Era*, Citadel Press, New York, 1971, p. 20.
11. See Allen W. Trelease, *White Terror: The Ku Klux Klan Conspiracy and Southern Reconstruction*, edited by Kenneth B. Clark, Harper & Row, New York, 1971, pp. 189-225, 336-348; and Richard L. Zuber, *North Carolina During Reconstruction*, North Carolina Archives, Raleigh, 1969.
12. Helen G. Edmonds, *The Negro and Fusion Politics in North Carolina, 1894-1901*, Russell (1973 reprint of 1951 ed.), p. 210.

13. C. Vann Woodward, *Origins of the New South, 1877–1913*, Louisiana State University Press, Baton Rouge, 1971, p. 195.
14. *The New York Times*, December 16, 1914, quoted in Edmonds, op. cit., p. 143.
15. William L. Patterson, ed., *We Charge Genocide*, International Publishers, New York, 1970.
16. In *Barriers to Black Political Participation in North Carolina*, Southern Voter Educational Project, Atlanta, 1972, the author William A. Towe gives the following dramatic figures: Of some 10,000 elected to fill all offices in North Carolina in 1970, only 10 were Black. In 1971, 63 of more than 2,000 mayors and councilmen and only 82 of 4,000 elected state and local officials were Black—a mere two percent. By 1976, there was not one Black mayor in North Carolina; only three Blacks sat in the 170-member General Assembly; a half-dozen were among the 468 county commissioners; and less than 20 occupied the more than 600 school board posts.
    Towe also points up the fact that the Voting Rights Act of 1965 had less effect in North Carolina on Black registration than in most southern states. By 1970, North Carolina was at the bottom of the ladder in southern Black voter registration.
17. Much of this material was gathered in interviews conducted by the author in the Spring of 1974. Those interviewed include then Lieutenant Governor James B. Hunt, February 20; then Attorney General Robert Morgan, February 22; Republican state senate leader Charles Taylor, February 28: Judges I. Beverly Lake, Joseph Branch and Dan K. Moore, April 17; then Chapel Hill Mayor Howard Lee, April 18; the late Governor Luther Hodges, April 19; former Governor Robert Scott, April 29; former Governor Terry Sanford, May 15; then Raleigh Mayor Clarence Lightner, May 20; U.S. Senator Jesse Helms, June 20.
18. "The Man North Carolina Needs for Governor," 1960 Lake campaign brochure.
19. *The News and Observer*, June 26, 1964.
20. Key, op. cit., pp. 208–09.
21. Quoted in ibid.
22. Interview with Frank Porter Graham by Charles Jones, Anne Queen and Stewart Wills, Chapel Hill, June 9, 1961, Southern Oral History Program, University of North Carolina.
23. Unpublished conversation with Jonathan Daniels and Mrs. Kerr Scott, Chapel Hill, June 10, 1962, Southern Oral History Program, UNC.
24. Samuel Lubell, *The Future of American Politics*, Harper & Row, New York, 1965, pp. 106–13.
25. Stephen Klutzman, *Sam J. Ervin, Jr.*, Grossman Publishers, Washington, D.C., 1972, p. 2.
26. Paul R. Clancy, *Just a Country Lawyer: A Biography of Senator Sam Ervin*, Indiana University Press, Bloomington, 1974, p. 152.
27. "The Watergate Committee Chairman's New Clothes," *Southern Voice*, March-April 1974, p. 8.
28. Klutzman, op. cit.
29. Los Angeles *Times*, March 17, 1974.
30. Broyhill's political career is charted in his official biography by a son-in-law, William Stevens, *Anvil of Adversity: Biography of a Furniture Pioneer*, Grosset & Dunlap, New York, 1968, pp. 116–32.
31. *The New York Times*, February 17, 1974.
32. "The New American Majority," a speech to the Dean Clarence Manion Testimonial Dinner, May 15, 1974.
33. Speech to Daughters of the American Revolution, April 16, 1974, as excerpted in *The News and Observer*, April 28, 1974.
34. Author's interview, May 21, 1974.
35. William H. Towe, op. cit.

Two

1. Luther Hodges, *Businessman in the Statehouse,* University of North Carolina Press, Chapel Hill, 1962.
2. Ibid., p. 83.
3. Ibid.
4. Ibid., pp. 84-100.
5. Raleigh *Times,* February 19, 1974.
   Years after the busing controversy died down in North Carolina, school desegregation remained a major issue. Under orders from the U.S. Department of Health, Education and Welfare to desegregate the University of North Carolina system by increasing Black enrollment at its predominantly white institutions by 150 percent, the University's Board of Governors proposed instead a plan that called for only a 32 percent increase. A Black member of the board resigned over the plan, a second Black member cast the lone dissenting vote against it, and a third abstained from the voting. HEW later rejected the university's proposal which had the support of Governor James B. Hunt, according to *The New York Times,* August 23, 1977.
6. Quoted by Ferrel Guilory, "Southern Republicans: Not That They Hate Watergate Less But They Love the Southern Strategy More," *Southern Voices,* loc. cit., p. 13.
7. Hodges, op. cit., Chapter 10.
8. Ibid., p. 239.
9. Boyd E. Payton, *Scapegoat—Prejudice, Politics, Prison,* Whitmore, Philadelphia, 1970, p. 31.
10. Ibid., pp. 51-52.
11. Ibid., p. 82.
12. Ibid., pp. 273-75.
13. Paul M. Gaston, *The New South Creed: A Study in Southern Mythmaking,* Louisiana State University Press, Baton Rouge, 1973, p. 17.
14. "The Development of Textiles, Tobacco, Furniture Industries in North Carolina," a paper issued by Burlington Industries, Inc., circa 1974.
15. *The American Tobacco Story,* American Tobacco Co., Durham, 1964. See also John Wilbur Jenkins, *James B. Duke, Master Builder,* Reprint Co., South Carolina, 1971.
16. Quoted in Woodward, op. cit., p. 130.
17. Ibid., p. 137.
18. Quoted in ibid., p. 307.
19. Ibid., p. 422.
20. Aptheker, *Afro-American History: The Modern Era,* loc. cit., p. 351.
21. Quoted in ibid., p. 20.
22. W.J. Cash, *The Mind of the South,* Random House, New York, 1941, p. 173.
23. Ibid., pp. 125-26.
24. W. McKee Evans, *To Die Game: The Story of the Lowry Band, Indian Guerrillas of Reconstruction,* Louisiana State University Press, Baton Rouge, 1971, pp. 3-4. See also Evans' work, *Ballots and Fence Rails: Reconstruction on the Lower Cape Fear,* University of North Carolina Press, Chapel Hill, 1967.
25. For the most complete study of the period, see Edmonds, op. cit.
26. Ibid., p. 10.
27. Ibid., p. 137.
28. Jack Riley, *Carolina Power & Light Company, 1908-1958,* Carolina Power & Light Company, Raleigh, 1958, pp. 276-78.
29. Woodward, op. cit., p. 330.
30. Edmonds, op. cit., chapters 6-9.
31. Ibid., p. 138.
32. Ibid., pp. 143-44.
33. Woodward, op. cit., p. 350.
34. Quoted in Edmonds, op. cit., p. 145.

35. November 17, 1898, quoted in ibid., pp. 151, 153.
36. Quoted in ibid., p. 165.
37. Ibid., p. 168.
38. Quoted in Herbert Aptheker, ed., *Documentary History of the Negro People in the United States,* Vol. 2, Citadel, New York, 1968, pp. 813-15.
39. Interview with John Coit, op. cit.
40. Author's interview with General John Tolson, state Secretary of Military and Veterans' Affairs, April 29, 1974.
41. Figures for military personnel and expenditures are available from the public information offices at Fort Bragg and Camp Lejeune. See also "Southern Militarism," *Southern Exposure,* Spring 1973, p. 82.
42. Letter released by Camp Lejeune public information office, Spring 1974.
43. *Camp Lejeune 74,* BP Industries, Midland, Texas, 1973, p. 56.
44. Author's interview with Major Harold Owens, public relations officer, Camp Lejeune, February 23, 1974.
45. Ibid.
46. *Fort Bragg: Ready to Serve the Nation,* BP Industries, Midland, Texas, 1973, p. 11.
47. Ibid.
48. *Helping Hands 72,* BP Industries, Fort Bragg, 1973, p. 26. All references on Domestic Action programs, unless otherwise noted, are from this annual report.
49. Interview, op. cit. Unless otherwise indicated, the following paragraphs are based on this conversation and official materials released by the DMVA.
50. Authors interview with District Judge John Walker, February 22, 1974.
51. Raleigh *Times,* August 26, 1975. See also *Counterspy* magazine, Winter 1976, pp. 45-59.

Three

1. Reprinted as "Attorney for the Defense," *Esquire,* October 1973, pp. 224-27.
2. *The New York Times,* November 6, 1973.
3. *The New York Times,* November 30, 1973.
4. *The New York Times,* October 15, 1973.
5. *Daily World,* June 8, 1974.
6. *The New York Times,* July 20, 1974.
7. Ibid.
8. *The New York Times,* July 13, 1974.
9. Quoted by Jessica Mitford, *Kind and Usual Punishment,* Random House, New York, 1974, p. 51.
10. Interview with the author, May 21, 1974.
11. James Baldwin. "Fifth Ave., Uptown," *Esquire,* October 1973.
12. "Charlotte Report," North Carolina Criminal Justice Task Force hearings, July 28-29, 1972, p. 5.
13. Payton, op. cit., p. 305.
14. "Raleigh Report," North Carolina Criminal Justice Task Force hearings, September 9, 1972, pp. 3-4.
15. "Charlotte Report," loc. cit.
16. Author's interview with N.C. Highway Patrol Commander Colonel Edward Jones, February 28, 1974.
17. *The New York Times,* December 10, 1974.
18. Interview, op. cit.
19. Charlotte *Observer,* March 11, 1976.
20. Raleigh *Times,* April 16, 1976.
21. Interview, April 16, 1976.
22. Richmond, Va., *Times-Dispatch,* February 2, 1974.
23. Speech by Dunn to Brotherhood of Winterville, N.C. Baptist Church, April 10, 1974.

24. Interview, op. cit.
25. *The News and Observer,* May 12, 1976.
26. See David M. Rorvick, "Bringing the War Home," *Playboy,* February 1974.
27. LEAA Fifth Annual Report, Fiscal Year 1973, Washington, D.C., 1973.
28. Information and quotations regarding the Durham police are from Mark Pinsky, "State of Siege, City of Siege," *WIN,* June 19, 1975.
29. According to James Donovan, public relations spokesman for the American Textile Manufacturers Institute, in 1974 there were 1,023,000 textile workers in the country, 293,000 in North Carolina. Interview with the author, April 23, 1975.
30. "The Textile Industry and Burlington's Position In It," mimeographed paper issued in 1974 by Burlington Industries, Inc., Greensboro.
31. *North Carolina Report: An Objective Study of a Southern State,* First Union National Bank of North Carolina, Charlotte, revised edition 1974, pp. 38, 40, 42, 55-56.
32. Author's interview with Dick Byrd, assistant director of public relations and community relations for Burlington Industries, April 22, 1974.
33. "Giant Burlington Faces Trying Time for Textiles," *Business Week,* March 2, 1974.
34. Author's interview with Leo Rossi, J.P. Stevens public relations official, June 10, 1974.
35. "Cannon," a brochure issued by Cannon Mills in 1974. Also, author's interview with Cannon Mills vice-president Edward L. Rankin, Jr., April 25, 1974.
36. Cash, op. cit., p. 222.
37. Mary Frances Barnes, "The Richest Man Who Ever Lived in Charlotte," *Charlotte,* February 1974.
38. Raleigh *Times,* February 28, 1974; Charlotte *Observer,* March 11, 1976.
39. United Mine Workers of America advertisement, *The New York Times,* July 17, 1974.
40. Transcript of testimony, N.C. Utilities Commission, Docket E-7, Sub. 159, Vol. 7, p. 112. See the brochure, "Duke Power: the un-friendly, un-neighborly power company!!" by the N.C. Public Interest Research Group, Durham, 1974.
41. "Duke Power," op. cit.
42. *The New York Times,* May 5, 1974.
43. For a complete examination of this interlocking corporate control, see *Southern Exposure,* Summer-Fall, 1973; and 1973 annual reports for Wachovia Bank, NCNB, Duke Power, C & L, Burlington Industries, J.P. Stevens Co., R.J. Reynolds Co.
44. Interview with author, April 25, 1975.
45. Key, op. cit., p. 211.
46. Barnes, loc. cit. See also "A Troublesome Legacy: James B. Duke's Bequest to His Cousins," *The North Carolina Historical Review,* October 1973, pp. 394–415.
47. "Public Relations Pointers," published by the American Textiles Manufacturers Institute, Charlotte, January 1974.
48. "Back to the Good Old Ways," special edition of *Duke Power Magazine,* 1974, p. 5.

Four

1. Figures released by the North Carolina Board of Conservation and Development.
2. Figures cited in interview with author by William Coley, industrial developer for Carolina Power & Light Co., May 21, 1974.
3. *North Carolina Statewide Development Policy,* North Carolina Department of Administration, Raleigh, March 1972, pp. 3-45.
4. Author's interview with Creed Gilley, April 24, 1974.
5. Interview with author May 1, 1974.
6. "Report on Existing Area Survey," Carolina Power & Light Co., April 1974.
7. Author's interview with William Coley, May 24, 1974.
8. Interview with author, April 19, 1974.

9. Interview with author, May 16, 1974.
10. "Report on Existing Area Survey," op. cit.
11. Op. cit.
12. See Kenyon Bertel Segner III, *A History of the Community College Movement in North Carolina,* 1927-1963, James Sprunt Press, Kenansville, N.C., 1974, p. v.
13. *North Carolina Community College System, Biennial Report 1970-1971,* North Carolina State Board of Education, Raleigh, p. 51.
14. *North Carolina Community College System Report 1963-70,* North Carolina State Board of Education, Raleigh, p. 87.
15. Terry Sanford, *But What About the People?,* Harper & Row, New York, 1966, p. 107.
16. Interview with the author, May 21, 1975.
17. "Glad You Asked That," distributed by the North Carolina Board of Education in 1974.
18. Ibid.
19. *North Carolina Report,* op. cit., pp. 22–28.
20. Emil Malizia, et. al., *Earnings Gap in North Carolina,* North Carolina State AFL-CIO, Raleigh, June 1975.
21. "North Carolina and the Southeast: A Bird's Eye Perspective and a Future Look," published by the Wachovia Bank and Trust Co., Winston-Salem, 1973, p. 5.
22. *General Social and Economic Characteristics, 1970 Census, North Carolina,* Washington D. C., 1972. (Hereafter, *1970 Census, N. C.*)
23. "Economic Outlook for North Carolina in the 1970s," a speech by Wachovia vice-president M.N. Hennessee, 1973, p. 6.
24. Ibid., p. 8.
25. Statistics quoted by Sol Stetin, then general president of the Textile Workers Union of America, *Daily World,* June 17, 1975.
26. *North Carolina State Government Statisical Abstract,* second edition, Raleigh, 1973. p. 209 (Hereafter referred to as *Statistical Abstract.*)
27. Ibid, p. 220.
28. Klutzman, op. cit., p. 5.
29. The North Carolina Fund, *Annual Review 1966,* Durham, 1967, p. B-14.
30. Ibid., pp. A-1, B-11.
   The following excerpted story from a North Carolina Fund article, "Domestics United: An Exercise in Free Enterpirse," indicates the Fund's approach to eradicating poverty: "When Domestics United first appeared, there were no smiles from the white housewives of Charlotte. They feared a maid's 'union' that would make militant demands without offering high quality services in return. Things have worked out differently. Higher wages and more benefits are indeed the goals of Domestics United, but better service rather than militant action is to be the means of getting there. For those who can profit by training and show their dependability, higher wages appear to be assured. Says Mrs. Adams [Wilhelmina Adams, president], 'We have people who promise to pay $1.40 an hour for a maid who has had real training in domestic skills.'" (*Blue Print for Opportunity,* The North Carolina Fund, Volume 3, Number 3, November 1967, p. 8.)
31. Michael P. Brooks, *The Dimensions of Poverty in North Carolina,* The North Carolina Fund, Durham, June 1964, pp. 3-4.
32. *North Carolina's Present and Future Poor,* The North Carolina Fund, Durham, 1966, p. 45.
33. *1970 Census, N.C.,* op. cit.
34. Ibid.
35. *Annual Review 1966,* op. cit., p. B-11.
36. James Baldwin, op. cit.
37. *Annual Review, 1966,* op. cit., p. B-14.
38. Jim Burns, "Dimensions of Poverty in North Carolina," *People,* published by State Department of Human Resources, Summer 1973.

39. Klutzman, op. cit., p. 6.
40. Raleigh *Times*, April 27, 1974.
41. *Statistical Abstract*, op. cit., p. 310.
42. Ibid., pp. 296-97.
43. Statistics and standards stated in interviews with June Stallings and with Dr. Rene Wescott, director of social services division, N.C. Department of Human Resources, February 28, 1974.
44. *Statistical Abstract*, op. cit., pp. 80-86.
45. *Adult Services in North Carolina*, special report number 16 of N.C. Department of Human Resources, February 1973, p. 4.
46. *Public Assistance Trends in North Carolina*, special report number 19, N.C. Department of Human Resources, August 1973, p. 33.
47. *North Carolina Local Health Department Budgetary, Economic and Other Pertinent Data, Fiscal Year 1972-1973*, January 1973, p. 7.
48. Author's interview with Dr. Jacob Kumen, Director, N.C. Health Department, February 27, 1974.
49. *Communicable Disease Morbidity Statistics, 1972*, N.C. Department of Human Resources Division of Health Services, Raleigh, 1973, pp. 2-3, 2-2.
50. *Statistical Abstract*, op. cit., p. 59.
51. *North Carolina Nutritional Survey, Part One*, Raleigh, 1974.
52. Klutzman, op. cit., p. 6.
53. Wesley George, "The Biology of the Race Problem," prepared by Commission of the Governor of Alabama, 1962.
54. Ibid., p. 18.
55. Ibid., pp. 22-23.
56. Ibid., p. 18.
57. *Psychology Today*, September 1972.
58. "Eugenical Sterilization in North Carolina," a pamphlet by R. Eugene Brown, Eugenics Board Secretary, issued by the Board, 1938, p. 3.
59. Ibid., p. 5.
60. Ibid., p. 9.
61. Published by the N.C. Eugenics Board, May 1948.
62. Ibid., p. 6.
63. Biannual Reports, 1954-1968, N.C. Eugenics Board.
64. Interview with author, February 28, 1975.
65. See Herbert Aptheker, "Racism and Human Experimentation," *Political Affairs*, January and February 1974, for a Marxist refutation of the ideological tenets of "eugenics."
66. Ibid.
67. *The New York Times*, March 13, 1975.
68. New York *Post*, April 10, 1974.
69. *The New York Times*, February 8, 1974.
70. New York, 1972, p. 2.
71. Quoted by Joseph Reynolds, "Behavior Modification: Psycho-Fascism in Disguise," *Political Affairs*, May 1974.
72. New York *Post*, March 18, 1972.
73. *Psychology Today*, April 1970.
74. *The New York Times*, February 15, 1974.
75. Testimony before House Committee on Government Operations, "Hearings on Federal Involvement in the Use of Behavior Modification Drugs on Grammar School Children," 91st Congress, Second session.

Five

1. Charlotte *Observer*, July 3, 1975; and the *Daily World*, August 29, 1975.

2. *Statistical Abstract*, op. cit., p. 360.
3. Ibid., p. 355.
4. Author's interview with David Jones, Secretary of the N.C. Department of Social Rehabilitation, February 27, 1974.
5. The figure and quotations are from David Jones, *A New Direction on Correction: Long-range Construction and Conversion Plan, 1974–1983,* North Carolina Department of Corrections, Raleigh, 1974, pp. 1, 3.
6. See Jesse F. Steiner and Roy M. Brown, *The North Carolina Chain Gang,* Patterson Smith, Chapel Hill, 1927, Chapter 2.
7. Ibid., pp. 12–13.
8. Ibid., p. 14.
9. Ibid., p. 15.
10. Ibid., p. 19.
11. Ibid., p. 24.
12. Ibid., p. 6.
13. Hodges, op. cit., pp. 140–44.
14. "North Carolina and the Southeast," op. cit., Appendix A.
15. Mitford, op. cit., p. 228.
16. See Steve Carlson, "Rehabilitation or Super Exploitation?," *World Magazine,* August 17, 1974.
17. Steve Carlson, "Super-Exploitation in the Prisons," *World Magazine,* August 10, 1974.
18. 1975 brochure issued by the State of North Carolina.
19. *Statistical Abstract*, op. cit., p. 357.
20. Author's interview with Ralph Edwards, N.C. Commissioner of Correction, February 28, 1974.
21. Ibid.
22. Ibid.
23. Jones, op. cit., p. 1.
24. *The News and Observer,* February 21, 1974.
25. As quoted in Mason P. Thomas, Jr., *Juvenile Corrections and Juvenile Jurisdiction,* Institute of Government, Chapel Hill, 1972, p. 4.
26. See *Tomorrow in Youth Development* by the N.C. Department of Social Rehabilitation, 1973, p. 7.
27. Ibid., p. 2.
28. Interview with the author, April 19, 1974.
29. Thomas, op. cit., p. 2.
30. Ibid., p. 3.
31. Ibid., p. 5.
32. Interview with Mason Thomas, op. cit.
33. Thomas, op. cit., p. 7.
In November 1973, 17-year-old Allan Foy wrote home from his cell in maximum-security Central Prison: "Mom and Dad, can I please come home? . . . I can't stand being locked up anymore and it won't be long until Christmas and it would not be pleasant at all to be here. I have been locked up so many Christmas days it's unforgetable. I just can't stand it any longer." Two days after Christmas, Allan Foy was dead, killed by a 4,300-volt electrical barrier, while trying to escape from Central. Allan Foy was serving a year-and-a-quarter on a misdemeanor charge of malicious damage, for having broken a window in his father's store. He was sent to prison "because everybody the judge, the police chief, his father and even Allan himself believed it was the only place he could get help for his mental problems . . . "At a pretrial meeting with his father, the chief and court-appointed attorney Earl Collins, Allan agreed to plead guilty with the understanding that he receive psychiatric help. 'The offenses didn't amount to a hill of beans—certainly not enough to give the boy an

active sentence,' Collins said. 'But we felt this was the only way to make sure he got help.' Collins said he considered having the boy committed to a state mental hospital by judicial order but 'he simply wasn't insane enough. He was a boy trying to find himself.'"(Charlotte *Observer*, January 13, 1974.)

34. Mason P. Thomas, Jr., *A Summary of Legislation Affecting Juvenile Corrections by the 1973 General Assembly*, Institute of Government, Chapel Hill, 1974, p. 4.
35. Ibid., pp. 6–7.
36. *As the Twig is Bent: A Report on the North Carolina Juvenile Corrections System*, prepared by the North Carolina Bar Association's Penal System Study Committee, Raleigh, 1972, p. 18.
37. Author's interview, op. cit.
38   *The News and Observer*, August 4, 1975.
39. The prosecution's use of hoods like Mitchell and Hall in the Wilmington 10 and Hood and Washington in the Charlotte Three and Chavis-Grant trials, had its precedents in the frame-ups of labor leaders from Gastonia to Henderson, in the decades-long attempt by the companies and the state to break the working-class movement. Boyd Payton, a leader of the Henderson strike in 1959, writes in *Scapegoat*, his memoir of the strike, his trial and his years in prison, of Harold Aaron, the petty crook who became a "hero" as the key witness against the union leaders. Payton quotes from a local news story of the time:
"'The bravest man I know.'
"This was the tribute prosecutor Robert Hight had for Harold Aaron more than a year ago.
"True, Aaron's testimony had just sent Boyd Payton and seven other union men to the penitentiary in the Henderson dynamite conspiracy trial.
"But it was a peculiar tribute, just the same. The only thing Aaron had heard from prosecutors for most of his adult life had been ugly charges of his guilt on charges of assault, assault with deadly weapons, drunkenness, reckless driving, theft, larceny of an auto, impersonation of an officer, etc.
"But this time Aaron, as a paid informer of the State Bureau of Investigation and with at least $1,100 [inflation has boosted the cost of informers, as it has gasoline and lamb chops, in the ensuing years – M.M.] of taxpayer funds in his jeans, was to bask in the role of Hero for the State." (p. 274.)
40. Cash, op. cit., p. 247.
41. Quoted in George B. Tindall, *The Emergence of the New South, 1913-1945*, Louisiana State University Press, Baton Rouge, 1967, p. 345. See also pp. 75, 318–77.
42. Broadus Mitchell, "Fleshpots in the South," *Virginia Quarterly Review*, III, 1927, p. 169.
43. Harry M. Douty, "The North Carolina Industrial Worker, 1880–1930," University of North Carolina Ph.D. thesis, 1936, p. 343.
44. See Tom Tippett, *When Southern Labor Stirs*, Jonathan Cape and Harrison Smith, New York, 1931.
45. "The Story of Gastonia," flyer issued by the International Labor Defense, New York, 1929.
46. See Samuel Yellen, *American Labor Struggles, 1877-1934*, Monad Press, New York, 1974, pp. 308–15.
47. Quoted in ibid., p. 310.
48. *The Nation*, September 25, 1929.
49. Liston Pope, *Millhands and Preachers*, Yale University Press, New Haven, 1965, p. 294.
50. Irving Bernstein, *The Lean Years*, Houghton Mifflin Co, Baltimore, 1966, p. 27.
51. Werner Jones, "Southern Labor and the Law," *The Nation*, July 2, 1930, as quoted in Pope, op. cit., p. 295.
52. *The Nation*, September 25, 1929.

53. Cash, op. cit., pp. 303–04.
54. Sinclair Lewis, *Cheap and Contented Labor*, pamphlet reprinted and distributed by the Asheville Area Central Labor Union, no date, p. 18.
55. Yellen, op. cit., pp. 316–21; also Pope, op. cit., p. 349.
56. Ibid., p. 321.
57. Tindall, op. cit., p. 523.
58. Ibid., pp. 526–27.
59. Ibid., pp. 572–73, 512.
60. Art Shields, "The Reynolds Strike of 1947," *World Magazine*, June 4, 1977.
61. Patterson, op. cit., p. 85.
62. Most of this account is taken from George Morris' column, "World of Labor," *Daily World*, July 13, 1974.
63. Author's interview with Wilbur Hobby, president of the N.C. AFL-CIO and a former tobacco worker, April 18, 1974.
64. Interview with author, April 23, 1974.
65. Herbert R. Northrup, "The Negro in the Tobacco Industry," in *Negro Employment in Southern Industry*, by H.R. Northrup and Richard Rowan, University of Pennsylvania Press, Philadelphia, 1970, Study 49.
66. Interview with author, April 25, 1974.
67. See Nina Bogomolova, *"Human Relations" Doctrine: Ideological Weapon of the Monopolies*, Progress Publishers, Moscow, 1973.
68. Ibid., p. 20.
69. Quoted in ibid., p. 60.
70. Robert Dubin, *The World of Work*, Prentice-Hall, New York, 1958, p. 245, as quoted in ibid., p. 91.
71. Ibid., p. 112.
72. Peter Drucker, *The New Society, the Anatomy of Industrial Order*, Harper & Row, New York, 1962, p. 283, quoted in ibid., p. 93.
73. News release issued by American Textile Manufacturers Institute, Charlotte, February 21, 1974.
74. Interview with author, May 16, 1974.
75. Pope, op. cit., p. 298.
76. Ibid., p. 292.
77. Ibid., pp. 30–31.
78. Baltimore *Evening Sun*, May 13, 1929, quoted in ibid., p. 282.
79. Author's interview with Professor Daniel Pollitt, April 21, 1974.
80. Author's interview with Duke Endowment spokesman Robert J. Salstead, April 25, 1974.
81. Author's interview with R.J. Reynolds vice-president Charles Wade, April 23, 1974.
82. Letter to constituents sent out on the letterhead of the "Americans Against Union Control of Government," undated 1975.
83. See Kenneth M. Jarin, *Earl B. Ruth*, Washington, D.C., 1972, pp. 2–3.
84. North Carolina Public Interest Research Group, *Caution: North Carolina OSHA May Be Hazardous to Your Health*, Durham, 1976.
85. Quoted in *The Guardian*, October 16, 1974.
86. *Action*, Durham, April-May 1974.
87. Henry P. Leiferman, *Crystal Lee: A Woman of Inheritance*, MacMillan, New York, 1975, pp. 46–49.
88. *The New York Times*, May 25, 1976.
89. Ed McConville, "How 7,041 Got Fired," *The Nation*, October 25, 1975.
90. *The New York Times*, September 1, 1977.
91. *The New York Times*, December 29, 1977.
92. McConville, op. cit.
93. Richard L. Rowan, "The Negro in the Textile Industry," Northrup and Rowan, op. cit.

94. *The New York Times,* June 30, 1976.
95. *New American Movement,* November 1974.
96. Interview with author, April 18, 1974.
97. Interview with author, May 16, 1974.

Afterword

1. Helms, whose idea of a man of vision seems to be someone who follows him, is something of a human divining-rod insofar as Jimmy Carter's human-rights principles are concerned. While the gentlemen's agreement with the Justice Department was being negotiated, Carter's State Department came to the defense of the fascist regime in Chile, which Helms had helped bring to power. Citing the fact that many of the functions of the Chilean secret police, DINA, had been transferred to other agencies, a department spokesman said that, "The image regarding human rights Chile has generally abroad is somewhat distorted and somewhat out of date." The transferred "functions" that went unelaborated upon included torture and murder of the regime's opponents. (Boston *Globe,* August 20, 1977.)

Two weeks after Helms' plea bargain was entered in court, he announced the opening of his new consulting firm that would advise U.S. businessmen on matters of trade between the United States and Iran. The new company, located two blocks from the White House, was named the Safeer Company. In Parsi, the Persian language, "safeer" means "ambassador." Helms had of course served as U.S. ambassador to Iran following his resignation from the CIA. The Iranian regime, perhaps the most barbaric in modern times if gauged in terms of widespread torture and political imprisonment, was brought to power by a coup d'etat engineered by Helms' colleagues at the CIA.

The day before Helms opened his business, that regime's head of state, the Shah of Iran, was welcomed by President Carter to Washington. The President praised the Shah for maintaining a "strong, stable and progressive Iran" under his leadership; and apologized to the dictator for "our temporary air pollution problem," referring to tear gas lingering in the White House air after the police dispersed peaceful anti-Shah demonstrators. (*The New York Times,* Nov. 16, 17, 1977.)